HIPPO
IN THE GARDEN
A NON-RELIGIOUS APPROACH TO HAVING A CONVERSATION WITH GOD

HIPPO
IN THE GARDEN

A NON-RELIGIOUS APPROACH TO HAVING A CONVERSATION WITH GOD

JAMES RYLE

FOREWORD BY JACK TAYLOR

CREATION
HOUSE
BOOKS ABOUT SPIRIT-LED LIVING
ORLANDO, FLORIDA

Creation House
Strang Communications Company
600 Rinehart Road
Lake Mary, FL 32746

First Printing, July 1993
Second Printing, April 1994

"In the last days, God says,
I will pour out my Spirit on all people.
Your sons and daughters will prophesy,
your young men will see visions,
your old men will dream dreams."
Acts 2:17

Dedicated to my sons and daughters:
Anna, David, Jonathan and Rachel—
that the Spirit of God may bring
this prophecy to pass in your lives.

Contents

Foreword 7

Preface 9

1 Encounters With the Living God 12

2 God Is Speaking Today 30

3 Learning to Listen 49

4 God Speaks Through Scripture 70

5 God Speaks Through Prophetic
   Ministry 93

6 God Speaks Through Dreams
   and Visions 117

7 God Speaks Through the
   Natural Realm 151

8 God Speaks Through the
   Supernatural 187

9 Discerning the Voice of the Lord 218

10 Sharing With Others What
   God Has Shown You 246

11 The Hippo in the Garden 258

Notes 293

For the thousands who are asking, have asked or soon will ask how and where prophecy fits in the church today, here is your answer.

It is strikingly simple, profoundly clear and powerfully illustrated in personal experience as well as in Scripture. The reading of it sparks in me a passion to know God more deeply, hear Him more exactingly and speak for Him with more anointing.

I knew James Ryle when he was fresh out of "hippie-dom" more than a score of years ago. When his star began to rise in recent years I did not recognize the new James Ryle. His is one of the clearest prophetic voices in the land. His gift is unique and priceless, packaged in humor and sparkling with practicality. All who are open enough to receive it will be blessed by it.

I am reading portions of *Hippo in the Garden* again and again and plan to give it wide coverage wherever I minister.

It is a "must" for the journey in these turbulent days and an intriguing insight into the kind of timber with which God is building His house today!

With excitement I commend both author and work to you!

Jack Taylor
President of Dimensions Ministries
Fort Worth, Texas

Preface

During the past twenty years of pastoral ministry, I have preached hundreds of sermons on a wide variety of subjects to a multitude of people. Over time, I have observed that the foremost topic of interest has been "hearing the voice of God." We intuitively recognize our need to know when and how God speaks to each of us, for it is foundational to the development of our personal lives — spiritually, morally, emotionally, intellectually and socially. This book was written to provide a sound pastoral perspective on this vital subject.

Much of what I have to say has been formed by intimate spiritual events of the past forty years of my life. Therefore, this book is personal in its style. It is written for inspiration as well as information. My goal in being so self-disclosing is to encourage you to expect God to do the same for you that He has done for me. The teachings set forth in this book are not mere opinions, but proven truths worthy of your attention. I offer them with no apology, for I am certain that they will enhance your pursuit of a personal relationship with the living God.

Finally, I am compelled to say a special thank-you to some significant people who have been very instrumental in my life:

To my mother, Ethel Jennings Ryle-Cottrell: Thank you for laying me on the altar those many years ago. Here is the Lord's return for your sacrificial investment of love and faith.

To my dad, Bert Eugene Ryle: Thanks for turning to the Lord before you died. Now we will have an eternity to know one another.

To Belinda, my wife: Thank you for your unending love that has filled my heart with trust and devotion. I count you as my dearest and deepest friend. While it is I who receives acclaim in the public forum, I know in my heart that the greater part belongs to you. Your faithfulness before the throne of God on my behalf is the undeniable cause for my steadfast pursuit of the Lord and for His grace so abundantly given to me. Therefore, I give you the honor that is rightly due you. You are an exemplary woman of God. "Many daughters have done well, but you excel them all" (Prov. 31:29, NKJV).

To my church staff and congregation, the Boulder Valley Vineyard: Thank you for allowing me the freedom to expand the boundaries of our ministry to the greater body of Christ. The light that shines the farthest shines brightest at home. Your flaming passion for Jesus Christ keeps the home fires burning and empowers me with faith to go to all the world and preach the gospel.

To Mary Guenther, my personal secretary: Thank you for knocking until the door opened. Your strength of faith carried us through the rigors of editing to complete this project. I would not have done it without you. May those who are blessed by these pages count you as more blessed for having labored so tirelessly to provide them.

To David Pytches, a mischievous and wonderful man of God: Thank you for threatening to take my material and write this book yourself. It proved to be the motivation I needed.

To you, the reader: Thank you for purchasing this book and giving me the chance to help you learn how to hear the voice of God.

James Ryle

Chapter 1

Encounters
With the
Living God

It was Saturday, January 7, 1989. I awakened in the early morning hours with a disturbing dream still vivid in my mind. In the dream I stood in the hallway at our church while a woman I did not know walked toward me. She was deeply troubled. She asked me if I knew a certain man who was attending our church at that time. When I acknowledged that I did, she said, "Well, he is having an affair with me, and I want him to stop." I told her I would take care of it for her, and the dream ended.

As the day began I felt impressed to go to my office, something I ordinarily do not do on Saturdays. While I sat at my desk wondering what I was doing there, I heard the church door open. Standing in the doorway of my office was the very man I had dreamed about. I was so stunned that I could do nothing but tell him the dream and ask him if it were true.

He turned pale, hung his head and said, "I knew that God was going to tell you."

I was speechless. He sat down in my office, and we dealt with the issues involved. Then I warned him that a more severe and public disclosure could happen if he sinned in this way again. The man repented and today continues to walk in faithfulness — and in the fear of the Lord!

That incident was amazing to me. Though the Lord had spoken to me in dreams many times before, none had ever been so specific and with such immediate fulfillment. I felt that this was something I should share with my friend John Wimber. When I told him the story, John responded by saying that just the day before the Lord had revealed to him that he was to pray for me to be released as a "seer" in prophetic growth and ministry. I cannot testify to feeling anything out of the ordinary as John prayed, but from that time forward there has been an increase of the word of the Lord in my personal life. The frequency, scope, accuracy and fulfillment of dreams, visions and prophetic words has been staggering. It is out of the overflow of this wonderful friendship with God that I have been moved to write down the things that make up this book.

The Bible teaches that peace will come to us as we become acquainted with God and treasure His words in our hearts (see Job 22:21-22). God Himself provides each of us with many opportunities for knowing Him and for hearing His voice. My life has been shaped by several encounters with the living God which have helped me learn to recognize how and when He speaks.

I will never forget the first time I heard the voice of

the Lord. I was a troubled young boy not given to the things of the Spirit, and when He spoke to me, it was unexpected and unsolicited.

I was raised in an orphanage, though I am not an orphan. My father was serving time in the state penitentiary, and my mother was hard-pressed trying to raise five children on her own. Finally Mom divorced my dad and married a wealthy oil man in hopes of a better life for us. But his unpredictable anger and addiction to alcohol created a highly volatile atmosphere at home. On one occasion my stepfather, in a drunken stupor, almost beat my brother to death. This was more than my mom could bear, so she left him to try to establish a new life for herself and her kids. The three youngest children were placed in an orphanage with the hope that things would work out for the best. I was seven years old then.

I remember how bewildered I felt the first few weeks in the strange and imposing dormitories of the orphanage. We were grouped together by age and sex, so I was housed with about a hundred other boys who had also been left by their parents. The atmosphere was charged with a sense of fear and abandonment. Although the orphanage provided food, clothing and shelter, it was poorly staffed and functionally incapable of giving personal attention and nurture to the hundreds of children within its care. So while I continued to develop physically, there was no positive shaping of my personality, nor anyone giving me any sense of my purpose in life.

The place had an inflexible religious mood about it. The older women working there often spoke of God, but the tone in their voices and the looks on their faces made a young boy wonder if God was someone you would really want to meet. The huge church sanctuary, large enough to hold fifteen hundred, was overwhelming to me when I first entered it. Painted on the walls in large, golden letters were the words, "Be still, and know that I am God" (Ps. 46:10) and "The Lord is in his holy temple: let all the earth keep silence before him" (Hab. 2:20, KJV).

I think now that the adults must have put those verses there as a means of keeping all of the kids quiet during church services! Whatever the reason, it had its effect on me: I was *afraid* of God. In fact, the first beating I received at the orphanage was for giggling during a church service. It didn't take me long to figure out that the best thing to do was to keep quiet and out of the way and to do what you were told. Otherwise, "God" might do something dreadful to you.

On one night in particular, I remember the uproar caused by two of the boys running away. After a couple of days they were caught and returned to the orphanage. I can still recall the chilling sounds of their screams echoing through the halls as they were beaten for having done something so foolish. As I lay in my bed, frightened by the sounds of punishment, I pulled the covers up over my face and timidly whispered a simple prayer to the God I did not know, but feared. "I promise, God," I said, "that I'll never run away." Bear in mind I was only seven years old.

The years passed, and I kept a low profile, avoiding trouble whenever possible. But with increasing exposure to the world that existed beyond the fence, I began to question the things that were taking place inside the orphanage. Finally, at the age of fourteen, I decided to run away. Two friends and I jumped the fence late one evening and scurried across a field into the darkened woods, thrilled by a sense of adventure.

Then something happened that I was not prepared for. The voice of the Lord spoke to me out of the silence, stopping me in my tracks: "You promised." That's all He said, but it was enough. I was dumbstruck.

My first thought was, I cannot believe that You would bring that up at a time like this! I didn't know what to do. My two friends, unaware of what was happening,

continued running into the darkness of the night while I
stood there wrestling with a choice I did not want to
make. Regrettably, I broke my childhood promise to
God that night. I've often wondered what would have
happened had I turned back — how different things
might have been. That was the first time I recall the
Lord ever speaking to me, but it certainly was not to be
the last.

The following few years were filled with trouble and
tragedy as I continued to run farther away from God.
When I was eighteen I was involved in an automobile
accident which killed a passenger in the car I was driving, yet I was miraculously spared from injury. I remember pounding my fists on the highway pavement as
I protested to God, "Why are You doing this to me?"

The death of my friend resulted in criminal charges
being brought against me, with a possible three-year jail
sentence pending the outcome of the trial. I was terrified and desperate. In an attempt to raise the money
needed to retain a good defense attorney, I turned to
selling drugs among my friends. But within a few weeks
I was arrested with drugs in my possession and indicted
on felony criminal charges that carried a possible life
sentence in the state penitentiary. Again, in anger and
bitterness, I struck out against God: "Why are You doing this to me?"

Obviously God was not doing any of this to me, but
that was the way I saw it at the time. The Bible says, "A
man's own folly ruins his life, yet his heart rages against
the Lord" (Prov. 19:3). It seemed that every foolish attempt I made at trying to get myself out of trouble only
made things worse, and in my mind, blaming it on God
seemed to be the right thing to do.

Evicted from my apartment as a result of being arrested and labeled as a "drug pusher" in my community,
I had nowhere to turn. Alone and afraid, I curled up
beneath a tree in the city park as night fell, hoping that

sleep would bring me some measure of relief from my troubles. I then heard my name being called by friends who knew of my difficulties and had found a place for me to stay at the house of a man they knew. Gratefully I moved in, and things seemed to start picking up for me.

Two months later I was scheduled to appear before the court for a pretrial arraignment. However, instead of representing me before the judge, my attorney used this occasion to withdraw from the case and return me to the custody of the state. Consequently I was immediately locked up in the county jail to await my trial.

That was the proverbial straw that broke the camel's back. I felt more rage, bitterness and hatred than I had ever known. With my fists clinched, my eyes glaring and my body trembling, I began cursing God and man for all the years of mistreatment and neglect I had suffered. With contempt and anger I again challenged God: "Why are You doing this to me? Why don't You just leave me alone? Why must You always interfere with my life? Why? Why? *Why?*"

After my senseless outburst I settled down in the dreadful environment of bondage and fear, surrounded by men even more desperate than I. Little did I know that God was about to speak to me again.

Morning came, and the sun shone through the tiny windows of the county jail. Shortly after breakfast I had a visitor. A friend had come to see me, his voice a welcome sound through the protective glass that separated us. We made small talk, nervously avoiding the subject of what was going to happen to me.

My friend casually told me that on Saturday night, the police had raided the house where I had been staying and arrested the man who had given me a room to live in. They had found over twelve pounds of marijuana and several bags of assorted drugs in the house. I remember nothing else of our conversation, for at that moment the Lord spoke to me very clearly, although He only said two words: "That's why!"

I was awestruck by the voice of God and stunned by the sobering realization that the One I had cursed and hated had literally saved my life. For if I had not been locked in the jail over the weekend, I would have been at the house when it was raided. The additional criminal charges which would have been filed against me would have undoubtedly resulted in a very long prison term.

I stood there overwhelmed with the realization that God had ignored my blasphemous disrespect and saved me from the worst possible thing that could have ever happened to me. A deep sense of shame came over me as I stood in the presence of the Lord. Suddenly a verse of Scripture that I must have read as a boy in the orphanage came clearly into my mind. "And we know that all things work together for good to them that love God, to them who are the called according to his purpose" (Rom. 8:28, KJV). I realized that God was speaking to me again as these comforting words extended their saving influence beyond the immediate circumstance to embrace my entire life.

The trauma of my early childhood, the turmoil of the years at the orphanage, the tragedy of the automobile accident, the timing of my arrest and confinement: "All things work together for good...." I suddenly realized how much God loved me, and I saw in that instant how He had worked all these things for my good.

My life was changed in that moment as I surrendered to the Lord Jesus Christ, saying, "Lord, I see that You are doing something in my life that is beyond my understanding. Please forgive me for the foolish way I cursed and blamed You. Go ahead and do whatever You are doing; I will not resist You anymore. Have Your own way, Lord."

The following day a state-appointed attorney from the public defender's office met with me to discuss my forthcoming trial. "James," he said, "you're guilty. You know it, I know it, and the prosecutor from the district attorney's office knows it. We have you, we have the evidence, we have the witnesses, and we have the case. What we do not have is the time to tie up a courtroom with a jury trial only to prove what we all know is true. I met with the judge in his chambers, and he proposed that if you waive your right to a jury trial and plead guilty as charged, he will give you the minimum sentence of two years."

To this day I view this as a judicial miracle performed on my behalf by God. The authorities could have locked me up for a very long time, but the Lord had greater plans for me than spending my life in prison. I agreed to their offer and within a few days was duly sentenced to serve two years in the Texas State Penitentiary.

The time I spent in prison gave me many opportunities for studying the Bible and drawing closer to the Lord. It was like being in seminary, and from what I've heard from those who have been to seminary, the similarities are remarkable! During this time I developed a deep love for the Word of God and began to cultivate a sensitivity to hearing His voice. The Bible says, "The entrance of Your words gives light; it gives understanding to the simple" (Ps. 119:130, NKJV).

I found this to be profoundly true as the Bible — a book somewhat familiar to me from my childhood at the orphanage — suddenly burst alive with new meaning. In its pages I found the comfort, direction and purpose in life that I had so desperately sought in other things.

Just as Jesus promised, the Holy Spirit became my Teacher. He opened my eyes to see great and wonderful things out of the Bible, causing my heart to burn within me as He talked with me along the way and gave me understanding to know the Scriptures. As the truth of God's Word entered my heart, healing and liberty began to fill my soul. How ironic that it took a prison cell to bring me to freedom.

After almost a year in prison, I was long overdue for a review with the parole board and was quite perplexed about why they hadn't contacted me. I began to pray earnestly about it, asking the Lord to give me favor with the officials so that I might be released early rather than having to serve the full two-year sentence. One night after specifically praying along those lines I picked up my Bible and opened it randomly to these words:

> [And Jesus] said to him, "Go home to your friends, and tell them what great things the Lord has done for you, and how He has had compassion on you" (Mark 5:19, NKJV).

I was impacted dramatically by this verse. It was as though the Lord Himself was standing before me in my prison cell speaking directly to me. I knew in that instant I would be going home, and within the week I was contacted by the parole board and granted an early release.

Just as the Lord had said, I went home and began telling the great things that He had done for me to all who would listen! That was over twenty years ago, and I am still at it to this day. In retrospect, one passage of Scripture says it better than my many words:

> I waited patiently for the Lord; and He inclined to me, and heard my cry. He also brought me up out of a horrible pit, out of the miry clay, and set my feet upon a rock, and established my steps. He has put a new song in my mouth — praise to our God; many will see it and fear, and will trust in the Lord (Ps. 40:1-3, NKJV).

At the time I was released from prison a mighty move of the Spirit of God was sweeping across the nation as thousands of young people were coming to Christ. In the summer of 1971, the impact of the "Jesus movement" (as it was called) came to Grand Prairie, the town where I was living, resulting in hundreds of conversions. A number of people joined together to establish a discipleship training ministry called "The True Vine" (from John 15:5). Suddenly I found myself regarded as one of the Bible study leaders and soon became a counselor on staff.

During the next year I witnessed firsthand the miraculous outpouring of God's love and power as over twelve hundred people came to know and accept the Lord Jesus as their personal Savior — an average of twenty-five people each week! It was a wonderful time of excitement, joy and growth as we watched God do remarkable things day after day.

It was at this time that I met Belinda, who was to become my wife. As we labored together in the presence of the Lord, we fell in love and became man and wife in the spring of 1972.

Meanwhile, the ministry was going as strong as ever, and we were swept up in the activity of it all. The excitement of seeing God at work caused the leadership of the True Vine to plan to reproduce in several major cities all the wonderful things God was doing in the town of Grand Prairie.

Thus Belinda and I were sent to Denver, Colorado, to be the directors of the Rocky Mountain regional branch of what was now pompously titled "The True Vine Ministries for Christ International Incorporated." We had big dreams and were going to do great things. It was going to be even more glorious than anyone could imagine!

The only problem with all of this was that nobody bothered to ask God if this was what *He* wanted. Well, as we came to find out, it wasn't.

The presence and favor of God lifted from the minis-

try so fast it made our heads spin! Consequently, over
the next year the entire True Vine ministry dissolved
and ultimately shut down — even in Grand Prairie,
where it had all begun. Out of this we learned a valuable
lesson about doing only what the Father is doing and
never assuming we can bottle the work of God and reproduce it at will.

With the obvious absence of God's blessings on our
labors, Belinda and I spent a year of frustration and
disillusionment in Colorado as we met with repeated
failure in attempting to recreate there what we had experienced in Texas. This put a great strain on our marriage, our faith and our enthusiasm. After a full year of
ineffectiveness, I was ready for a special touch from
God — and God was more than ready to touch me. It
came during a youth camp meeting sponsored by area
churches in the summer of 1973.

I had agreed to serve as camp counselor at the invitation of the pastors, despite my own sense of spiritual
barrenness and emptiness. Driven only by a sense of
duty, I arose early the first morning of camp and pos-
tured myself in a traditional "attitude of prayer." This
was done completely for the sake of the youngsters who
were looking to me for a pattern of spiritual maturity —
I did not feel spiritual, nor did I even care. As I knelt by
my bedside with my hands folded and my Bible open
(though my heart was quite closed), my eyes settled on
this verse of Scripture.

> You, O God, sent a plentiful rain, whereby
> You confirmed Your inheritance, when it was
> weary (Ps. 68:9, NKJV).

My heart suddenly ignited with faith, filling me with
a compelling sense of expectancy. I knew that the verse
I had read would be my testimony before the week was
over.

The very next day God fulfilled His promise in a dramatic way. A supernatural and overwhelming outpouring of the Holy Spirit came upon me during our evening prayer session. I laughed and wept simultaneously as the power of God surged through every part of my being, bringing forgiveness, cleansing, healing, restoration, renewal and joy. Although the experience seemed to last only a few moments, when I was able to compose myself I looked around to find I was alone. I had been so caught up in the awesome presence of God that I was completely unaware of everything and everyone else around me. How thankful I am that they didn't interfere with what God was doing. He truly sent a "plentiful rain" and confirmed His work in my life as He filled me with the Holy Spirit that night.

A few weeks after my encounter with God at camp, the Lord directed Belinda and me to return to Texas. As we left Colorado I had the strongest impression that God would bring us back in His timing to pastor a particular church where I had preached on a few occasions. Belinda and I buried that hope within our hearts.

We spent the following year working through the harsh realities of mediocrity as we struggled to make ends meet. We had lived in the spotlight of ministry, always on the go, always on the front line. Now we labored through the loneliness of separation from all our cherished activities. It was a time of testing and proving and a time of preparation for future ministry. After more than a year of silence, we were invited to return to Colorado to pastor the very church that God had said we would come back to. We knew it was the Lord's will for us to go.

With our newborn daughter Anna, Belinda and I entered the ministry of this church with the usual enthusiasm and expectation that had come to characterize our relationship with the Lord. Over the next six years the Lord blessed us with three more wonderful children —

David, Jonathan and Rachel. Each child brought a deeper sense of joy and fulfillment into our lives. Yet, while it was a time of great blessing and maturing, our stay at this church also became a time when we experienced the worst discouragement and heartbreak we had ever known.

The senior pastor of the church, a highly respected minister and trusted friend, began to exhibit signs of no longer walking with the Lord. A growing sense of God's absence permeated the church, and many of the people who could see this happening left. Yet the pastor had a persuasive charisma that commanded loyalty, and he was forceful in his claim of authority and anointing.

As a result, the "chosen few" (about fifteen from a previous congregation of over one hundred) remained true to the pastor and to the church. I am ashamed to say that I stood among them as a defender of the pastor's attitudes and actions. Perhaps I could say that I was trying to honor leadership and authority, and maybe in my own immature way I was, but the real truth is that a strong deception had blinded our eyes to the appalling condition of our sickly church and pastor.

Then the Lord mercifully intervened and revealed to me what we had become a part of and how it had happened. I attempted to bring about a recovery in the situation by addressing the glaring errors in the pastor's character and conduct, but instead my family and I became outcasts and were labeled as "rebellious and disobedient." It became intolerable for us to remain any longer with the church. Heartbroken and devastated, I resigned from the pastorate, and we moved to a neighboring city, trusting that God would provide for our family.

Two weeks after we left, God exposed the pastor by bringing to light several instances of gross sexual misconduct and deliberate attempts to keep it hidden. It was revealed that he had repeatedly made aggressive sexual advances toward another man's wife, telling her that if she said *anything* to *anyone* he would deny it, and she would appear as a fool. You can imagine how devastated I was to discover that this woman was *my wife!* Our leaving the church somehow freed Belinda from his grip and made it possible for her to report courageously what he had been doing. The pastor was ruined, and the church was destroyed by these disclosures. To this day, neither has recovered.

I felt betrayed by the pastor and became overwhelmed with anger and vengeance. All the time that I had been defending him from others who questioned his character and challenged his truthfulness, he was forcing himself on my wife and tormenting her with manipulative mind games! It is no exaggeration to say that I wanted to kill this man or, at the very least, do him great bodily harm.

I was alone on a hill outside the city, crying out to God, when I again heard the voice of the Lord. "James," He said, "I know this man has sinned against you and that you feel it would be unjust of Me to ask you to forgive him." That was, in fact, how I was feeling.

The Lord continued, "There is a time when it is right in my eyes for you not to forgive another."

I was all ears because I thought that this surely was such a time. The Lord seemed to pause as if to ensure that He had my full attention, then He delivered the knockout blow.

"You are right to withhold forgiveness from another whenever he sins against you more than you have sinned against Me!"

I gasped as those words hit squarely in my heart. I broke before the Lord, admitting that such a thing could never be and crying out, "I forgive him, Lord. I forgive him!"

I learned three valuable lessons from that encounter with God. First, forgiveness is a matter of *focus*. As long as you look at what others have done against you, it will be virtually impossible to forgive them. But when you keep your eyes on all the Lord has forgiven you — the great debt you owed and could not pay — it becomes remarkably easy to release them into the Lord's hand.

Second — and this is very important for victims to understand — forgiveness does not mean that what the person did against you is now all right. Rather it is your acknowledgment before God that the execution of judgment and justice is not your responsibility, but His.

Third, forgiveness does not change your past, but it does unlock your future.

Now with four children, Belinda and I moved to Boulder, Colorado, in June 1981, again in need of healing and restoration for the bitter failures we had experienced during the previous six years.

The Lord gave us loving care through a group of believers known as Bethel Fellowship, a small church with a family atmosphere. The pastor was fatherly and wise, and the body of believers was close-knit and very loving. Beyond this there was not much structure, nor was there any similarity to the traditional model of church government. During the following year the Lord restored us to faith, joy, vision, love and wholeness through the worship, fellowship and ministry of the church.

Then, in June 1982, a most marvelous thing happened. The pastor of the church resigned to move to a church in Texas. Before making this known to the congregation, he asked me to pray about what the Lord would have me do concerning Bethel Fellowship. I did as he asked, and the Lord assured me it was His will for me to become the pastor of this church.

Accepting the appointment from God, I couldn't help but wonder if the next six years would end with the same kind of loss and disappointment that we had experienced at the previous church. I asked the Lord earnestly about this, and He comforted me with these promising words, "There [referring to the former pastorate] you saw what kills a church; here I will show you what brings one to life!"

With that, Belinda and I once again entered into fulltime ministry — confident in the Lord and His promise!

Nine months later at a healing seminar hosted by the Denver Vineyard Christian Fellowship, I met John Wimber, Tom Stipe and several other Vineyard pastors. This event was to have a lasting impact on my personal life and on my direction in ministry. During the next eighteen months Belinda and I developed relationships with the Vineyard pastors and cultivated a deep appreciation for what God was doing in and through the Vineyard churches.

Then, in August 1984, after a year and a half of prayer, the Lord revealed to me in a dream that it was His will for us to become a part of the Vineyard movement. In the dream I saw myself and about ten other men dressed as Marines in a small rowboat, straining against the waves as we tried to row toward a beach about two miles away. We were being tossed back and forth by the waves, even though it seemed as if we were moving toward the land. Fatigue and frustration mounted with each futile stroke. Suddenly, towering battleships appeared on both sides of our little rowboat, cruising at full speed to the very land we were trying to reach. This powerful armada was supplied fully with troops, armor and weaponry. On the sides of the ships were the words "The Vineyard."

I awoke from the dream and sensed the Lord was saying to me, "The choice is up to you." Accordingly, and with little delay, Bethel Fellowship became the Boulder Valley Vineyard.

The deep significance of this imagery became even clearer two years later as our church relocated to its permanent home. I was meeting with several Vineyard pastors from the area for fellowship and ministry to one another. As we were praying, one of the brothers laid hands on me and said, "James, I don't understand what this means, but I am to tell you that the ships have landed on the shore, and you are about to raise the flag of victory on the land the Lord has brought you to."

This amazed me. This pastor had no knowledge of my dream, and I was overcome with joy in the Lord for the word I was receiving at that moment. No longer were we trying to make it to the shore — we were there! And we were there not just for battle, but for victory!

Shortly after this I awoke one morning from a dream in which the Lord had spoken a Scripture text to me: "Isaiah 5:1." He said this five times, and I was puzzled because I was unfamiliar with the verse. I got up from my bed and opened my Bible to read these words:

> I will sing for the one I love a song about his vineyard: My loved one had a vineyard on a fertile hillside (Is. 5:1).

The full impact of this didn't strike me until later in the day when a man from the church phoned me at home. He said he had been driving along the highway when the Lord spoke to him, telling him to call and have me read Isaiah 27:2-3. Now you can bet that I was intrigued. How coincidental that yet another verse from Isaiah should be brought to my attention. Curious, I turned to the passage in my Bible and read:

> In that day — Sing about a fruitful vineyard: I, the Lord, watch over it; I water it continually. I guard it day and night so that no one may harm it.

The Spirit of God put the two passages together in my mind and showed me how God saw our church —

"a fruitful vineyard on a fertile hillside!" This has been our motto from that day. The extraordinary fact is that since then we have increased our number by over ten times. Just as God promised, the past years have been filled with great blessings, wonderful growth and tremendous experiences in the Lord as He continues to show me the things that "bring a church" to life.

Looking back over my life fills me with wonder. Only God could have done the many things necessary to bring such depths of healing. Only God could make the bitter water sweet and then turn the water into wine. Only God could give a man whose life was destined for despair such a wonderful message of hope and then provide the audience to hear that message. I testify that the underlying dynamic throughout the entire process has been the faith that comes from hearing the voice of God.

The words of Isaiah have become a personal testimony for me:

> The Sovereign Lord has given me an instructed tongue, to know the word that sustains the weary. He wakens me morning by morning, wakens my ear to listen like one being taught (Is. 50:4).

How merciful is the Lord who continues to speak to me through a variety of ways, ever broadening my vision as He sets before me open doors to tell my friends the great things He has done for me. I count it a great privilege to do this, for it not only honors the Lord, but it also stirs the hearts of His people to believe that He will speak to them just as He speaks to me. My heart's cry is that everyone might experience the joy of knowing the Lord and hearing His voice every day. To that end I offer in this book the few things that I have discovered along the way. ❀

Chapter 2

God Is Speaking Today

How often have you heard someone say casually, "The Lord spoke to me," or "The Lord told me" to do this or that? Undoubtedly many times, for Christians seem to speak this way habitually, perhaps even to a fault.

While these expressions may sound reasonable to many of us, others might consider them preposterous — the most pretentious claims that a mortal man could make. In some cases those who feel this way would be exactly right, for many within the church use these terms to justify their own desires and opinions. Possibly they feel that this puts what they are saying beyond challenge. After all, how does one argue with a "word from the Lord"?

In light of this problem I have found it a good policy to avoid such expressions and simply say, "It occurred to me" when I am sharing some insight which I've received in prayer or devotions. This removes unnecessary stumbling blocks and allows more people to hear the message without being distracted with the way the word is being presented.

Nonetheless the Lord *does* speak to us today. We should not become overly concerned about unbelievers who may argue against the peculiarities of our faith; we expect that. However, the divisions within the body of Christ over this issue of hearing the voice of the Lord are more disturbing. In some places the controversy is heated, and the criticism is sharp, pitting brothers and sisters against each other to the delight of the powers of darkness.

I appeal to all who embrace Jesus as Lord and Savior to display the character of Abraham, God's friend, when he turned to his opponents and said, "Let's not have any quarreling between you and me...for we are brothers" (Gen. 13:8). Surely this would please the Lord greatly. It is my hope that the things I share will provide some answers to those who honestly ask for proof that God is speaking today. I also hope to encourage those who instinctively believe and sense that God is speaking to them but feel inadequate when they try to explain it to others.

In the West we live in a rational world of facts and figures, categories and logical conclusions. These shape the fundamental beliefs we hold about life itself. Many find it extremely difficult to accept spiritual things which cannot be rationally explained or understood. Even we as Christians, though we are born again of the Spirit, may retain much of our cultured ways and struggle with the things that God says or does. This prejudice

must be forsaken or else we — along with the world —
will scoff at the mysteries of the Spirit. We must take
great care not to mock and reject the ways in which God
speaks to us by the Holy Spirit, especially when they do
not come in the manner that we have determined to be
the only way that a word from God can come.

For example, what does one do when God talks
through a jackass? (You can ask my church, for they
have heard Him do this many times!) Or how well does
it sit with us that God led astrologers to the birthplace of
Jesus by means of a heavenly star? And what do we say
to the word of the Lord coming through Caiaphas the
high priest at the very moment he was conspiring *di-
abolically* to murder the Son of God? (See John 11:51.)
These are but a few of the many ways in Scripture that
God has used to give revelation to man. As God is broad
and creative in His choices of revelation, so we must be
in our appreciative embrace of all the ways through
which He makes His Word known.

God speaks, and it is imperative for us to learn how
to listen to His voice. Jesus said, "Man shall not live by
bread alone, but by every word that proceeds from the
mouth of God" (Matt. 4:4, NKJV). Not only do we receive life itself by the Word of God, but through His
Word He also gives us the faith we need to live that life.

> Faith comes by hearing, and hearing by the
> word of God (Rom. 10:17, NKJV).

The importance of faith cannot be overlooked, for the
Scripture says that "without faith it is impossible to
please God" (Heb. 11:6). It also says that "whatever is
not from faith is sin" (Rom. 14:23, NKJV). Since faith
is such an essential feature of a righteous life, and since
it can only be obtained by hearing the voice of the Lord,
doesn't this in itself demonstrate God's great readiness
to speak to all who will listen and obey? Certainly it

would be contrary to the character of God if He were to require of us what we do not have. The Scripture says, "What do you have that you did not receive?" (1 Cor. 4:7). God gives us faith by speaking to us, and that faith enables us to live a life that pleases Him in every aspect.

God wants us to hear His voice, know His words and discern His ways. However, He often acts or speaks in such a way as to train us to search, investigate and scrutinize what we are seeing or hearing. Yet we are instructed to temper these examinations with a bias toward the positive.

> Do not put out the Spirit's fire; do not treat
> prophecies with contempt. Test everything.
> Hold on to the good (1 Thess. 5:19-21).

This is important counsel because we are naturally conditioned to have a bias for the negative. In other words we are more likely to examine something for the purpose of proving that it is *false* than confirming that it is true. Most of us make better prosecutors than we do defenders. While we say a person is innocent until proven guilty, we nevertheless *believe* the opposite.

This seems to be especially — and shamefully — true within the broad circles of Christian faith. Come on, you Bible-believing Baptists, how do you really feel about those holy-rolling charismatics (and vice versa)? And you faithful Anglicans, what do you think about those ambiguous house churches?

We need not even ask Pentecostals the questions because, as we all know, they're the only ones going to heaven anyway, unless, of course, you discuss this with a Nazarene. (They'll at least admit that Pentecostals are indeed going *somewhere* for eternity!)

Now how about you traditional Lutherans and Presbyterians: Have you invited any liberal Methodists over for dinner lately? Dare I even mention the Catholics?

And you passionate evangelicals, come on and tell us the real story about those flamboyant Assemblies of God pastors.

But wait — there's more! Forget about how suspicious we are of those who differ from us; just look at what we do even to those who belong to our own particular denomination. Yikes!

We are so filled with opinion, criticism, debate, legalism and harsh judgments that we are unlikely to hear a word from God — even if He shouted it from heaven.

It is hoped that this challenge will sufficiently stir each of us to get past those things that hinder us from receiving the word of the Lord with childlike faith. Jesus said, "I tell you the truth, unless you change and become like little children, you will never enter the kingdom of heaven" (Matt. 18:3). Children display great fascination for the things they encounter every day. Surely the Lord takes great delight when we regard Him with appropriate childlike wonder.

The psalmist wrote, "The works of the Lord are great, studied by all who have pleasure in them" (Ps. 111:2, NKJV). The more fascinated we become with the ways of the Lord, the more we will seek to know them for ourselves. And as we seek, so shall we find (see Jer. 29:13).

The greatest single argument for those who hold to the belief that God speaks is found in the person of Jesus Christ:

> In the beginning was the Word, and the Word was with God, and the Word was God (John 1:1).

Leaving no doubt about whom this was referring to, Scripture then says,

> The Word became flesh and made his dwell-

ing among us. We have seen his glory, the
glory of the One and Only, who came from
the Father, full of grace and truth (John 1:14).

Jesus Christ is the Word of God to mankind! He came
and showed us that God is alive and intimately involved
in the lives of men and women. The very presence of
Jesus Christ on the earth proves God's passion for
speaking to mankind.

Here lies one of the many great distinctions between
Christianity and other religions of the world. Others
worship gods they themselves have made after their
own images. Their gods have hands that do not bless,
eyes that do not see, ears that do not hear and mouths
that do not speak. But it is not this way with our Lord.
He who made the eye, shall He not see? He who made
the ear, shall He not hear? And He who made the mouth,
shall He not speak? The questions are rhetorical, for the
answers are self-evident (see Ps. 94:9).

When the religious leaders challenged His provoca-
tive disregard for their vain and empty customs, Jesus
answered,

> I tell you the truth, the Son can do nothing by
> himself; he can do only what he sees his Fa-
> ther doing, because whatever the Father does
> the Son also does. For the Father loves the
> Son and shows him all he does. Yes, to your
> amazement he will show him even greater
> things than these (John 5:19-20).

Many others have taught us about almighty God, but
Jesus showed us the Father. Everything He said and did
was a perfect revelation of the heart and character of
God. Jesus taught us that God was approachable, compassionate, loving and friendly. He proved that we can
now relate to God on a personal level without diminish-

ing the sovereign majesty of His awesome greatness
and holiness. Jesus revealed to us that knowing God is a
delightful joy and a never-ending adventure.

Now — and brace yourself for this — here is the
great thing which is called the gospel (the good news):
Jesus came not only to show us the Father, but to bring
us into the same relationship with the Father that He
Himself enjoys! Surely we would not dare to believe
such a thing except that we have these treasured words
from His very lips:

> Father, the time has come. Glorify your Son,
> that your Son may glorify you. For you
> granted Him authority over all people that he
> might give eternal life to all those you have
> given him (John 17:1-2).

Now this is the part I want you to see: Jesus said,
"This is eternal life: that they may know you, the only
true God, and Jesus Christ, whom you have sent" (John
17:3). We may know God as Jesus knew Him, and God
will speak to us as He spoke to Jesus.

Jesus was very clear on this matter with His disciples
the night before He was crucified.

> I tell you the truth: It is for your good that I
> am going away. Unless I go away, the Coun-
> selor will not come to you; but if I go, I will
> send him to you (John 16:7).

Earlier that same evening Jesus had told them what to
expect from the Holy Spirit: "The Counselor, the Holy
Spirit, whom the Father will send in my name, will
teach you all things and will remind you of everything I
have said to you" (John 14:26). "He will testify about
me" (John 15:26), and "He will guide you into all truth.
He will not speak on his own; he will speak only what

he hears, and he will tell you what is yet to come" (John 16:13). Jesus was telling the disciples that they, too, would hear the voice of God by the ministry of the Holy Spirit, just as He had. Indeed, after the Holy Spirit came on the day of Pentecost, we see numerous examples in the book of Acts demonstrating that what Jesus promised is now being experienced.

Philip the evangelist heard the angel of the Lord say, "Arise and go toward the south along the road which goes down from Jerusalem to Gaza" (Acts 8:26, NKJV). As Philip followed these directions he came upon a man who had great authority under the queen of the Ethiopians. The man happened to be reading from the writings of Isaiah and needed someone to explain to him what the prophet was talking about.

The Bible says that Philip, beginning with that scripture, "opened his mouth, and...preached Jesus to him" (v. 35, NKJV).

The Ethiopian man was so impacted by the truth that he exclaimed, "I believe that Jesus Christ is the Son of God" (v. 37, NKJV).

Philip then baptized him and sent him on his way. There can be little doubt that this influential man subsequently swayed many in his own nation to trust in Jesus as their Savior. Philip's obedience to the voice of the Spirit led him directly into a divine appointment which had eternal results. This story is especially encouraging because Philip was just an ordinary disciple like you and me. He was not one of the apostles; he wasn't in the upper room the night Jesus made the promise about the Holy Spirit; yet he received the fulfillment of that promise and heard the voice of the Lord. So can you and I.

Peter was told by the Spirit to go to the house of a Gentile named Cornelius.

While Peter was wondering about the mean-

ing of the vision, the men sent by Cornelius
found out where Simon's house was and
stopped at the gate. They called out, asking if
Simon who was known as Peter was staying
there.

While Peter was still thinking about the
vision, the Spirit said to him, "Simon, three
men are looking for you. So get up and go
downstairs. Do not hesitate to go with them,
for I have sent them" (Acts 10:17-20).

Peter did as he was told and as a result witnessed the
outpouring of the Holy Spirit upon the Gentiles in the
same way that the Spirit came upon the Jews.

In the church of Antioch a group of prophets and
teachers was worshipping the Lord and heard the voice
of the Holy Spirit. He told them to recognize and ordain
Barnabas and Paul for the work to which God had called
them (see Acts 13:1-3). Later, as he was preaching in
the face of much opposition, Paul was told by the Lord
to stay in Corinth and minister because the Lord had
many people in that city (Acts 18:9-11). Paul's obedience gave birth to one of the greatest Christian churches
in history.

These are only a few of the many recorded cases in
which ordinary people heard the voice of God in the
early days of the church. Jesus said, "My sheep listen to
my voice; I know them, and they follow me" (John
10:27). Time and time again the early believers proved
that He was right. But this is a "present-tense promise
for a present-time people!" We are not merely to look
back and sigh at how wonderful it must have been to
hear God's voice and be led by His Spirit. No! God still
speaks to us today.

The writer of Hebrews brings this point home with
power:

So, as the Holy Spirit says: "Today, if you hear his voice, do not harden your hearts as you did in the rebellion, during the time of testing in the desert..." (3:7-8).

And again in the following verses:

See to it, brothers, that none of you has a sinful, unbelieving heart that turns away from the living God. But encourage one another daily, as long as it is called Today, so that none of you may be hardened by sin's deceitfulness (3:12-13).

The operative word here is "today." It would be difficult to deny that God spoke in the past, for we have the infallible record of that Word, the Bible. The issue in question among some seems to be whether or not the Lord speaks today. The writer of Hebrews says, "Today, if you hear his voice," and it seems clear enough that he means "today."

Jesus taught us to pray that our Father would give us each day our daily bread. Since He declared that man should not live on bread alone but on every word that comes from the mouth of God, doesn't this imply that He wants us to hear His voice every day of our lives? I think so.

The Bible says, "God is light; in him there is no darkness at all" (1 John 1:5). It is a natural fact that light reveals. God, who is light, is therefore willing to reveal Himself to anyone who will look. The Bible also says, "God is love" (1 John 4:8). Just as light reveals, so love communicates. When you love someone, you will open up and share yourself in many meaningful ways. God is love, and He therefore will speak to anyone who will listen for His voice. Furthermore, God's light and love are in abundance today.

But someone says, "I never hear God's voice, so He must not be speaking!" The breakdown of communication with God is always on our side, never on His. We can hear the very heart of the Lord in the tender words of the apostle Paul:

> We have spoken freely to you, Corinthians, and opened wide our hearts to you. We are not withholding our affection from you, but you are withholding yours from us. As a fair exchange — I speak as to my children — open wide your hearts also (2 Cor. 6:11-13).

The Lord's arm is not shortened that it cannot save. The Lord's ear is not dull so that it cannot hear, nor is His mouth closed so that He cannot speak. Failure to hear the voice of God is our doing, not His.

The book of Job gives us wonderful insight on this matter of hearing the voice of God:

> For God does speak — now one way, now another — though man may not perceive it (Job 33:14).

This Scripture verse reveals three significant facts.

Fact 1: God Does Speak

In one sense this is surprising because God does not owe us anything; it is remarkably merciful that He would speak to us at all. Remember, we are the ones who have broken His covenant over and over again, beginning with eating the forbidden fruit in the garden of Eden. If we talk about what God "owes" us, then we should brace ourselves for death, for that was His promise to Adam in the garden.

> And the Lord God commanded the man,
> "You are free to eat from any tree in the gar-
> den; but you must not eat from the tree of the
> knowledge of good and evil, for when you
> eat of it you will surely die" (Gen. 2:16-17).

Yet God is not willing that any should perish, but that all should be saved and come to a knowledge of the truth. His purpose in making us was that we might know Him and Jesus Christ whom He has sent. He has graciously forgiven our sins through the atoning death of His Son — the innocent dying for the guilty — so that we might now be restored to unbroken fellowship with Him. And in this restored relationship we ourselves may hear again, as it were, "the voice of the Lord God walking in the garden in the cool of the day" (Gen. 3:8, KJV).

I shall never forget how the Lord answered me when I complained how unfair it seemed that I should be counted as a sinner because of Adam's transgression in the garden. The text that was before me was Romans 5:19: "For just as through the disobedience of the one man the many were made sinners, so also through the obedience of the one man the many will be made righteous." This was an enigma. Why should I be made a sinner because of Adam's sin? I wasn't there. I didn't eat the forbidden fruit, and I presumptuously complained about that to the Lord. He responded with direct and profound simplicity.

First He assured me that had I been there, I would have done exactly as Adam did. Conviction struck my heart as the Lord reminded me of the several occasions in which I had indeed "eaten the forbidden fruit." Then He surprised me by saying, "You're right, James. It is not fair that I should count you as a sinner because of what Adam did." (I knew I was in for something at that point so I waited silently for the Lord to finish.) Finally

He spoke these words, and I have never forgotten them: "Neither is it fair for Me to count you righteous because of what Jesus did! If you want the forgiveness that comes through Jesus Christ, you must first acknowledge the guilt that came through Adam."

God has reconciled us to Himself through Jesus Christ, no longer holding our sins against us. He has revealed this glorious news in His written Word, which has been preserved faithfully, that through it we might have faith to experience His living Word. Yet mere knowledge of the Scripture is not enough. The Scripture was given as a testimony to Jesus, to cause us to come to Him that we truly might live. Those who come find Him faithful to His word and fully disposed to revealing the secrets of His heart. Yes, God did speak in times past, and we have the Bible to confirm it. Yes, God will speak on the day when He judges men's hearts by Christ Jesus. But the text in Job says that God does speak! His very name is I AM, and if we accept Him fully as the God of the present in all matters of life, He would certainly speak to us daily, even moment by moment.

Fact 2: God Speaks in Many Ways

Job's friend Elihu did not simply say that God speaks and leave it at that. No, he expanded it considerably when he stated that God speaks "now one way, now another" (Job 33:14). This reveals how committed God is to communicating with the sons of men. He has not limited Himself to one language. Think for a moment what a great burden it would be if God spoke only Swahili or some other rare and distant dialect! Thankfully His Word is not for the chosen few, but for the masses. God does not speak obscure mysteries that only eccentric, asocial "holy men" can solve after years of secluded navel-gazing.

The heavens declare the glory of God; the skies proclaim the work of his hands. Day after day they pour forth speech; night after night they display knowledge. There is no speech or language where their voice is not heard. Their voice goes out into all the earth, their words to the ends of the world (Ps. 19:1-4).

As broad as the sky and as bright as the sun, so is the Word of God to the hearts of men. "I publicly proclaim bold promises," the Lord said through the prophet Isaiah. "I do not whisper obscurities in some dark corner so that no one can know what I mean. And I didn't tell Israel to ask me for what I didn't plan to give! No, for I, Jehovah, speak only truth and righteousness" (Is. 45:19, TLB). God is fully resolved to speak to as many as will hear His voice, and He uses everything at His creative disposal to give His words an opportunity to be heard.

However, mankind exhibits an habitual and sinful preference for independence from God. We like to think that we can function with self-sufficiency. For this reason, many of the ways of the Lord are often untraceable — mysterious and enigmatic — requiring the guidance of the Holy Spirit each step of the way.

God speaks in different ways to keep us seeking Him for the meaning of what He is actually saying. Furthermore, how God speaks to one person is not always the same way that He speaks to another. This creates the necessity of healthy interdependence upon one another. "We know in part and we prophesy in part" (1 Cor. 13:9). When we put our parts together the puzzle is solved, and we have the whole picture.

The writer to the Hebrews says,

In the past God spoke to our forefathers

through the prophets at many times and in
various ways, but in these last days he has
spoken to us by his Son, whom he appointed
heir of all things, and through whom he made
the universe (1:1-2).

God speaks in many ways, and all of them are
summed up in Jesus Christ. We will examine this in
greater detail in later chapters.

Fact 3: God Speaks, Though Man May Not Perceive It

This is most astounding. People are programmed to
think that the voice of God is so awesome that it would
be unmistakable. After all, creation itself is the direct
result of God's speaking. What power there must be in
the voice that can not only light the fires of a million
suns, but keep them burning for eternity! Appropriately,
Amos cried,

The lion has roared — who will not fear? The
Sovereign Lord has spoken — who can but
prophesy? (Amos 3:8).

How terrified the children of Israel were when the
audible voice of God thundered forth from the trembling mountain in the wilderness! They said to Moses,

Speak to us yourself and we will listen. But
do not have God speak to us or we will die!
(Ex. 20:19).

Rightly did the psalmist declare:

The voice of the Lord is powerful; the voice
of the Lord is majestic. The voice of the Lord

> breaks the cedars; the Lord breaks in pieces
> the cedars of Lebanon....The voice of the
> Lord strikes with flashes of lightning. The
> voice of the Lord shakes the desert; the Lord
> shakes the Desert of Kadesh. The voice of the
> Lord twists the oaks and strips the forests
> bare. And in his temple all cry, "Glory!" (Ps.
> 29:4-9).

These are but a few examples in Scripture that show
the awesome majesty of the voice of God. How then can
He speak and man not perceive it? Simple. These passages reveal only one aspect of God's voice. Elsewhere,
the Bible shows that the God who thunders also speaks
in a "still, small voice" (1 Kin. 19:12, KJV). In fact, this
is how He speaks more often than not, and it is precisely
at this point that man fails to perceive it. In order to hear
the still, small voice, we ourselves must become still
and small — still from doing our own works and small
in our own opinions.

A member of my church recently shared a story that
illustrates what I am saying. She and her husband were
building a new home for their family. Throughout the
building process she had been going to the construction
site and writing verses, prayers and blessings with very
small letters in the walls and along the foundation. It
was her special way of acknowledging the Lord as the
builder of their home. One day, she was going happily
from room to room writing her words when she noticed
a construction worker watching her in a peculiar way.
Thinking nothing of it, she finished what she was doing
and went home.

The following day she received a phone call from the
foreman at the job site. "You have just changed a young
man's life," he said.

When she asked him what this meant, he continued,
"A man who works for me left his wife and young child

some time ago, and his life has been filled with darkness. Yesterday he watched you sitting on the floor and writing things on the walls of your new house. After you left he went from room to room, getting down on his knees so he could read what you had written. The verses from the Bible and the prayers you wrote touched him deeply. He gave his life to the Lord and returned home to his wife and baby this morning!"

To satisfy his curiosity, the young man had to become "still and small" by kneeling down on the floor. The Lord spoke to his heart in the quietness of those moments and brought salvation to his life and family. Truly the Lord is wonderful!

> The Lord is my shepherd; I shall not want.
> He makes me to lie down in green pastures;
> He leads me beside the still waters. He restores my soul (Ps. 23:1-3, NKJV).

How often we would find restoration if we drew aside with the Lord by the still waters. Doesn't the Lord say to each of us, "Be still, and know that I am God" (Ps. 46:10)? Surely the Holy Spirit will come alongside us in our busy schedules and say to us, even as Samuel said to Saul, "Stand thou still a while, that I may shew thee the word of God" (1 Sam. 9:27, KJV). The cares of life and distractions of the world often crowd out the still, small voice, leaving us destitute of faith and power; yet the Lord is speaking to us at all times.

The Pig and the Billboard

Some time ago, I was invited to conduct a training seminar in a neighboring city. I arrived at the pastor's house the evening before the event was to begin and settled down for a good night's rest. But just before I fell asleep, I sensed the presence of the Lord suddenly fill the bedroom. I asked aloud what He desired of me, and in a vision I saw a billboard alongside a road. Standing in the grass beside this billboard was a little pink pig. I looked at the pig and asked the Lord, "What does that mean?" He did not answer me, so I began to think of all the verses in the Bible that mentioned pigs, trying to come up with a plausible interpretation on my own.

I thought maybe the Lord was trying to tell me there would be demons in the meeting tomorrow, and I was to cast them into pigs (Matt. 8:31-32); or perhaps the people would be like pigs that went back to wallow in the mud after they were cleansed (2 Pet. 2:22); or that maybe I shouldn't even teach because it would be like casting my pearls before swine (Matt. 7:6). I even thought He might be telling me not to look at any pretty girls who were there, because they would be like a gold ring in a pig's nose (Prov. 11:22)! But I could not come up with anything that made sense out of this strange vision.

Finally, I stopped and asked the Lord what He was trying to say to me.

"James," He asked, "did you read the billboard?" (Oops. I hadn't considered that.)

"Lord, I'm sorry," I said. "I was so taken by the pig that I didn't even look at the billboard. What did it say?"

He showed me the vision again, and I read the words written on the billboard: "Don't Be Distracted!" I felt so foolish. The very thing that the Lord was trying to tell me not to do was exactly what I was doing! The Lord continued, "I am speaking to My people in 'billboards' all of the time, but they are so distracted by the little pigs that they seldom notice what I am saying."

Indeed God speaks, now one way and now another, though man may not perceive it. Nevertheless, He still says,

> Here I am! I stand at the door and knock. If
> anyone hears my voice and opens the door, I
> will come in and eat with him, and he with
> me (Rev. 3:20).

It seems that the question is not, Does God speak today? but, Do we listen to what He is saying? If we do, great blessings will fill our lives.

> Blessed is the man who listens to me, watch-
> ing daily at my doors, waiting at my doorway
> (Prov. 8:34).

Once we get past the barriers of unbelief, we will discover that every circumstance of life becomes an opportunity to have a conversation with God. And the benefits of listening to His voice are immeasurable. ❀

Chapter 3

Learning to Listen

That God speaks today is an issue forever settled on the authority of the Scripture and validated in the lives of countless men and women throughout the world. God is light and will reveal Himself to anyone who will look; God is love and will communicate to anyone who will listen.

There is, however, a significant difference between hearing and listening, just as there is a difference between noise and music. While it's true that the natural ear may hear the sound of God's voice, it is the ear of the *heart* that listens to the substance of what He says. God is looking for the listeners, those who will be both attentive and obedient to His revealed will. To such as these He will surely speak,

> For the eyes of the Lord range throughout the earth to strengthen those whose hearts are fully committed to him (2 Chron. 16:9).

Although the Lord is looking for the listeners, He rarely finds them — a long-standing problem that has characterized the people of God throughout history. The Lord Himself lamented Israel's indifference to His words, revealing that their defeats in battle were directly tied to their neglect in listening to His voice.

> If my people would but listen to me, if Israel would follow my ways, how quickly would I subdue their enemies and turn my hand against their foes! (Ps. 81:13-14).

Charles H. Spurgeon, the distinguished prince of preachers, once commented on this verse, saying, "Our enemies find their greatest weapons against us in the stockpile of our own disobedience. They could not defeat us were we not first to defeat ourselves"[1] The foremost cause of our many defeats is failure to heed the word of the Lord. How much grief do we experience simply because we do not listen to what He says?

More than once, Jesus reprimanded His disciples for their dullness of hearing and slowness of heart.

> "Can't you understand? Are your hearts too hard to take it in? 'Your eyes are to see with — why don't you look? Why don't you open your ears and listen?' Don't you remember anything at all?" (Mark 8:17-18, TLB).

The apostle James was moved of God to write this

now-familiar charge in his epistle to the early Christians: "Do not merely listen to the word, and so deceive yourselves. Do what it says" (1:22). And it is still the same today as it was with ancient Israel and with the first disciples in Galilee. A stupor in the hearts of many believers blocks their discernment and appreciation of spiritual things. As a result, more than a few are slow to listen to the word of the Lord.

The hectic pace of modern life seems to have made listening a lost art and replaced it with "much ado about nothing." In your next conversation, notice how much of it consists of your actually listening to what the other person has to say. Go a step further and watch people as they are absorbed in conversation. It should not surprise you to find that most people would rather hear themselves than consider what another has to say. Indeed, to entertain some people, all one needs to do is listen! Permit me to alter slightly a familiar nursery rhyme:

> Old MacDonald loved to hear
> The sound of his own words.
> And if he ever caught your ear
> That's all you ever heard!
> With a yak-yak here and a yak-yak there...!

You get the idea. A Chinese proverb cleverly observes that God gave man two ears and one mouth so that he might listen twice as much as he speaks.

As an experiment, why not stop for a moment and just listen. Try to identify the many sounds around you. Listen past the obvious clamor for the subtle tones and sounds so often overlooked. Go for a walk and count how many times you hear a bird sing. Listen for the sound of wind rustling through the trees. Can you hear children playing in the distance? As you pass through a shopping center, take note of the chatter caused by many voices talking all at once. Then try to pick out individual conversations. Identify as many songs as you know in the music being piped into the shops. Then see if you can hear the hum of the fan or central heating as it keeps the room at a comfortable temperature. And do all of this while you are actually carrying on a meaningful discussion with a friend! Your ability to listen will expand as you begin to pay attention to the many things you might otherwise ignore.

While *sensitive* listening increases what we are hearing all about us, *selective* listening draws our attention to the things we consider most important. For example, when a mother puts her newborn baby in its bed and goes to sleep herself, most noises throughout the night fail to wake her from her rest. But let that baby squeak even once, and the mother is out of bed in an instant, standing by the crib like a guardian angel! The great value she places on her child determines her sensitivity to the baby's softest cry, while at the same time shuts out the nonessential racket of other things.

Hearing the voice of God is much the same. The value we place on hearing Him causes us to focus on His speaking, which in turn cultivates our sensitivity for hearing Him when He does speak. In addition to enhanced sensitivity through godly values, there are at least three other prerequisites essential for hearing God's voice: a pure heart, a hearing ear and a responsive life. Let's take a closer look at each one.

Prerequisite 1: A Pure Heart

Jesus said, "Blessed are the pure in heart: for they shall see God" (Matt. 5:8, KJV). In another place the Bible says, "To the pure all things are pure, but to those who are defiled and unbelieving nothing is pure; but even their mind and conscience are defiled" (Titus 1:15, NKJV). We must turn to the Lord for cleansing whenever we are defiled by the awful things that happen in a fallen world. Otherwise we will carry the defilement within our hearts and find ourselves unable to receive the words of the Lord, much less believe them. A wounded heart can distort God's words just as a defective radio receiver distorts a good signal: The signal from the station is perfectly clear, but the message being heard in the living room is garbled and irritating.

Suppose, for example, that a man had a particularly cruel father who treated him with such harshness that it warped the way he viewed himself and the world around him. One can imagine the difficulties that would arise within that person's heart as he was introduced to the notion that God wanted to be his Father! God wants to be my Father? he might ask, while at the same time thinking, He wants to beat me and belittle me!

Many mistreated sons and daughters unwittingly project onto God the awful failures of their own earthly fathers in just this way. Aloof, absent and angry men have done so much to give God a bad name through their distorted examples of fatherhood. As a result, the world is filled with broken children who are trapped in this awful deception and in desperate need of a true revelation of the Father-heart of God. Perhaps you are one of them.

It is precisely at this point that purity of heart becomes a vital issue because whatever you inherently believe about God's character, whether right or wrong, ultimately determines the kinds of things you would receive from Him as His word. This accounts for some of the unsuitable and outrageous "prophecies" sometimes spoken in certain gatherings.

I recall one church service in which our hearts were stilled with quiet expectancy for the Lord to reveal Himself in some wonderful way. The worship songs had done much to prepare us to receive from the Lord, so we waited in deep adoration for several moments, yearning for Him to speak to us. Then the silence was broken by a man who bellowed out his "word from God."

It began with a forceful, angry shout: "O My people!" A word of advice: brace yourself when a prophetic utterance starts with "O My people," because what usually follows is seldom wonderful.

The man continued, straining with every word, "How long must I tolerate your wicked, vile and contemptible sinfulness! Oh, I am so upset with every one of you! Know that if you do not repent I will surely visit you with My terrible and swift sword, and you will be undone! Repent at once and humble yourselves before Me, for I am God!"

Needless to say, a long pause of awkward silence followed after he had finished. I came so very close to following that "word" with one of my own: "Thus says the Lord, 'That wasn't Me!' " Obviously this troubled man was speaking out of the fears and foolishness bottled up within him, trumpeting aloud the awful discord of his own inner agony.

This is not to say that the Lord does not rebuke sinful man, for He does. But the situation discussed here was one of surrendered worshippers, captivated with love for the Lord Jesus Christ as we waited for Him to speak so that we might obey. It is most unlikely that the Lord would answer such devotion with an angry rebuke! Furthermore, the Bible says that prophecy is for "strengthening, encouragement and comfort" (1 Cor. 14:3), and the above "prophecy" provided none of these.

Let's bring this to a personal level. Have you ever prayed, "Lord, I know what You must be thinking about me right now," and then begun to tell Him what you were actually thinking about yourself? We all do this. We condemn ourselves for the mistakes we have made and conclude that this must be what the Lord thinks of us. This is a wrong thing to do! This type of "praying" comes out of the same polluted pool as the so-called prophecy above. We must stop putting our own words in

the Lord's mouth. We must come to know the Lord as
He is and not as we assume Him to be. Scripture alone
is our sure foundation. Listen to what the Lord says
about Himself in the words of Jeremiah:

> "For I know the plans I have for you," de-
> clares the Lord, "plans to prosper you and not
> to harm you, plans to give you hope and a
> future" (29:11).

And in the writings of Isaiah:

> "For My thoughts are not your thoughts, nor
> are your ways My ways," says the Lord. "For
> as the heavens are higher than the earth, so
> are My ways higher than your ways, and My
> thoughts than your thoughts" (55:8-9,
> NKJV).

God's plans for us are greater than the plans we
would make for ourselves. God thinks more highly of us
than we think of ourselves.

Yet something within us makes us believe that God is
always angry with us, always ready to clobber us for the
slightest mistake. We tread softly in His presence and
cower when we pray, for we dare not rouse Him from
slumber lest He strike us with His rod of righteous judgment — O bless His holy name! Now, I ask you honestly, how in the world can you have any kind of a
meaningful relationship with someone like that? You
can't! And that's precisely why so few really know the
Lord. They are more caught up with what they fear Him
to be like than knowing and loving Him as He really is.

Writing with inspired brilliance, the apostle Paul addressed this very issue through a series of rhetorical
questions in his letter to the Christians in Rome. "What,
then, shall we say in response to this?" he asked. And

then he gave his own answer: "If God is for us, who can be against us?"(Rom. 8:31). The logic of his reasoning is simple, yet profound. God is for us, so much so that He did not spare His own Son but gave Him up to save us from our sin. Having justified us at so great and costly a price, God also graciously decided to give us all things together with His Son. Now then, do you really think that He will cast all that aside and bring criminal charges against us simply because we bumble and stumble along the way?

What about Jesus? Will He go against His Father and condemn us? Of course not! He died to forgive us; further, He was raised to life and is at the right hand of God this moment interceding for us. Jesus paid so dearly for us and now prays tenderly for us — could He really be so double-minded as to set His affections aside and hurl accusations and condemnations against us? Paul asks,

> Who shall separate us from the love of Christ? Shall trouble or hardship or persecution or famine or nakedness or danger or sword? (Rom. 8:35).

Again he answers his own question:

> No, in all these things we are more than conquerors through him who loved us. For I am convinced that neither death nor life, neither angels nor demons, neither the present nor the future, nor any powers, neither height nor depth, nor anything else in all creation, will be able to separate us from the love of God that is in Christ Jesus our Lord (Rom. 8:37-39).

The one great revelation of Scripture is that God is love. One day as I was reading my Bible the Holy Spirit showed me just how staggering this truth is. As I was

reading 1 Corinthians 13, the love chapter, I suddenly
realized that those verses were nothing less than a character description of God Himself. In other words, since
God is love, and love is patient, God is patient. I followed this pattern throughout the text, putting the name
of God in the place of the word *love* and discovered
aspects of His personality I never dreamed of!

You will see what I mean as you read the paraphrased
list: God is very patient and kind, and He looks for ways
of being constructive and helpful. God is not possessive
or envious. He does not cherish inflated ideas of His
own importance. God is not selfish or rude, nor does He
ever demand His own way. He is not irritable or touchy,
and He does not hold grudges. In fact, He hardly even
notices when He is wronged! God is loyal no matter
what it costs Him. He always believes in me, expects
the best of me and will stand His ground defending me.
God is love! A few of these phrases may stretch some of
you more than a little bit, but this is what the Bible says.
The more we get to know this wonderful God, the better
we will be at introducing others to Him.

One of my favorite verses for revealing the Lord's
personality states:

> The Lord your God is with you, he is mighty
> to save. He will take great delight in you, he
> will quiet you with his love, he will rejoice
> over you with singing (Zeph. 3:17).

The richness of the Hebrew words used in this verse
portrays the Lord in a most riveting way. According to
Strong's concordance, the phrase "rejoice over you with
singing" literally means "to jump up, whirl about and
shriek at the top of your voice." Can you see the bound-
less joy and celebration in those words? Can you sense
the sheer delight and the victorious jubilation of the
Lord? And can you imagine the Lord actually feeling

that way about you? Believe it or not, it is the truth.

The Trash Can Dream

Some time ago, I had an interesting dream. Driving along a narrow road, I came upon a large trash can blocking my way. It had been toppled and its contents were strewn about the road. I stepped out of my car to clean up the mess when suddenly a face appeared on the trash can, giving it the appearance of a man's head with garbage coming out of the top. The Lord then spoke clearly from above me, "Stop filling your head with trash!" I awakened with little doubt about what the Lord meant. I made a quick work of repentance that day as I scrutinized everything I was doing, making certain that I was obedient to what the Lord had said, and I continued faithful in this resolve for some time.

However, we Christians are a predictable lot. It seems almost inevitable that after a period of intense devotion and painstaking faithfulness, we somehow decide to reward ourselves for being so good by giving ourselves permission to slacken our vigilance.

Some months later I found myself at a conference in which John Wimber was preaching a sermon titled "Pure Hearts Before the Lord." As I listened, I suddenly came under the conviction of the Holy Spirit, being reminded of the word the Lord had spoken to me. I reflected over the recent months and had to confess that I had "left my first love." I was so grieved for having offended the Spirit of God that I could hardly endure the moment. Later, as I sat in my hotel room praying about the revelations of the evening, the Lord spoke to me again. "If you had responded to my rebuke, I would have poured out my heart to you and made my thoughts known to you" (Prov. 1:23).

At first this was more than I could bear, for I thought that the Lord was saying it was over for me. I feared I

had failed a critical test and thereby missed the privilege
to be commissioned for prophetic ministry. My spirit
sank in despair as I concluded that I would never be
entrusted with knowing the Lord's intimate thoughts —
at least, that's what the proverb seemed to say to me.
But even as I struggled with condemnation and guilt,
the Lord spoke to me in my room as He had in my
dream: "Stop filling your head with trash!"

At last I got the message. I realized that my own
carnal fears, my unbelief and my self-doubt were themselves polluting my heart; that was the trash the Lord
wanted out of my mind. The Lord was cleansing me by
His word (see John 15:3). As I began to worship and
thank Him, He spoke again: "If you will stop filling
your head with trash, then I will start filling your heart
with treasure!" The Scripture says it this way:

> Do not conform any longer to the pattern of
> this world, but be transformed by the renew-
> ing of your mind. Then you will be able to
> test and approve what God's will is — his
> good, pleasing and perfect will (Rom. 12:2).

Prerequisite 2: A Hearing Ear

In Scripture we find no fewer than fifteen times the
expression "He that has an ear, let him hear." Clearly
this does not refer to the ears on the sides of our heads
but to the ears within our hearts. This distinction is noteworthy for the word of the Lord comes from within, not
without. The prayer of Scripture is that the "eyes of our
heart" would be opened that we might see the things of
God. Indeed, "the heart of the discerning acquires
knowledge; the ears of the wise seek it out" (Prov.
18:15). The Bible teaches us that the kingdom of heaven
does not come with outward manifestation, but that it is
"within" us. In order to perceive and experience it, we

must be transformed from the inside out. This is why Jesus said, "I tell you the truth, no one can see the kingdom of God unless he is born again" (John 3:3). The natural man cannot receive the things of the Spirit of God for they are foolish to him; they must be discerned *spiritually*. That is, the things of the spirit must be perceived, examined, scrutinized, assessed, tested and decided upon *in a spiritual way* by the observer.

The religious leaders of Jesus' day had great difficulty with this process. They were constantly missing the point of what Jesus was saying and doing. Their spiritual blindness and dullness of heart revealed that they did not have "an ear to hear." In fact, Jesus Himself confronted them on this point:

> He who belongs to God hears what God says.
> The reason you do not hear is that you do not
> belong to God (John 8:47).

A hearing ear is given to each of us when we are born again. Now, although the capacity to hear the Lord is *develop* present, we each must develop the ability to do so. And the Lord is most gracious to give us help in this happy endeavor.

Isaiah said, "The Sovereign Lord has given me an instructed tongue, to know the word that sustains the weary. He wakens me morning by morning, wakens my ear to listen like one being taught" (50:4). Have you ever watched a classroom of students eager to learn about a particular subject? They focus on the teacher and screen out the insignificant babble of background noise. They take notes on what is being said, ask questions and nod with enthusiasm and affirmation when they grasp something which excites them. This is what it means to "listen like one being taught." If we will show this same attentiveness to the Lord, He will awaken us every morning to more revelation of Himself!

> Does not wisdom call out? Does not under-
> standing raise her voice? On the heights
> along the way, where the paths meet, she
> takes her stand; beside the gates leading into
> the city, at the entrances, she cries aloud: "To
> you, O men, I call out; I raise my voice to all
> mankind" (Prov. 8:1-4).

What a fascinating thought! Wherever we may be,
we can hear the cry of Wisdom, the voice of God. At the
busy crossroad in the crowded city, above the clamor of
carnality, Wisdom calls to the sons of men. Or in a field
far removed from the hustle of a busy life — amid the
chatter of birds, squirrels, crickets and frogs — there
Wisdom speaks to those who will listen. All about us,
Wisdom is speaking in an unending dialogue, and, mind
you, she is not whispering.

To develop a "hearing ear" we must regard the word
of the Lord as a vital feature of our daily lives. Hearing
God's voice must become more than a fond desire, more
than something interesting to do and more than a means
of giving us some sense of spiritual status. Frankly, it
must become a matter of life or death to us. Job said it
in the clearest of terms:

> I have treasured the words of his mouth more
> than my daily bread (Job 23:12).

In the West, so much of our lives revolves around
eating. When we wake up in the morning, the first thing
we do is *eat*. Then it's off to work, and the morning has
hardly begun when we take a coffee break so we can
eat. This gives us what we need to make it through the
rest of the morning to lunchtime when we can really
"chow down with a mega-meal!" After lunch, we return
to work and count the moments until our afternoon
break when, once again, we *eat*.

Ah! At last, it's quitting time. We jump in our cars and trains to go home. On the way we may make a quick stop so we can *eat* a little something to tide us over until supper time. Later at home the table is set; the aroma wafts throughout the house; we take our places and *eat*.

Our evenings are filled with an assortment of family events and homey things, with snacks thrown in here and there. And then it's bedtime. But wait! Let's take one more opportunity to *eat*! How about a nice piece of toast and jelly? Finally, it's off to bed in hopes that our dreams will be filled with "visions of sugar plums" dancing around in our heads or, at the very least, pepperoni pizza with extra cheese. I once asked a man what he did for a living, and he answered, *"I eat!"*

Jesus said, "It is written: 'Man does not live on bread alone, but on every word that comes from the mouth of God' " (Matt. 4:4). None of us would dare deprive our bodies of food the way we deprive our spirits of God's words. We must change this. We cannot settle for hearing God's voice only in times of convenience or crisis, but rather we must treasure it as the indispensable highlight to our everyday lives. This alone will enable us to hear His voice regularly.

> You will seek me and find me when you seek me with all your heart (Jer. 29:13).

Just as a matter of practical reminder, why not make the cover of your Bible look like a kitchen cupboard door — that way you'll be sure to open it more often!

Once we have a deep regard for God's Word in our personal value system, we will give ourselves to the discipline of daily devotion in the Scriptures — with far-reaching rewards. Paul informed Timothy that "all Scripture is God-breathed and is useful for teaching, rebuking, correcting and training in righteousness, so that the man of God may be thoroughly equipped for every good work" (2 Tim. 3:16-17).

By reading and meditating on Scripture we can increase our understanding of God's "vocabulary" and gain knowledge of both His words and His ways. This enables us to understand not only what God is saying, but even why He is saying it. In other words, the more familiar we become with the Bible, the more personally we will know the Lord; and, as an inevitable result, the more readily we will discern when something that is being said or done is truly of the Lord or not.

Who among us would go fishing in a swimming pool? (What's the catch? you may be asking. Well, there is no catch because there are no fish!) However, stock the pool with as much fish as it can hold, then we will catch plenty. In the same way, our spirits could be likened to pools of water before the Lord. If we have stocked the pond by spending time with Scripture, God is more likely to speak to us. To put it rather cleverly, when there are fish in the pool, God often drops us a line! Perhaps the reason God has never spoken to you can be traced to your never having taken time to put His Word in your heart.

> I have hidden your word in my heart that I
> might not sin against you (Ps. 119:11).

There are no shortcuts to a meaningful relationship with God. Each of us is personally responsible to study the Scriptures so that we might know the Lord. We cannot expect someone else, such as our pastor or Bible study leader, to do this for us. Nor can we excuse ourselves by saying we do not have the time to do it for ourselves. That is one argument that will not stand in the presence of the Lord.

In the parable of the two men who built houses, one on rock and the other on sand, both took the same amount of time to do the actual construction of their respective homes. The man who built his house on the sand could not say, "I didn't have time to build my house on the rock." The question was not one of time, but of treasure. The fact is that our values determine our priorities, which in turn determine our practices. We do what we take time to do, and we take time for what we value.

If we say, I don't have time to read the Bible, we need to stop deceiving ourselves. The truth is that we do have the time, but we do not have the values to make it a priority in our lives. This is a grave mistake because our negligence is detrimental to our own well-being. The storms of life are indiscriminate, periodically hammering us with winds, pummeling us with rains and blasting us with floods, just as in the parable. Only those whose lives are "built upon the rock" will survive the storms (see Matt. 7:24-27). By depriving ourselves of God's Word we become increasingly disabled for life's great challenges. So why do that?

If the negative consequences are not enough to stir you to action, how about looking at the positive benefits?

> Blessed is the man who does not walk in the counsel of the wicked or stand in the way of sinners or sit in the seat of mockers. But his delight is in the law of the Lord, and on his law he meditates day and night. He is like a tree planted by streams of water, which yields its fruit in season and whose leaf does not wither. Whatever he does prospers (Ps. 1:1-3).

This is almost verbatim the covenant promise God made to Joshua,

Do not let this Book of the Law depart from

> your mouth; meditate on it day and night, so
> that you may be careful to do everything
> written in it. Then you will be prosperous and
> successful (Josh. 1:8).

Prosperity and success await the man or woman who
is devoted to God's Word!

Prerequisite 3: A Responsive Life

Obedience is a critical factor in hearing the voice of
God. Jesus said, "Whoever has my commands and
obeys them, he is the one who loves me. He who loves
me will be loved by my Father, and I too will love him
and show myself to him" (John 14:21). Notice the pro-
gression in this verse. First, "he who has my commands"—that's all of us. Now let's narrow the field
down just a bit. "He who has my commands and *obeys*
them" (italics added)—that's not all of us, although it
should be. These are the ones to whom the Lord reveals
Himself; those who respond to His Word in faithful obedience.

Take a good look at the word *obedience*. Did you
notice the letter *I* is right in the middle? Can you guess
where the Lord wants us always to be? That's correct!
We should always be right in the middle of obedience,
in the center of His perfect will. And how does He get us
there? Look again at the word *obedience*, paying special
attention to the three middle letters: die. We must die to
ourselves that we might come alive unto the Lord.

> If anyone would come after me, he must deny
> himself and take up his cross daily and fol-
> low me (Luke 9:23).

Jesus Christ extends an open invitation to any who
will follow Him, and the first step in obedience requires

us to deny ourselves and opt for the prerogatives of the Lord.

We "take up our cross daily" when we accept the fact that, in Jesus, we died not only to sin, but also to our own desires and dreams. And it is right to do this, for we are not our own but have been bought with a price that we should glorify God with our lives.

> For none of us lives to himself alone and none of us dies to himself alone. If we live, we live to the Lord; and if we die, we die to the Lord. So, whether we live or die, we belong to the Lord.
>
> For this very reason, Christ died and returned to life so that he might be the Lord of both the dead and the living (Rom. 14:7-9).

But dying to self is not always an easy thing to do, as I was once reminded only too clearly.

The Golf Ball Incident

I'm an avid golfer. I thoroughly enjoy the game. I even like to watch it on television! One day I was playing nine holes by myself and decided to use this opportunity to work on "keeping my head down" (a technical golf term too complicated to explain). Standing on the second tee, I resolved I would not look to see where my ball went after I hit it. Whack! Surely the ball had to be straight down the fairway because I had done everything according to the book! Well, I'll have you know that I walked all over that place trying to find my golf ball, but it was nowhere in sight. So much for that theory. I finished the round and turned to go home.

As I passed the club shop, the Lord spoke to me about the manager behind the counter. "Go inside and tell that man I love him and that I will see him through the difficulty he is facing."

My response was very original: "Is that You, Lord? It sounds like You, but I'm not sure." I kept walking to my car.

The Lord spoke again, saying the same thing, but more emphatically.

That almost sounds like it could really be the Lord, I said to myself. But it's probably not. I think that's just me feeling spiritual all of a sudden. Yeah, that's what it is. And with that, I got into my car and drove away.

I was only a few hundred yards away from the golf course when the Lord spoke clearly to me: "Look to your right, and you'll find a lost golf ball."

Sure enough, to my utter amazement, there alongside the road was the very ball I had lost on the second tee shot! How it got there I'll never know. (And if I did, I'd never tell because I would not hear the end of it from my golfing buddies.) Well, I got back in my car and said politely, "Thank You, Lord, for telling me to look there so that I could find my lost ball."

At that moment the Lord spoke to me and said, "If it was I who told you to look for the golf ball, then it was also I who told you to go inside and talk to that man!"

Have you ever felt the "tractor beams" of the Holy Spirit? The conviction upon me was so strong that I could go no farther. I turned the car around and drove back to the golf course, quite certain that God was about to do something really special — you know, the kind of thing that makes a great illustration when you're preaching about power evangelism. My faith was growing with each step as I drew closer and closer to the shop door.

I found the room filled with people — *lots* of people — who had not been there earlier. It surely would have been easier had I done it then. (Hmmm, make a note of that.) Well, I stalled in hopes that everyone would clear out and give me a moment of privacy to deliver my message from God to the man. Suddenly, he turned to me and said, "Is there something on your mind?" Of course, he said it just loud enough so that everybody in the room was now looking directly at me.

There was no way around it, so I decided just to say it. "I'm a pastor, and, uh, I believe in God, and, uh, well, uh, I read the Bible and, uh, sometimes He, well, He talks to me, and uh...." I stumbled through all my qualifying remarks and finally said what the Lord had told me to say.

When I finished I expected this man to fall to his knees, declaring, "Surely God is in our midst!" or "What must I do to be saved?" I would have settled for either one. Instead he stared blankly at me for a moment and then said, "Thank you very much," as he turned back to his work.

That was it? I wondered. I ambled slowly out to my car, giving the Lord "the silent treatment." I drove away again, only this time I was pouting. When I passed the spot where I'd found my lost ball, I actually looked the other way out of spite! I continued along the road until I came to the place where I had felt those irresistible "tractor beams."

Unable to maintain my stewing silence I finally blurted out, "Lord, what was that all about?"

He answered in an instant with one word only: "Obedience."

The young boy Samuel, whose name means "he will hear the Lord," gives us a wonderful model for obeying the word of the Lord. He was only a child when the word of the Lord came to him in the tabernacle at Shiloh. Having never heard the Lord's voice before, the perplexed Samuel thought Eli was calling him, so he awakened the old man. Eli had enough sense left to realize that the Lord was speaking to the boy, so he told him, "Go and lie down, and if he calls you, say, 'Speak, Lord, for your servant is listening' " (1 Sam. 3:9).

Young Samuel did as Eli instructed him, and the Lord's word came to him in the night. His obedient response to what God said inaugurated one of the most distinguished prophetic ministries of all time.

> The Lord was with Samuel as he grew up, and he let none of his words fall to the ground. And all Israel from Dan to Beersheba recognized that Samuel was attested as a prophet of the Lord. The Lord continued to appear at Shiloh, and there he revealed himself to Samuel through his word. And Samuel's word came to all Israel (1 Sam. 3:19–4:1).

Yet another compelling example of a life responsive to the Lord is Mary, the mother of Jesus. When the angel Gabriel informed her of the Lord's purpose for her, she replied with humility and obedience: "I am the Lord's servant....May it be to me as you have said" (Luke 1:38). Her reaction was quite different from Zechariah's. Standing in the holy of holies ministering unto the Lord, he saw the angel Gabriel appear before him to tell him that his wife would have a son. The old priest doubted the angel and questioned the authenticity of his message. His reluctance and unbelief resulted in prolonged silence. He was unable to speak for nine months, and it seems highly probable that no angel showed up with any more messages for him!

Samuel and Mary exemplify all the essential components for hearing God: sensitivity, godly values, purity of heart, a devotion to hearing Him and obedience to His words. We would do well to devote ourselves to responding to His words with similar faithfulness. Surely the Lord is pleased with such listeners and quick to make His voice known in their hearts. ❧

Chapter 4

God Speaks
Through
Scripture

The first and foremost way that God speaks is through the Scriptures. There should be no controversy over this claim among those who adhere to historic Christianity, for the Bible is the Word of God. Any discussion concerning the means by which God makes Himself known must therefore begin with the Bible as a matter of priority, for it alone stands as the final authority on all revelation. The Bible is our highest court of appeals on all matters of faith and doctrine.

There is no oracle, vision, revelation or any other thing that man claims as being from God which stands above or apart from the Bible or is unanswerable to its sovereign scrutiny. All other means through which God may speak must themselves align perfectly with what the Bible says, or we must dismiss them forthrightly as not being from the Lord. "To the law and to the testimony!" Isaiah cried. "If they do not speak according to this word, it is because there is no light in them" (8:20, NKJV). Clearly the Scripture is vastly superior to all other means of revelation.

A dear friend of mine was once approached by a man asking him for a "word from the Lord."

My friend thrust his Bible into the man's hand and said, "Here, sir, is a whole book of words from the Lord! Read it!"

During the first few years of my present pastorate I worked in an auto paint and body shop to supplement the small income our church was able to pay me at that time. One of my workmates had a horrific addiction to alcohol. By his own estimate he spent no less than $10,000 a year intoxicating himself. Each weekend he would frequent his favorite bar and drink until he literally became unconscious! Many times he would spend the night curled beneath a table in the bar. This compulsive drinking was slowly taking a dreadful toll on him.

One day at work he was fumbling through the phone directory when he turned to me and asked, "James, how do you spell 'psychiatrist'?"

I realized that he was reaching out for help, but I also knew that going to a psychiatrist, though valid in itself, was not the answer to my friend's problems. He needed Jesus. The Holy Spirit led me in my response to his question.

"I have a friend who is a pastor of a nearby church," I said. "He is very professional and is good at helping people through these kinds of problems." I felt that since he was seeking professional help I should accommodate him by directing him to someone he would regard as a "real" pastor. I asked if he would permit me to make an appointment for the two of us to go together.

As it happened, my pastor friend was going out of town for the weekend and was not able to see us until the following Monday evening. I felt some urgency for my fellow worker, since it was noon on Friday and the weekend was when he had his worst battles, so I went to a store during my lunch hour and bought him a Bible. As I handed it to him, I suggested he read it in preparation for our meeting. He thanked me warmly and said that he would. I went back to work and started praying for God to perform a miracle in this man's life.

The weekend was unbearably long, for I was filled with great anticipation of the forthcoming meeting — so much was at stake. I knew Satan would waste no time trying to thwart the work of God in my friend's life. As the hours passed, I wondered how he was doing and if he would make it through the weekend. I feared the worst when he did not show up for work on Monday. As the workday ended, I quickly cleaned up and, as we had agreed, went to his house to pick him up for the appointment. To my great relief I found him ready and waiting when I arrived. There was something different about him, but I was so excited that my plan was coming together I didn't really notice. We arrived at the pastor's office and sat down to talk. That's when I heard the most wonderful news.

My friend had experienced a dramatic conversion by the power of the Holy Spirit while he was reading the Bible during the weekend! Not only was he truly born again, but the addiction to alcohol was completely gone. He was instantly delivered and healed by the power of God, without any human intervention! That was over ten years ago, and to this very day the man walks in freedom and ministers to others.

Our church recently invited Dick Mills to minister to us. He is a seasoned prophetic minister of thirty years who relates verses from Scripture to an individual's life

by the leading of the Holy Spirit. The obvious impact on
the lives of those receiving this ministry gives unmistakable witness to the accuracy and power of these
timely words from the Bible. To illustrate what I mean,
let me recount a story Dick shared with our congregation.

Dick and his wife, Betty, had concluded a time of
ministry in a church and were walking down the aisle to
the pastor's office as the service was being dismissed.
Dick told us that his eye was riveted to a young man
who was crouched in the pew, curled into a fetal position, shaking feverishly. As he saw that pitiful specimen
of humanity, a word from the Lord came to him. Dick
leaned over, put his arm around the man and whispered
quietly so as not to distract from the pastor's closing
prayer. "I have a word from the Lord for you, friend. It's
Isaiah 3:10: " 'It will be well with you.' "

Dick walked on and didn't give this incident another
thought until two years later when he got a letter.

> Dear Dick and Betty,
> I am pastoring a church, and I want you to
> come and minister to us. Let me refresh your
> memory. I was the young man you spoke to
> in church one night. I had overdosed on her-
> oin and didn't even know I was in a church; I
> was totally out of touch with reality and
> didn't have a clue as to how I got there. Sud-
> denly, I was dimly aware that somebody had
> walked up to me, put an arm around me and
> whispered something to me. In my fogged
> mental condition, I heard these words from
> Scripture: "It will be well with you."
> My head was like an echo chamber, and
> those words reverberated through my mind.
> Every time they echoed, my mind got clearer.
> The words continued to bounce back and

forth — "It will be well with you. It will be
well with you. It will be well with you...."
My mind was clearer and clearer until finally
I was completely sober. When I looked
around, I realized that I was in church. The
pastor was dismissing the congregation, but
he suddenly stopped and said, "God just
spoke to me and said there is a miracle happening out there. Who is it? Make yourself
known because you need further ministry."

I acknowledged that it was I. The pastor
and others who were there laid hands on me
and prayed. Right there in front of all the
people, I became born again and Spirit-filled.
I was also immediately set free from addiction to heroin. While I was speaking in
tongues, the Lord called me to preach the
gospel. God is good! Dick, will you come
and minister at my church?

Of course, Dick and Betty went, and they had a wonderful time.

What wonder-working power resides in God's Word!

Then they cried to the Lord in their trouble,
and he saved them from their distress. He
sent forth his word and healed them; he res-
cued them from the grave. Let them give
thanks to the Lord for his unfailing love and
his wonderful deeds for men (Ps. 107:19-21).

Glory to God for the Bible! If only all men and
women would devote themselves to reading and obeying it, honoring it and advancing its claims.

However, the Bible is not an end in itself; rather it is
the God-given means to an end. Indeed, we have been
"born again, not of perishable seed, but of imperishable,

through the living and enduring word of God" (1 Pet. 1:23). Yet the goal of this new birth is not that we might have a relationship with the Bible, but that we might have relationship with God — its Author! In other words, the written Word was given to lead us into relationship with the living Word.

We must not assume that academic knowledge of Scripture is the same as a personal relationship with Jesus Christ. Otherwise we ourselves would become a new breed of Pharisees, presuming that we have life through searching the Scriptures, while never coming to know the Lord.

Jesus said, "You diligently study the Scriptures because you think that by them you possess eternal life. These are the Scriptures that testify about me, yet you refuse to come to me to have life" (John 5:39-40). Even in the time of Christ, the most ardent, God-fearing men reasoned that their understanding of Scripture was equivalent to knowing God, and they therefore settled into the false security of their religious knowledge. The apostle Paul would later write of these people:

> For I can testify about them that they are zealous for God, but their zeal is not based on knowledge. Since they did not know the righteousness that comes from God and sought to establish their own, they did not submit to God's righteousness (Rom. 10:2-3).

How tragic it is that people have taken the very book which should lead them to God and used it as a means of functioning apart from Him in self-righteousness!

God has given us His Word that we might know Him. As we take time to read the Bible, God will reveal Himself to us on at least two levels: historical truth and personal revelation.

Historical Truth

The Bible is the historical revelation not only of God's words but also of His ways, His works and His will. In fact, all we may know about God is revealed to us in the Bible. Even when nature shows us something of His character, we will still find a proof text for it in the Scripture. Jesus Christ is "the Word of God made flesh," giving us the full revelation of the Father. However, we still only know of Jesus Himself through the Scripture. There is simply no way around the Bible in getting to God. It is the historical revelation of Himself to mankind. For that reason we are to obey wholeheartedly as though God looked us directly in the eye and spoke the words audibly right to our face.

When, for example, Jesus said to take up your cross and follow Him (Luke 9:23); He did not leave it open for discussion. And when He said to seek first the kingdom of God (Matt. 6:33), He meant for each one of us to take it personally. It is God's Word. We do not need some special witness from the Spirit, some confirming token whereby we finally understand that He is actually speaking this to us. When asked for a supernatural witness to prove His claims, Jesus answered, "If they do not listen to Moses and the Prophets, they will not be convinced even if someone rises from the dead" (Luke 16:31).

Jesus commanded His disciples to go into all the world and make disciples of all nations (Matt. 28:19). No one could deny that we are each accountable to do this even though Jesus did not actually say those words to us, but to the eleven disciples on the mount before He ascended. It is the historical Word of God and, as such, has resident authority that does not change with time, place or recipient. When the Bible says clear things, we are to clearly do them!

A person once said, "The Bible troubles me because there are parts of it I just don't understand!"

Upon hearing that remark, Will Rogers, the famous American humorist, responded, "The Bible troubles me because there are parts of it that I do understand!"

This is historical revelation. God has spoken; we are to obey. Any questions?

Personal Revelation

Personal revelation occurs when the Spirit of God shows us a verse or portion of Scripture that impacts us dramatically. While the verse may, in fact, be taken completely out of its historical context, it nevertheless has direct bearing on some immediate situation we are facing, giving us much-needed insight, patience and hope. All believers could give many examples of the Lord speaking to them in this way because it is common throughout the body of Christ — not only in modern times, but in early Christian experience as well. Take, for example, fourth-century Augustine of Hippo.

After years of searching for God, Augustine lay crying under a fig tree in his garden. Suddenly he heard a childlike voice repeating, "Take it and read." He thought children were playing next door, but he could not remember any such phrase in a child's game. Finally, he decided that God was speaking to him, so he picked up his Bible, opened it at random and read Romans 13:13-14.

> Let us behave decently, as in the daytime, not in orgies and drunkenness, not in sexual immorality and debauchery, not in dissension and jealousy. Rather, clothe yourselves with the Lord Jesus Christ, and do not think about how to gratify the desires of the sinful nature.

These words spoke so directly to Augustine that he later wrote, "My heart was filled with the light of confidence and all the shadows of my doubt were swept away." This climactic narration of Augustine's conversion is found in the story of his life, *Confessions*, and serves as a credible example of God speaking to us intimately from the Scripture.

In 1517 Martin Luther was twenty-six years old. Burdened with guilt, trying desperately to find forgiveness for his sins, he submitted himself to the ordinances of the church and went to Rome on a pilgrimage. Wherever he turned for help, all anyone could tell him was, "Pray harder; be more devout; deny yourself."

Then, in a show of complete desperation, Martin Luther crawled on broken glass and bones up the chapel steps as an act of contrition. All of a sudden, the Holy Spirit brought to his mind a verse of Scripture. "The just shall live by his faith" (Hab. 2:4, KJV). The power of those words brought him to his senses. He swept the bones and glass off the steps, stood to his feet as a man and lit the fire of reformation!

Now we tell everyone, "You can get to heaven. You don't buy your way in; you don't earn your way in; you don't crawl from here to eternity to get in. You stand up and walk by faith in the name of Jesus!"

It was after this that Martin Luther wrote one of the great hymns of the Christian faith, "A Mighty Fortress Is Our God." The third verse shows how impacted he was by the revelation that God had given him.

> And though this world, with devils filled,
> Should threaten to undo us,
> We will not fear, for God hath willed
> His truth to triumph through us.
> The prince of darkness grim —
> We tremble not for him;
> His rage we can endure,
> For lo! his doom is sure.
> One little word shall fell him.

More than a century later, God spoke "one little word" to John Wesley. In his day, it took a whole year to become a Christian in the Church of England. Those who desired to be converted were required to sign up for a one-year Bible course. At the end of the year, the prospective convert was drilled with three hundred questions called the catechism. If the answers were correct, then the individual went through confirmation and was thereafter considered a Christian.

John Wesley was struck by the unreasonable difficulties this process posed to many. What would happen, for instance, if someone had an incurable disease and did not have a year to live? Or what about those who were struggling long hours at work just to survive, with no time in their lives to devote to studying the faith? And consider the countless illiterate: how could they come to know the Lord if they were unable to meet the requirements of this course? The catechism was only for the educated, the affluent — those people capable of disciplined study.

Pressed with conviction from the Lord and perplexed by the confusion of the religious system, Wesley gave himself to prayer and fasting. The Lord answered him at Aldersgate. A flame from heaven came down and burned into his heart a great passion to see people come into the kingdom of God. The Lord gave him a word — one little word: " 'In the time of my favor I heard you, and in the day of salvation I helped you.' I tell you, *now* is the time of God's favor, *now* is the day of salvation" (2 Cor. 6:2, italics added).

Wesley wrote later in his journal:

> About a quarter before nine, while he was describing the change which God works in the heart through faith in Christ, I felt my heart strangely warmed. I felt I did trust in Christ, in Christ alone, for my salvation; and

an assurance was given me that he had taken
away my sins, even mine, and saved me from
the law of sin and death.[1]

John Wesley was so compelled by this revelation that
he told people they didn't have to wait for a year before
they could be saved. They could be converted right now
— today! He introduced the church to "instantaneous
conversion" and lit the fires of revival that spread
around the world!

Today we preach to all who will listen: The door is
open. Come in! You don't have to sign up for a year's
course of study. You can meet Jesus now because *now* is
the accepted time; *today* is the day of salvation. Glory to
God for that one little word.

In the late 1800s Charles G. Finney, a renowned law-
yer, had a dramatic conversion. He described it as liquid
waves of fire flooding him. During this transforming
experience with the Holy Spirit, God called him to be an
evangelist. Afterward, Finney went to western New
York to tell a Presbyterian pastor friend what had happened to him. His arrival coincided with a large conference this pastor was hosting. With excitement he
attended the conference and watched as his friend
preached to fifteen hundred people about the advan-
tages of righteousness, the beauty of holiness and the
bliss of being in heaven with God forever. He sensed the
presence of the Holy Spirit brooding over the congregation, causing conviction in many hearts. To Finney's
astonishment, the pastor then concluded and dismissed
the service.

After the meeting, Finney expressed his perplexity
to his friend. "I don't understand," he said. "You told
everybody how beautiful it is to be with the Lord for
eternity, but you didn't give anybody a chance to respond."

The pastor told him, "Charles, you are young and

have a lot to learn. God has sovereignly designed this whole thing. The people who are going to be saved are going to be saved, and nothing can keep them away from the Lord. The people who are not going to be saved can fast and pray, join the church, give, sacrifice, deny themselves, but they can never change God's mind. The reason I didn't give an altar call is because the wrong people might have come forward."

Finney was dumbfounded. To call people to church, preach the gospel and not give them a chance to become converted seemed the most illogical thing in the world. He spent three sleepless nights and three foodless days out in the woods, waiting on God, questioning, "God, I don't understand all this." On the morning of the third day, as the sun came up, Charles Finney heard a word from God that rolled the stone away and brought him forth to life.

> The Spirit and the bride say, "Come!" And let him who hears say, "Come!" Whoever is thirsty, let him come; and whoever wishes, let him take the free gift of the water of life (Rev. 22:17).

Finney came out of the woods with an evangelistic anointing that challenged and changed a nation. His first sermon was titled "I want to tell you why you are not a Christian."

He explained to people that God willed everyone to be saved and come to the knowledge of the truth. He told them that the only reason they were not saved was because they had not done what God had said: "Come to me, all you who are weary and burdened, and I will give you rest" (Matt. 11:28). Finney's message was simple. If men would come to Jesus, the Lord would do the rest. In colonial America over the next nine years, three million people were born again!

And now, as we stand on the threshold of the twenty-first century, we proclaim boldly to all, "Come, all you who are thirsty, come to the waters; and you who have no money, come, buy and eat! Come, buy wine and milk without money and without cost" (Is. 55:1).

What power there is in "one little word" from God. Solomon said, "Where the word of a king is, there is power" (Eccl. 8:4, NKJV). Certainly, therefore, when the King of kings speaks, awesome things happen. What "one little word" might God speak to you that could change the course of history yet again? Take your Bible and read it with expectation for the Lord to speak such a word to you.

Yet the excitement of faith must be balanced with the caution of wisdom. For sometimes these "personal words" are subjective and must be regarded with utmost honesty.

> The heart is deceitful above all things and beyond cure. Who can understand it? (Jer. 17:9).

It is therefore very easy for people to fabricate the Scripture into a cleverly woven "word from the Lord," only to be led into deception and heartbreak. The sad stories of those who have done this could fill volumes. Shattered lives, broken homes and divided churches all bear witness to the destructive power of deceptive revelation.

> There is a way that seems right to a man, but in the end it leads to death (Prov. 14:12).

Jesus Himself was tempted in this regard when Satan said, "If you are the Son of God...throw yourself down. For it is written: 'He will command his angels concerning you, and they will lift you up in their hands, so that you will not strike your foot against a stone' " (Matt. 4:6).

Notice how Satan will seek to use the Scripture against us when he sees that we rely so much upon it. By doing so he hopes to seize us with perplexity, apprehension and isolation, making it easier for him to defeat us in any situation. Indeed, how many great warriors has he vanquished through the misquoting of Scripture? It is imperative that we know the Bible well enough to answer his twisted texts in the same way Jesus answered him, "It is *also* written" (Matt. 4:7, italics added).

A great safeguard against this form of deception is to certify whatever "revelation" we have received with other Scripture passages that support it strongly. The Bible says, "Every matter must be established by the testimony of two or three witnesses" (2 Cor. 13:1).

Another safeguard is submission. Let others examine your "words from God" and heed their input. If the Lord is indeed speaking to you, the words will always have these three distinguishing traits. First, the word you have received will be *relevant* to what you are facing, without having to be forced to fit — and others will see it as clearly as you do. It will also bring *revelation* — a clear understanding of what the Lord wants you to do and the faith and wisdom to do it. Finally, it will be *redemptive* — leading you into a deeper relationship with the Lord Jesus Christ and to more commitment to His church. Any so-called word from God that fails in any of these three tests, even if it comes through the Scripture, is to be discarded as fictitious and deceptive.

The Chains Are Gone!

Recently I received a word from the Lord that serves as an excellent example of a relevant, revealing and redemptive use of "personalized" Scripture. I cele-

brated my fortieth birthday in October 1990 with a thoroughly enjoyable party with many of my friends — despite the black balloons, corny jokes and funeral dirges
of those who "mourned my passing." Yet I had a deeper
reason to look forward eagerly to this significant time.

A few months earlier the Lord brought to my mind all
that had transpired in my life over the years, both before
and after I had come to know Him. I sensed Him saying,
"For you, James, life really does begin at forty. In the
second twenty years of your life I have undone all that
Satan did against you during the first twenty years of
your life, and I have given you 20/20 vision to know the
things of My Spirit and My Word."

I somehow understood that the date which would
mark the timing of this promise would not be my actual
birthdate in October, but rather December 22, 1990 —
the twentieth anniversary of my release from the Texas
State Penitentiary.

When that day arrived I was filled with anticipation
that the Lord would speak to me in some unmistakable
way, and I was not disappointed. Reading in the book of
Jeremiah during a devotional quiet time, I came to chapter 40 (an interesting number in light of my expecta-
tions), and the word of the Lord ignited in me when I
read the fourth verse: "Today I am freeing you from the
chains on your wrists."

Now as a matter of contextual accuracy these are the
words of the captain of the guard upon the occasion of
Jeremiah's release from the dungeon of Malchiah (see
Jer. 38:6, KJV). Clearly, the historical circumstance of
this verse had no bearing on my life at all. Nevertheless,
in my heart it was the Lord speaking to me personally,
confirming my release into His purposes for my life as
a man of God.

How truly marvelous that the Holy Spirit would
show me this verse on the very day when I was celebrat-
ing the twentieth anniversary of my release from prison!

(On second thought, maybe it was just a coincidence!)

Drawing me even deeper, the Holy Spirit then reminded me of the passage in Isaiah 26:13-14:

> O Lord our God, other masters besides You have ruled over us, but we will acknowledge and mention Your name only. They [the former tyrant masters] are dead, they shall not live and reappear; they are powerless ghosts, they shall not rise and come back. Therefore You have visited and made an end of them, and caused every memorial of them [every trace of their supremacy] to perish (AMP).

How amazing that these words of Scripture written so very long ago would have such a timely and uncanny application to my life. And as anyone who knows me would attest, I do not bear any marks of my former life. The "chains" are no longer upon my hands; the "other lords" are indeed gone. The Lord Jesus has visited my life and destroyed the works of darkness. Like the Hebrew children who were redeemed from the fiery furnace, I — by the grace of God — have come forth from the furnace of adversity without even the smell of smoke on me (Dan. 3:27). Glory to God in the highest!

Honor Your Father and Your Mother

Growing up the way that I did naturally left large holes in my personality which the Lord has patiently and lovingly healed and filled. The Bible says, "When my father and my mother forsake me, then the Lord will take me up" (Ps. 27:10, KJV). I received a deep revelation of God as my Father at a crucial point in my Christian life.

Sitting in a seminar listening to a teacher discuss fatherhood, I felt distant and depressed. I had no framework for relating to what the man was saying. His illustrations, while delighting everyone else attending the session, made little sense to me. I couldn't wait for the teaching to end so I could get away. Then, right before he closed, this man said, "It occurs to me that there might be a man here who did not know his father and perhaps feels that he is missing out on something." That statement captured my attention, to be sure; but what he said next captured my heart!

He rolled off a list of names of men from the Bible who had been used greatly by God throughout biblical history. Among the names he mentioned were Moses, Samuel and Jesus. He pointed out that one thing these men had in common was that each was raised apart from his natural father (even Jesus was raised by a step-father). Then this teacher said, "You see, you have not missed out on anything. For it seems that when God destines a man for greatness, He Himself does the fathering by placing him in situations apart from the normal course of everyday life!" That single statement opened wide a door of hope for me. I ran through it into the affirmation of God, who has been even more than a Father to me.

Later I had an experience while on a ministry trip to Holland which confirmed my heavenly Father's faithfulness in my life. I was part of the ministry team and was scheduled to preach on the final evening of the conference. I spent my free time in the afternoons walking about the retreat grounds, visiting with various people and taking in the sights. When my turn to minister arrived, I felt led to share my testimony with the people there. The Holy Spirit touched many men and women with the love of God, setting them free and filling them with much joy.

The following morning as we were preparing to leave for the airport, an old gentleman approached me to say good-bye. He took a firm hold of my hand, politely refusing to let go, and he began to weep softly as he said to me in broken English, "I must ask your forgiveness."

"Whatever for?" I asked in return.

"All week I have watched you walk about the campus, smiling and laughing, being so happy; and I judged you in my heart," he said. "I thought that you were a typical 'all-American boy' who always had everything he ever wanted, who never knew hardship of any kind and who had nothing to say to me. I wondered who you thought you were to come here and talk to us. I am ashamed to say that I did not like you very much!"

I smiled as he said these things because I knew God had done something in his heart.

"Last night when you told us your story," he continued, "I realized how terribly wrong I was. I am so sorry for judging you as I did. Please forgive me."

I hugged this dear man and assured him of my forgiveness. Then he said these parting words which I shall never forget: "You said last night that God was your Father, and you are right. He has done an excellent job in raising you as His son, for there is no trace left of what you used to be!" The Scripture is true. "When my father and my mother forsake me, then the *Lord* will take me up" (Ps. 27:10, KJV, italics added).

But the story doesn't end here. A couple of years later, during a tender time of worship at a Vineyard healing conference, I felt troubled. "God," I said, "You are a great Father, and I love everything You have done for me, and I wouldn't change anything that has happened — but don't I get to have a mother? Most people have a father and a mother. What about me?"

That is when the Holy Spirit showed me a truth I prize to this day. "James," He said, "the church has been your mother."

I saw it as soon as He spoke those words. The people of God have indeed been like a mother to me. They brought me forth at my new birth and held me close in loving acceptance and affirmation. They drew me near to their hearts and nursed me on the milk of the Word. They hushed my crying and filled me with laughter time and time again. They even changed my soiled diapers in the early days when I made a mess everywhere I went! They endured my insufferable sermons as I tried to find exactly what it was I was trying to say. They watched me grow and encouraged me every step of the way. I stand as a man of God today, greatly indebted to His people, who patiently loved me toward wholeness.

What a revelation that was to me. I have never recovered from it, nor shall I. As I knelt there, staggered by love, I heard the Holy Spirit clearly saying, "James, honor your Father and your mother that your days may be long upon the earth!" That was when I fell irretrievably in love with God and His church — my Father and my mother — and for all of my days I will live to bring them honor!

Entrusted With the Gospel

Several years ago I awakened one morning with a terrible pain in my upper right jawbone. It would not subside despite prayer and medicine. The dentist informed me that I had an abscess and that he could do nothing until the infection cleared up. He put me on antibiotics and gave me strong pain relievers, but the medicine had no measurable effect on the pain. Rather it increased to excruciating levels.

I was deeply distressed and confused because this came at a time when my relationship with the Lord was particularly strong and vital. I could think of no reason why this affliction should be unattended by His merciful intervention. As I earnestly sought Him concerning this, He recalled to me an incident that had occurred several years earlier.

At that time my young daughter had fallen ill with a

fever, and I'd prayed God would heal her. My prayers seemed totally ineffectual, so, in my immature anger, I literally flung the Bible across the room, accusing God of never doing what the Bible says He will do. Well, after a few days my daughter did recover, and I repented before the Lord for how I had handled the situation. Now the Lord brought up that incident and asked me if I remembered it. I answered, "Yes, I remember that, Lord, but I thought You were supposed to forget it" (see Jer. 31:34).

The Lord assured me that He indeed had "forgotten" it, but that Satan had not. On that night so long ago, Satan saw me throw my Bible in anger as I challenged God's faithfulness, and he took note. Now that I was doing well in my walk with the Lord, the evil one sought an occasion against me. Armed with a weapon that I had given him, Satan issued this challenge to the Father: "I know what will make him curse You to Your face. Let me afflict him, and then withhold Your hand when he calls to You. You will see that he will act as before. Nothing has changed!" Satan had assaulted Job in a similar way (see Job 2:5).

Having revealed this to me in the spirit, the Lord then said to me, "My son, be wise, and make my heart glad, that I may answer him who reproaches me (Prov. 27:11, NKJV).

The Father gave Satan permission to do this to me in order to give me the opportunity to take back what I had given up so long ago. The battle was on. Despite all attempts to ease it, the pain increased. Words cannot describe how awful it was. My only cry was that my faith fail not, regardless of how long this was to last. I was set in my resolve to honor the Lord through the duration of this terrible trial, finding comfort in Job's confession, "Though he slay me, yet will I trust in him" (Job 13:15, KJV).

Late one evening, I became so angry with Satan that

I opened my window and shouted out at him, "If you
think this pain is going to make me curse the Lord, then
you are sadly mistaken! Just listen to this," I yelled, and
then I began to sing at the top of my voice, "All hail the
power of Jesus' name; let angels prostrate fall!" Just at
that moment the porch lights turned on at my neighbor's
house. Not meaning to wake anybody up, I continued
undaunted, though in a much softer voice: "Bring forth
the royal diadem, and crown Him Lord of all!" I'm not
afraid of the devil, but as for my neighbor — that's a
different situation altogether!

The terrible ordeal continued with little relief for several days. The pain was so dreadful that I was unable to
eat or sleep. The only rest I got was when I would mo-
mentarily pass out in total exhaustion, merely to be
awakened again by the piercing throb of relentless pain.
What I'm trying to tell you is, It hurt! After two full
weeks I was physically drained. My face was ashen, my
eyes bloodshot, my hair stringy. I sat on the bed with a
blanket draped over my shoulders, rocking slowly back
and forth, unable to muster much more than a moan.

Suddenly and wonderfully, my bedroom filled with
the presence of the Holy Spirit. I could sense the life-
giving breath of God sparking my frail spirit with
strength. I reached for my Bible and opened it randomly
to these words:

> At Gibeon the Lord appeared to Solomon
> during the night in a dream, and God said,
> "Ask for whatever you want me to give you"
> (1 Kin. 3:5).

Joy floods my heart even now as I relive those precious moments. It was as if the Lord stood right before
me, saying those very words to me! I was overcome
with great emotion and prayed through broken sobs,
"Lord, all I ask of You is that my faith fail not. However

much longer this affliction has to last, my prayer is that my faith fail not!"

I was suddenly filled with the sense of God's great pleasure. How pleased the Lord was with what I had asked Him to do. I was so overcome with joy that I began to laugh uncontrollably. My dear wife entered the room thinking I had surely lost my mind! I tried to assure her that I was really quite all right, but the joy was so full I could hardly speak. I also knew in that moment that I had beaten Satan; I had successfully taken back from the enemy what I had given him those years ago. In the peace of those moments I drifted off to sleep. When I awakened the following day I noticed a measurable decrease of the pain. By mid afternoon it was all but gone. The battle was indeed over. And I had won!

The next morning as I was reading in the Scripture, the Lord quickened these words to me:

> We have been approved by God as worthy of being entrusted with the Good News, that approval being based upon the fact that we had met His requirements. Thus we are speaking, not as pleasing men but as pleasing God who puts His approval upon our hearts after we have met the test to which He has subjected us (1 Thess. 2:4, Wuest).

Having read these words I sensed the Holy Spirit say to me, "James, I have tested you and found you trustworthy. I now entrust you with the ministry of proclaiming the gospel of Jesus Christ." I treasure these words from the Lord, holding them in my heart with the deepest regard, for they marked the moment of my commission. He who ordained me and called me had now authorized me to preach the word of the Lord. And He has never failed to back up that authorization with His presence and His power.

As a footnote to this story I should add that I did go back to the dentist after this. He injected my gums with an abundance of novocaine and extracted five teeth at once — and that's the closest I've ever come to being an "empty-headed numbskull"! Yet, despite what I'd lost, it is what I gained through that experience that causes me to hold it so fondly in my memories.

These few personal examples illustrate how God can and does speak to us intimately through the Scriptures. Over and over again I have found the truth of Paul's words:

> For everything that was written in the past was written to teach us, so that through endurance and the encouragement of the Scriptures we might have hope (Rom. 15:4).

My prayer then is that God will fill your life with even more wonderful testimonies of how He speaks through His Word. Regardless of your circumstances, I encourage you to read the Bible expecting the Holy Spirit to speak to you. There will be no doubt in your mind when He does, for the message will be relevant, revealing and redemptive. And the testimony you give to others will fill them with faith and hope in God! ❀

Chapter 5

God Speaks Through Prophetic Ministry

In Ephesians 4:7-13 we read, "But to each one of us grace has been given as Christ apportioned it. This is why it says: 'When he ascended on high, he led captives in his train and gave gifts to men.' (What does 'he ascended' mean except that he also descended to the lower, earthly regions? He who descended is the very one who ascended higher than all the heavens, in order to fill the whole universe.)

"It was he who gave some to be apostles, some to be prophets, some to be evangelists, and some to be pastors and teachers, to prepare God's people for works of service, so that the body of Christ may be built up until we all reach unity in the faith and in the knowledge of the Son of God and become mature, attaining to the whole measure of the fullness of Christ."

Apostles, prophets, evangelists, pastors and teachers: according to Scripture, these are the ministries which Jesus Christ gave to His church to equip her for service. There does not appear to be any rank or preference of one ministry above another, for each is as essential as the other. That is how the Lord gave them, and that is how they were to be received.

Yet today, only three of these five gifts are widely accepted throughout the body of Christ (that is, evangelist, pastor and teacher). The remaining two are held at arm's length and viewed with awkward suspicion by many within the mainstream of evangelical Christianity. In other words, if I were to describe myself as a pastor, a teacher or an evangelist, most Christians would not think twice about my claim. But should I say that I am a prophet, or be so bold as to say I am an apostle, I would raise more than a few eyebrows. For the record, I am not saying I am either.

Perhaps the reluctance to embrace apostolic and prophetic ministry is because of the confusion that often surrounds both the theological and practical expressions of these gifts, as well as the generally bizarre characteristics exhibited by some of those who minister in these giftings. This is an understandable caution that can be addressed through sound teaching and example.

However, another basis exists for rejecting apostolic and prophetic ministry — one which is not so easily corrected. There are a few who believe that these ministries are no longer needed and therefore denounce any claim of their validity in the modern era of church life. Those holding this view cite as a proof text the often-quoted verses of 1 Corinthians 13:8-10:

Love never fails. But where there are prophecies, they will cease; where there are tongues, they will be stilled; where there is knowledge, it will pass away. For we know in part and we prophesy in part, but when perfection comes, the imperfect disappears.

The interpretive key here seems to be "when that which is perfect" (KJV) has come. Some argue strongly that this refers to the Bible and go so far as to insist that since we now have the sacred canon of Scripture, we no longer need the prophetic ministry. That position seems highly questionable and extremely weak. If the Bible is indeed "that which is perfect," then exactly which translation are we talking about? How can something "perfect" come in so many differing versions? Furthermore, if indeed the Bible is "that which is perfect," does this mean that we now know even as we are known — that we now see the Lord face-to-face as the Corinthian text clearly states? I think not.

To reject the prophetic ministry is to reject the Lord who deemed it a worthy gift for strengthening His body on the earth. And, according to the passage at the opening of this chapter, this ministry is to take place "until we all reach unity in the faith and in the knowledge of the Son of God and become mature, attaining to the whole measure of the fullness of Christ" (Eph. 4:13).

This clearly has not happened yet, so the ministry must still be — by the unalterable decree of God — a valid work of the Holy Spirit within the church today! Therefore, let us give place to it. Then, when that which is perfect is come (that is, the return of the Lord Jesus Christ to earth), all these ministries — apostle, prophet, evangelist, pastor and teacher — will be done away with. But the "doing away with" them will be because they are *unnecessary*, not because they are *unwanted*.

I believe much confusion could be cleared up by viewing each of these ministries as functions to be fulfilled rather than titles or offices to be held. When a title is bestowed upon an individual, it carries with it inherent authority. And certainly the issue of authority is critical as it relates to the question of the apostolic and prophetic ministry. We all affirm the divine inspiration and authority of the holy Scriptures written by the prophets and apostles of old. But it must be understood that those who function today in the apostolic and prophetic ministries in no way aspire, nor are they destined, to be counted as equal in authority and inspiration with those we historically embrace as the holy prophets of God and the apostles of the Lord Jesus Christ.

In fact, there are clear examples in Scripture which, upon close examination, show that even the prophets of the New Testament did not always speak with divine authority or with 100 percent accuracy. The disciples of Tyre said to Paul "by the Spirit" that he should not go to Jerusalem (see Acts 21:4), but Paul went anyway. Evidently he did not consider this to be disobedience to the word of the Lord even though the word was spoken "by the Spirit." The prophet Agabus gave further insight into what awaited Paul in Jerusalem.

> After we had been there a number of days, a prophet named Agabus came down from Judea. Coming over to us, he took Paul's belt, tied his own hands and feet with it and said, "The Holy Spirit says, 'In this way the Jews of Jerusalem will bind the owner of this belt and will hand him over to the Gentiles' " (Acts 21:10-11).

We know as a matter of historical fact (see Acts 21:33) that it was the Romans, not the Jews, who bound Paul. Also, the Jews did not voluntarily hand him over but rather tried to kill him (Acts 21:31), causing the Romans to take Paul from them by force just to save his life! Clearly the circumstances did not happen exactly as Agabus prophesied. Yet, despite these inconsistencies, Agabus is nonetheless acknowledged as "a prophet" by the Holy Spirit in the New Testament.

Prophetic ministry clearly played a crucial role in the life of the first-century church. Paul even says that the church's foundation is built upon the apostles and the prophets, Jesus Christ Himself being the cornerstone (Eph. 2:20). From the very outset of the church's empowerment on the day of Pentecost, we are told to expect our sons and daughters to "prophesy" (Acts 2:17). It seems that one of the principal distinctions of the church at its inception was that we would be a prophetic people — a group of men and women, old and young alike, who could hear and speak words from God.

Further experiences in the book of Acts show the unchallenged presence of prophets. Agabus is one of the more notable, gaining credibility by prophesying a great famine that occurred during the reign of Claudius Caesar (Acts 11:28). Besides Agabus, there were also Judas and Silas, who said and did much to encourage and strengthen the churches (Acts 15:30-33).

Paul himself was no stranger to the prophetic word. The first Christian ever to greet him was Ananias, who said that Jesus appeared in a vision and told him to lay hands on Paul (Acts 9:10-18). Then it was the prophets in the church at Antioch to whom the Holy Spirit said, "Set apart for me Barnabas and Saul [whom we know as Paul] for the work to which I have called them" (Acts 13:2). Finally, Paul's own teachings make it very clear that God set prophets in the church, along with the other ministry gifts, as it pleased Him.

> God has arranged the parts in the body, every one of them, just as he wanted them to be....And in the church God has appointed first of all apostles, second prophets, third

teachers, then workers of miracles, also those having gifts of healing, those able to help others, those with gifts of administration, and those speaking in different kinds of tongues (1 Cor. 12:18, 28).

The prophetic ministry that has continued since the New Testament era must not be despised. We need to be told this because our natural inclination is to do this very thing. When someone approaches you saying, "I have a word from the Lord for you," what is your first tendency? And how many times have you rolled your eyes and moaned quietly as brother Joe or sister Sue timidly shared a "word from the Lord" with the church? Paul admonishes the Christians of Thessalonica, "Do not treat prophecies with contempt. Test everything. Hold on to the good" (1 Thess. 5:20-21).

Rather than dismissing prophecy as insignificant, we are to "test" prophetic words for the purpose of holding on to what is of the Lord, kindly disposing of that which is not. In light of this, consider the word which the Lord spoke to Jeremiah:

> Therefore, thus says the Lord, "If you return, then I will restore you — before Me you will stand; and if you extract the precious from the worthless, you will become My spokesman" (Jer. 15:19, NAS).

As we hear prophetic words, we are responsible to extract the precious from the worthless in order that we may have a proven and trustworthy "word from the Lord" to pass on to others.

The fundamental goals of true prophetic ministry are edification, exhortation and comfort. Paul said that we are all to aspire to prophesy because it would edify and strengthen the church.

> Follow the way of love and eagerly desire
> spiritual gifts, especially the gift of prophecy
> (1 Cor. 14:1).

As we pursue this gift for the good of the body, some among us will undoubtedly exhibit a distinctive anointing from God for greater insight and accuracy. We ought to give these their place, understanding that while they do not hold the historic stature of the prophets of old, their ministries are nevertheless as valid and as vital to the church today as those of their predecessors were. As God is pleased to speak through prophetic ministry, we for our part should receive it with grateful hearts.

But how does prophecy come? The Holy Spirit inspires us to speak through any number of means. Sudden memory of a relevant text from Scripture, intuitive knowledge, inward impressions or spontaneous utterance — these are but a few of the ways.

When we speak of prophetic ministry, it is to be understood that we mean the communication of the word of the Lord by preaching, teaching or other forms of inspired utterance such as singing, praying and specific revelation, to an individual or to an entire congregation. Think for a moment how many times the word of the Lord has impacted you through a sermon your minister was preaching. How could he have known the things you were struggling with all week? How could he have known that you had asked the Lord a question during the morning prayer time and were now getting a direct answer through the message he was preaching?

Going the Distance

Not long ago, I received a letter from a family in my congregation telling me of a remarkable thing the Lord had done as a result of my Sunday sermon. A friend of the family had recently experienced the heartbreak of divorce. Her twenty-one-year marriage had come to an abrupt end when her husband had left her late that autumn. The emotional anguish and terrible depression moved this broken lady to seek the Lord's help in her life. When she turned to her friends for direction and comfort, they brought her to church. She was warmly greeted and made to feel at home and so continued attending for the following few weeks.

One Sunday morning she awoke with mixed feelings about going to church that day. As she would later describe it, she forced herself to get out of bed and get dressed. It was a battle for her every step of the way. Even as she drove toward the church, she was still being torn between going or turning back home and succumbing to depression. The struggle grew so intense that she drove right past the church, deciding not to go after all. About a mile down the road, she said, "No, Satan! I'm going to go to church today!" With that she turned her car around and went to the worship service.

My sermon on that Sunday morning was titled "Going the Distance." It addressed the importance of enduring hardship as good soldiers of Christ Jesus. I introduced my remarks by reading, "Blessed is the man who perseveres under trial, because when he has stood the test, he will receive the crown of life that God has promised to those who love him" (James 1:12). Then I gave a stirring example of endurance by recounting the life of a man who attained greatness in American and world history:

> This man failed in his first attempt at business. He then tried politics and within only one year failed there also. He went back to business for yet another try and failed again. Three failures in three years. He asked his fiancée to marry him after four years of courtship, but she said no. Later, another

sweetheart died. He struggled for the next two years and suffered a nervous breakdown. After taking two years to recover, he tried once again in the political world and was defeated in his bid to be elected as speaker of the House.

Two years later he sought to be appointed as the elector and was again defeated. Three years after this, he ran for a seat in Congress and was defeated. He waited another five years to run for office again and was defeated. It was during this time that his four-year-old son died. He spent the next seven years in relative obscurity and then ran yet again for a political office — this time in the Senate. Again he was defeated. The following year, he was nominated by his party to be the candidate for vice president, but he was defeated along with his running mate in the general election. After two more years he tried again for the Senate seat but was defeated. Then, two years later in 1860, *Abraham Lincoln* was elected as the sixteenth president of the United States! Twenty-four years of sheer endurance!

After the story, knowing nothing of the woman's inner battle, I quoted Emerson, "There is no difference between heroes and ordinary people; the hero just fights five minutes longer."[1] I challenged the people never to stop believing that God would come through for them — even in the darkest of circumstances. "Just fight for five more minutes!"

Can you imagine how captivated by the Holy Spirit this dear lady had become? Her friends who first brought her to church reported later that she cried through the entire message. Never had a sermon been so fitted to her immediate need. The love of God filled her heart with such comfort and strength that it defeated the work of the evil one in her soul. For me it was another sermon; but for her it was the very word of the Lord!

In addition to God's use of sermons, consider also the impact of a prophecy being spoken directly, perhaps even unexpectedly, to any particular person. I have heard hundreds of prophetic words given to individuals and can hardly recall a single instance in which they were not positively and dramatically affected by the love of God, responding with adoration and dedication to the Lord Jesus Christ.

This then is why we are instructed to desire earnestly that we might prophesy. And speaking as one who prophesies, I can attest to the undeniable power of this ministry to build up those to whom it is directed. The prophetic word is truly a wonderful blessing in the lives of God's people. If for no other reason than this, I am resolved to give myself to it wholeheartedly for the rest of my life.

One great purpose of the prophetic ministry is to bring restoration into the lives of men and women. Historical examples of this are men like Haggai and Zechariah, who preached to the people of God as they were returning from captivity and helped them rebuild the destroyed temple of the Lord.

Malachi, a contemporary of Haggai and Zechariah, prophesied the coming of "Elijah" before the return of the Lord, saying that he would "turn the hearts of the fathers to their children, and the hearts of the children to their fathers" (Mal. 4:6). We know from the New Testament that, in one sense, John the Baptist was the fulfillment of Malachi's prophecy (Matt. 11:14). This is the closing promise of the Old Testament.

Whatever this may come to mean in its final fulfillment, one thing is clear: "Turning the hearts" of men and women toward one another in the purposes of God is a principal task of prophetic ministry.

A Reconciled Family

A dramatic example of this work of restoration occurred recently at a prophetic conference in Northern California. The pastor of the church that hosted the conference had been praying with his wife for over a year that their estranged daughter would return. She had run away without a trace. Months passed before the family heard from a minister in another city that their daughter was now married to a young man whom they knew. Still they had no address, nor any means of contacting them. They continued praying that God would intervene with His mercy and work a wonder of love on their behalf.

Meanwhile, in what seemed to be an unrelated turn of events, the young man who had married the pastor's daughter received a few of my teaching tapes in the mail from friends who thought he would enjoy hearing them. He was so touched while listening to the sermons that he asked the Lord to make it possible somehow for him to meet me. While he was praying, the Lord impressed upon him that it was time to repair the relationship with his wife's parents. The young man knew it was the Lord's will and made the commitment in prayer to take care of the matter.

Three days later, the young man received a brochure in the mail inviting him to register for this conference, which was in a city just forty miles away. I was to speak on "Hearing the Voice of God." His heart leapt within him upon seeing God answer his prayer so immediately. Then he noticed the venue for the conference and received the shock of his life: It was the very church where his father-in-law was the pastor! Now he knew that God was indeed up to something. He and his young wife filled in the registration form and sent it to the church. Imagine the joy of the parents when they saw those names on the registration sheet. They began praising God for what they knew was about to happen, sharing with their close friends the wonderful news that their daughter and son-in-law were coming home.

With great excitement they answered the knock at the door on the afternoon their children returned. There was much embracing and confession, repentance and forgiveness on everyone's part. They spent the day telling one another all that had happened over the past months. It was a wonderful time of reconciliation.

Later that evening, I was invited to the house for dinner. There in the dining room of the pastor's home, God answered many prayers. There I was, sitting across the table from the young man who had asked God for the opportunity to meet me. There, seated next to one another, were the children these parents had asked God to bring back into their lives. And there the prophetic word of Malachi came true dramatically as the heart of the father turned to the children, and the hearts of the children turned to the father. The Lord removed the curse that hung over that situation and, in its place, bestowed His blessing!

> How good and pleasant it is when brothers live together in unity! It is like precious oil poured on the head, running down on the beard, running down on Aaron's beard, down upon the collar of his robes. It is as if the dew of Hermon were falling on Mount Zion. For there the Lord bestows his blessing, even life forevermore (Psalm 133).

Before leaving, I shared this passage of Scripture with the family and prayed that God would bring it fully to pass in each of their lives.

The personal nature of most prophetic words, combined with the essential privacy of the individual, make it rather difficult to give examples of prophetic ministry. Yet the necessity of providing uncontrived illustrations is equally compelling. It is with the utmost care and discretion (and with the permission of the people identified) that I relate the following few testimonies of how God has spoken to His people through the rightful employment of the gift of prophecy.

Big Ed, the Evangelist

I was ministering in Southern California at a church pastored by Ed McGlasson. Ed and his wife, Jill, are close family friends. During a time of personal prophetic ministry, I looked at Ed and received an impression from the Lord to share with him.

"Ed, the Lord shows me that the cabinets are finished and, not many days from now, the goods will be in the cupboards. I see that the Lord is putting a mantle upon you for world evangelism such as we have seen faithfully accomplished in the ministry of Billy Graham. As you have played in the great stadiums of the world in times past, so you shall preach in those stadiums in the time to come."

Ed had been a professional athlete with the National Football League and throughout his career was in numerous stadiums. The power of the Lord came on him noticeably as these words were being shared, but beyond that there was not much else to show for the moment.

However, a few months later Ed called me to relate a most amazing testimony. His church had scheduled a men's retreat in the California mountains at a place called "Forrest Home." While they were there preparing for the evening session, a man informed the group casually that several years ago Billy Graham had been at this very retreat center and had experienced a powerful touch from God as he dedicated himself to preach the

Word of God to the world.

The man went on to say that there was a commemorative plaque on a large rock beside the lake at the top of the mountain, suggesting that the men might want to see it during their stay there. Ed was stunned to hear this and felt compelled to go at once to the top of the hill to see what God might say to him.

In the darkness of night Ed labored through the thick forest and up the steep hill. Although he found the lake easily enough, he could not find the rock which marked the place of Graham's encounter with God. At length he became exasperated. Feeling pressured for time, he chose simply to kneel at a great rock near him and cry out to God for the outpouring of the Holy Spirit. He knelt in the darkness, drawing his face near the surface of the large boulder. He then saw that it was the very rock he had been searching for! Upon the rock was a plaque with this inscription:

> To the praise of God for the life and ministry of Dr. Billy Graham, who had a life-changing encounter with God here at Forrest Home when, as a young preacher, he knelt with a Bible in his hand and promised God he would take the Bible by faith and preach it without reservation.

Suddenly the power of the Holy Spirit came upon Ed as he wept and rejoiced in the presence of almighty God. After the outpouring was complete, Ed rose to his feet and began making his way back down the mountain to meet with his men. The hike down took about half an hour. Ed told me that as he was descending the hill, the voice of God spoke to him: "Ed, the goods are in the cupboards!"

We find this passage about goods in Matthew 25:14 (KJV): "For the kingdom of heaven is as a man travelling into a far country, who called his own servants, and delivered unto them his goods." Again the Holy Spirit came upon him, confirming the work God was doing.

Ed arrived at the chalet and found all the men from his church, along with the worship leaders, lying prostrate upon the floor in silent adoration of the awesome presence of the Lord. Ed asked what was going on, and one of the men replied, "About thirty minutes ago the power of God came upon us in a mighty way, and we have been like this ever since." It happened at the same time God was touching Ed at the top of the hill!

I share this as an example of the prophetic word touching one man's life, but I must quickly add that this particular word is, in fact, for many whom the Lord is raising up in this hour to be "world-class" evangelists — men and women who will display the passion, integrity and faithfulness which have always characterized the life and ministry of Billy Graham. Let me explain why I believe this.

In May 1990 the national news service reported that Billy Graham had undergone surgery to remove a rib from his side. I found this report too significant to overlook. The biblical symbolism alone beckoned flights of inspired imagination. And the fact that it was Billy Graham compelled me to ask the Lord if He was possibly speaking through this incident. I believe that the Lord showed me this insight in response to my prayer.

Billy Graham, like Adam in the garden, is a representative, a prototype. He exemplifies all those who aspire to faithfulness and fruitfulness in the call to world evangelism, but in many ways he has been "alone in the garden," having no peers. Others have fallen from those great heights of visibility and influence, but he has stood.

The Lord said of Adam, "It is not good for the man to be alone. I will make a helper suitable for him" (Gen. 2:18). So it could also be said of Billy Graham. To

Adam the Lord gave Eve, and I believe that to Billy
Graham the Lord will give a legacy of faithful "Eve-an-
gelists"! Even in this very hour, the Lord is calling forth
men and women to a new commitment in world evangelism. I believe that Billy will be able to look upon this
great army of faithful witnesses and say as a spiritual
father, "They are bone of my bone; flesh of my flesh!"
Perhaps, dear reader, you are one of the very ones the
Lord is calling. If that be so, then may the power of the
Holy Spirit fall upon you as you read these words!

Olive Oyl and Popeye

Not long ago I concluded an evening sermon with
prophetic ministry directed toward various individuals
present in the church. As I was looking at the congregation, a lady on the right side of the platform caught my
eye. I looked at her and saw the cartoon character Olive
Oyl superimposed upon her face!

What's this? I thought and quickly looked to the
other side of the room to see if the Lord would show me
anything there. I ministered to a few people, but I could
not shake the vision I had seen.

Finally I turned to the lady and said, "I don't know
how else to say this, but when I look at you I see Olive
Oyl."

She was shocked. "That's what kids called me all
during my school years!" she exclaimed. "I can't stand
to hear that name anymore!"

The Lord then gave me remarkable insight into what
He was saying to this dear woman. I told her that the
name Olive Oyl symbolized something very precious in
the eyes of the Lord. He designated the clear oil of the
pressed olive as the principal ingredient in the holy
anointing oil of the Old Testament (Ex. 30:24). It was
also the very oil used to light the holy place in the temple of the Lord (Lev. 24:2). I shared with her that, just as

the olive was crushed to bring forth the precious oil that was so useful to the Lord, so had she been through many crushing experiences. But now the Lord was bringing light and anointing into her life as a blessing not only unto herself, but to many others as well.

I continued by saying that, like the cartoon character Olive Oyl, she had been fought over by the brute Bluto but that "Popeye" had come to the rescue! Here the Lord permitted me to turn the phrase into a pun that carried special meaning for her. I emphasized the word so that it came out as "Pop's Eye" (that is, the eye of the Father), further encouraging her by saying that she was the "apple of His eye" (Deut. 32:10; Ps. 17:8-9).

I could see that she was being impacted by what I was saying, but at the time I had no idea of how deeply this was touching her heart. I was simply prophesying according to the measure of faith I had at that moment, describing as best I could the things I was seeing. My only motive was to bless her life.

After the ministry time she related her story to me, and I saw the wonderful thing the Lord had done for her. Apart from being called Olive Oyl throughout her school years, this woman had a much deeper connection with the cartoon characters of this unusual prophecy.

She had, in fact, been married to a man who had beaten her on many occasions, keeping her in a prison of fear. This was the Bluto who had fought over her. That traumatic relationship ended mercifully when the state police arrested the man and sent him to prison for committing several rapes in the area where they lived. After his conviction and sentencing, she divorced him and moved to another state to start life anew. God then blessed her with a Christian husband who has done much to restore her in many ways. Amazingly, his nickname is Popeye!

What a wonderful word this prophecy was to this lady. How tender of the Lord to take what appeared to be foolish in the eyes of man and fill it with such personal healing and affirmation for her! Not only did the Lord bring healing to painful memories of the past, but He also affirmed His blessing upon her marriage and future. Of course, I realize how ridiculous all this may seem to those with critical minds, but God was pleased to bless one of His children by this means. And I, for one, count it an unspeakable privilege to have been used by the Lord in such an unusual and unforgettable way.

"Jan, It's Over!"

An extraordinary example of God's love and power revealed in prophetic ministry came at a conference hosted in Irvine, California, in the summer of 1990. Several eminent leaders and preachers shared the speaking. Among them was Paul Cain, a man of significant prophetic endowments from the Spirit of God. At the conclusion of his message he prophesied to several individuals throughout the great crowd of over thirty-five hundred in attendance. Just when it seemed that Paul had finished, he abruptly turned to his right, pointed to a woman seated in the first balcony above the arena floor and said, "Jan, it's over! The Lord says, 'It's over, Jan.' You must go on. Your young child is in the presence of the Lord, beholding His glory. It's over, Jan; you must go on!"

From where I was seated I could see the woman and her husband. She immediately bowed over in her seat and began to cry, while her husband jumped to his feet with his hands upraised, saying, "Thank You, Jesus! Thank You, Jesus!" An awesome hush fell over the crowd. The multitude of men and women sat there stunned by the magnitude of the Lord's presence at that moment. When the meeting concluded, one of the ministers made his way to this couple to find out what this was all about.

Months earlier, this couple had tragically lost their young son in a terrible hunting accident. To make matters worse, the boy had died at the hands of his brother, who was now struggling with the trauma of what had occurred. Jan felt especially responsible because she had insisted that her husband take the youngsters with him on the hunting trip. As for the father, he continually had to cope with the painful memories of carrying his dead son out of the woods and the added burden of trying somehow to console his other son, who was crushed with what he had done accidentally. The entire situation was filled with nearly insurmountable difficulty.

As the devastated couple had entered the conference arena that morning, overwhelming grief once again seized Jan's heart. She stopped in the lobby and cried as she had on many other occasions, "I can't go on! It will never be over! Never!"

The deep anguish in the heart of that bereaved mother touched the depths of the great heart of God. He sovereignly revealed that couple's heartbreak to Paul and released him to speak a staggering word of comfort and encouragement in their moment of greatest need!

Through this anointed encounter God brought deep healing and added a new memory into the scenario of that long-standing tragedy. Jan and her husband would never again have to relive those awful memories alone. Now, each time their minds recall the unforgettable moments surrounding their son's death, they will also remember the wonderful word which the Lord gave them in the presence of many witnesses.

But the story doesn't stop here. A few months after this, I was with a group of ministers at another conference on prophetic ministry, discussing the various ways we had each seen God work in the prophetic gifts. I felt strongly impressed to share the story of Jan. When I did so, I inadvertently pointed to one of the ministers seated at my right as I illustrated how Paul Cain had pointed to Jan in the balcony. I said, as Paul had said, "It's over! You must go on!"

Immediately, the power of the Holy Spirit came upon the minister at whom I pointed. He began to weep. When I paused to ask what was happening, he said, "This is too unbelievable! When I was sixteen my cousin was killed in a terrible hunting accident. I had to carry his body out of the woods. With every step I took, I felt more and more inadequate. Those awful memories and feelings have haunted me for the past twenty-five years; I have been unable to get them out of my mind. But just now God is speaking to me as I hear that testimony, and He's telling me that it's over!"

God had sovereignly touched and healed another of His children with a prophetic word, piercing the very core of his being with an arrow of light and truth. We laid hands on this brother and confirmed the work the Holy Spirit was effecting within him as we watched the heavy burden roll away. Blessed be the name of the Lord!

I later spoke with Paul Cain and teased him, "Paul, even your 'used prophetic words' have more anointing in them than my first-hand ones!"

Perhaps someone reading this may need a special touch from the Lord to help you get past your own painful memories. For such a person I pray that the Holy Spirit will flood your heart with the love of God and fill your mind with the wisdom which comes from seeing things through God's eyes. I strongly encourage you to seek pastoral counsel and to bring to light those secret burdens which you have borne for so long. A joy shared is doubled; a grief shared is halved. God comforts us most often through one another, but we must be willing to open the door.

Praise be to the God and Father of our Lord

> Jesus Christ, the Father of compassion and
> the God of all comfort, who comforts us in all
> our troubles, so that we can comfort those in
> any trouble with the comfort we ourselves
> have received from God (2 Cor. 1:3-4).

May the healing grace of the Lord Jesus Christ be
upon you abundantly!

Angela and the Story of Naaman the Leper

One Sunday morning as I ended the sermon, I felt led
by the Lord to allow time for prophetic ministry. As I
looked to see if He would reveal anything, my eye fixed
upon a woman in the middle of the congregation. I
shared with her what I sensed the Lord was doing in her
life. These were the exact words I was given for her:

> Angela, the Lord has a wonderful word for
> you this morning! Do you remember the
> story of Naaman the leper? He came to the
> prophet Elisha for healing and was told to dip
> seven times in the Jordan river. When he had
> done this, God healed him as he came out of
> the water on the seventh time. The Bible says
> that his flesh was restored as a child. Angela,
> the Lord's love for you is so strong and so
> great.

At this point a powerful surge of compassion flooded
my heart, almost bringing me to tears. I struggled to
continue with the words I was speaking.

> Angela, you had "leprosy" at one time, and
> you know what I'm referring to, but in your
> pursuit of Jesus you have obeyed Him fully;
> you have dipped seven times. The Lord says

to you that your flesh is restored as a child.
There is an innocence and a purity which the
Lord is putting upon you. It is as though
nothing has ever happened previous to now!
Amen!

When I ended this prophecy the congregation erupted
in spontaneous praise and applause to the Lord. It was a
wonderful moment in the life of our church, but even
more wonderful in the life of Angela. It is with her
permission that I now tell you what this prophetic word
meant to her and what God has done for her since.

Before she became a Christian, Angela had given
herself to a life-style of promiscuity. The abuse and
abandonment she had suffered in her early years evidently led her to pursue love and acceptance among her
peers. A very physical, outgoing person, Angela took
every available opportunity to go rock climbing, skiing
and white-water rafting. An inordinate affection for
physical beauty drove her to sunbathe for long hours in
order to have a tanned, golden body that would surely
turn the heads of male admirers.

The excessive exposure to the sun through all of Angela's outdoor activities slowly began to take its toll.
She contracted telangiectasia, an abnormal dilation of
capillary vessels that often results in tumors. In addition, Angela also developed extreme photosensitivity;
she burned within two minutes of exposure to sunlight.
Her condition was so critical that she had to use special
skin cream and wear protective clothing (long sleeves,
hat and dark glasses) just to be outside. This ailment
was intensified by the fear which it naturally spawned,
as well as the social discomfort of being ill in a society
in which physical fitness is so highly valued. Feeling as
if she had been "robbed" of the only things she enjoyed,
she became deeply bitter, which only compounded the
problems.

Even worse than all of this was the emotional, mental and physical devastation Angela suffered one dreadful night as she was violently raped. In the aftermath of that awful event she discovered the prolonged terror and anguish rape victims suffer. After seven hellish years and spending thousands of dollars on counseling and therapy, the pain worsened rather than being alleviated. Angela was much like the woman described in the Gospel:

> She had suffered a great deal under the care of many doctors and had spent all she had, yet instead of getting better she grew worse (Mark 5:26).

The torment of her memories and the distress of her weakened health ultimately turned Angela's heart to seek the Lord. When she accepted Christ as her Savior, there was an immediate change in many areas of her life. Most notable was her ardent dedication to sexual purity. Angela became a new person. We are reminded of 2 Corinthians 5:17: "Therefore, if anyone is in Christ, he is a new creation; the old has gone, the new has come!" However, despite the many measurable changes, Angela still required much counsel and encouragement in the slow process of long-term healing.

One of the great moments in my years as a pastor came the day that Angela announced her engagement and asked me to perform the wedding ceremony. What a witness to the healing power of the Lord Jesus Christ! His patient love had effected a deep and lasting change of attitude in Angela's heart toward men. And how good the Lord is, for He brought Angela the perfect man of God for her: strong and caring, a defender and champion. In his arms she has found all that she had been searching for during her dark and lonely years.

Angela had been a full three years in the healing process when the prophetic word from the heart of the

Lord was spoken to her that Sunday morning. Her wedding was only two months away, which made the timing of this word most appropriate. Here, in Angela's own words, is the testimony of how God has blessed her.

> God washed me clean of all the sexual sin from those years of promiscuity. He told me on my wedding night that my virginity was restored. One of the greatest things the Lord did was to show me that women can indeed be healed of the emotional devastation of rape. The healing can come through Jesus Christ alone. This was part of the "leprosy" from which God has healed me. Also, my skin has been restored to its original sensitivity. I was able to enjoy my honeymoon in Maui and get a normal suntan! Although my broken capillaries are still present, the severe photosensitivity is not. God also healed me of the emotional bondage I was in because of the fear of being exposed to the sun. I praise the Lord for the wonder of His lovingkindness and His tender mercy.

I continue to be struck by the truth of Paul's ageless words, "But everyone who prophesies speaks to men for their strengthening, encouragement and comfort" (1 Cor. 14:3)! What a wonder it is to see the dramatic power of a prophetic word from the Lord. And what a great privilege to deliver such a word by faith.

Truly, God speaks through the prophetic ministry and invites each of us to seek earnestly for opportunities to hear His voice in this way. Those who seek will find. Those who listen will hear. May the Holy Spirit find each of us with hearts that are yielded and still, willing and ready to become "spokesmen" for the Lord! ❊

Chapter 6

God Speaks Through Dreams and Visions

From Genesis to Revelation, the Bible abounds with instances of God's speaking to people through dreams and visions. No student of the Scriptures would argue with this claim. The format of this book does not provide adequate time and space for us to examine the many revelations given in dreams and visions to such men as Jacob, Joseph, Isaiah, Daniel, Ezekiel, Zechariah and John (just to name a few). In fact, there is such an abundance of biblical examples that I could rightly borrow the words from the writer to the Hebrews:

And what more shall I say? I do not have
time to tell about Gideon, Barak, Samson,
Jephthah, David, Samuel and the prophets
(Heb. 11:32).

While we cannot here research every dream and vision recorded in the Bible, it will be helpful at least to
consider a small sampling of the many from which we
have to choose.

From Abraham to Paul

The first record of God's speaking to man through
dreams and visions was to Abram.

After this, the word of the Lord came to
Abram in a vision: "Do not be afraid, Abram.
I am your shield, your very great reward"
(Gen. 15:1).

The use of this particular word *vision* suggests that
Abram actually fell into a trance yet had his eyes open
to see the sight before him (compare Num. 24:4 where
the same word is used). It means to gaze upon, to perceive with the mind and to contemplate with pleasure.
Given the content of God's greeting to Abram, there can
be little doubt that he certainly found pleasure in this
visitation!

The Bible then says that God took Abram outside and
showed him the stars of the heavens, saying, "Look up
at the heavens and count the stars — if indeed you can
count them....So shall your offspring be" (Gen. 15:5).
Following this we read the classic text which became a
cornerstone of the New Covenant, "Abram believed the
Lord, and he credited it to him as righteousness" (Gen.
15:6). Shortly thereafter God made a covenant with him
and changed his name to Abraham, patriarch of Israel

and father of nations. The descendants of this man have indeed become many nations in the earth. How astonishing that it all began with a *vision*. And also how appropriate, for the Scripture says, "Where there is no vision, the people perish" (Prov. 29:18, KJV).

Another early example of God's speaking to man through dreams occurred with Abimelech, king of the Philistines. Genesis 20 records that God came to Abimelech in a dream one night and said to him, "You are as good as dead because of the woman you have taken; she is a married woman" (v. 3). Now Abimelech had taken Sarah, Abraham's wife, not knowing who she was. Furthermore, he had not gone near her, so he said, "Lord, will you destroy an innocent nation? Did he not say to me, 'She is my sister,' and didn't she also say, 'He is my brother'? I have done this with a clear conscience and clean hands" (vv. 4-5).

God then said to him in the dream,

> Yes, I know you did this with a clear conscience, and so I have kept you from sinning against me. That is why I did not let you touch her. Now return the man's wife, for he is a prophet, and he will pray for you and you will live. But if you do not return her, you may be sure that you and all yours will die (vv. 6-7).

Early the next morning Abimelech summoned all his officials, and when he told them all that had happened, they were very much afraid. And, of course, they made quick work of their repentance!

The story of this Philistine king dramatically attests to the veracity of Elihu's words to Job.

> I tell you, in this you are not right, for God is greater than man. Why do you complain to

> him that he answers none of man's words?
> For God does speak — now one way, now
> another — though man may not perceive it.
> In a dream, in a vision of the night, when
> deep sleep falls on men as they slumber in
> their beds, he may speak in their ears and
> terrify them with warnings, to turn man from
> wrongdoing and keep him from pride, to pre-
> serve his soul from the pit, his life from per-
> ishing by the sword (Job 33:12-18).

God mercifully spoke in a dream to Abimelech and saved him from wrongdoing.

Centuries later God showed similar mercy to Pontius Pilate during the events surrounding the crucifixion of Jesus Christ.

> While Pilate was sitting on the judge's seat,
> his wife sent him this message: "Don't have
> anything to do with that innocent man, for I
> have suffered a great deal today in a dream
> because of him" (Matt. 27:19).

Subsequently, Pilate exercised great care in handling the matter of Jesus' trial and sentencing, even trying to release Him. But when the Jews demanded His crucifixion, Pilate took water and washed his hands in front of the crowd.

> I am innocent of this man's blood....It is your
> responsibility (Matt. 27:24).

In response the angry crowd retorted, "Let his blood be on us and on our children!" (Matt. 27:25). Pilate's dramatic compliance to the message his wife received now stands in history as an indisputable confirmation that God speaks through dreams and visions. The imperial authority of the Roman Empire was swayed by the impact of that single dream because, within it, a man heard the voice of God almighty.

In another place and time, Gideon was strengthened by the Lord when he overheard two Midianite soldiers expressing their terror about a dream which had shown that Gideon would be triumphant over their army (Judg. 7:9-15). Little did they know that Gideon's army numbered only three hundred men against more than fifty-eight thousand Midianites. God used the dream to instill fear in their hearts, while at the same time it brought faith and courage to Gideon and his band of warriors. And the dream came to pass, giving us one of the great stories of the Bible.

In the New Testament, Peter was directed by a vision to go and preach the gospel to the Gentiles gathered in the house of Cornelius, a commander of the Italian troops in the Roman army (Acts 10:1-23). Peter found this very difficult because it contradicted his traditional Jewish upbringing of separatism and brought to the surface his own religious prejudice. Nevertheless, Peter obeyed the word of the Lord and saw a great outpouring of the Holy Spirit upon the Gentiles as on the day of Pentecost. This marked the initial fulfillment of Joel's prophecy, "I will pour out my Spirit on *all* people" (Joel 2:28, italics added) — and this prophecy is still being fulfilled today.

Peter had been present when Jesus had told His disciples:

> But you will receive power when the Holy Spirit comes on you; and you will be my witnesses in Jerusalem, and in all Judea and Samaria, and to the ends of the earth (Acts 1:8).

Standing in the home of Cornelius and watching him

overflow with joy in the Holy Spirit, Peter understood more clearly than ever before exactly what Jesus had meant! And let's not lose sight of this one great fact: God chose a *vision* as the means by which He inaugurated the spread of the gospel to the Gentiles.

The apostle Paul was stymied in his missionary zeal until, in a night vision, he saw the men of Macedonia begging him to come across the Aegean Sea and help them. Paul and his companions got up and left immediately, "assuredly gathering that the Lord had called [them]" (Acts 16:10, KJV). There is no hint in the text that they were surprised at all that God would speak to them in this way. They accepted the dream as a word from God, and they obeyed because they believed it was the will of God. Thus did Europe open up to the advance of Christianity: God spoke through a dream.

One dream of particular interest is that which came to Joseph prior to the birth of Christ.

> An angel of the Lord appeared to him in a dream and said, "Joseph son of David, do not be afraid to take Mary home as your wife, because what is conceived in her is from the Holy Spirit. She will give birth to a son, and you are to give him the name Jesus, because he will save his people from their sins" (Matt. 1:20-21).

It is fascinating to note that while the angel of the Lord appeared to Zechariah in the sanctuary (Luke 1:11) and to Mary in her dwelling (Luke 1:28), he came to Joseph *in a dream*. Zechariah and Mary were both awake and saw the angel of the Lord with their natural eyes, but to Joseph the supernatural encounter occurred in a dream! Was this any less real? Certainly not. For everything the angel said to Joseph came to pass exactly as foretold. Even today we speak the Lord's name as the angel gave it to Joseph in that dream: "You shall call his name Jesus." Now I ask you, how real is that?

King Solomon's encounter with God at Gibeon is an authoritative case study of the reality of spiritual experiences in God-given dreams. Solomon, a young man, had just been established as the king of Israel in rightful succession to his father, David. Following his coronation the Lord appeared to Solomon and said, "Ask for whatever you want me to give you" (1 Kin. 3:5). Solomon humbled himself before the Lord and asked not for riches or power or for the life of his enemies. Rather he entreated the Lord for wisdom.

> Now, O Lord my God, you have made your servant king in place of my father David. But I am only a little child and do not know how to carry out my duties. Your servant is here among the people you have chosen, a great people, too numerous to count or number. So give your servant a discerning heart to govern your people and to distinguish between right and wrong. For who is able to govern this great people of yours? (1 Kin. 3:7-9).

The Lord was greatly pleased with this request and not only gave him discernment, but promised him riches and honor as well (see 1 Kin. 3:11-14). Then came the remarkable conclusion of Solomon's dramatic meeting with God. "Then Solomon awoke — and he realized *it had been a dream*" (1 Kin. 3:15, italics added)! From the early days of my childhood to the present I have read and studied the story of Solomon many times. Yet in all those years I had never noticed that this phenomenal encounter with God happened in a dream.

It occurs to me that some would discredit the reality of this episode simply because it was a dream. Oh, they might say, we thought you were talking about something that *actually* happened. We didn't know it was *only a dream.*

We may well answer with the plain facts of history:

> God gave Solomon wisdom and very great insight, and a breadth of understanding as measureless as the sand on the seashore. Solomon's wisdom was greater than the wisdom of all the men of the East, and greater than all the wisdom of Egypt. He was wiser than any other man....And his fame spread to all the surrounding nations. He spoke three thousand proverbs and his songs numbered a thousand and five. He described plant life, from the cedar of Lebanon to the hyssop that grows out of walls. He also taught about animals and birds, reptiles and fish. Men of all nations came to listen to Solomon's wisdom, sent by all the kings of the world, who had heard of his wisdom (1 Kin. 4:29-34).

King Solomon was endowed with wisdom such as the world had never known. He also had wealth, power and fame of such measure that to this day his achievements maintain their legendary status. The incontrovertible record of history shows that Israel enjoyed its greatest period of peace under his reign. All this issued forth as a result of that night in Gibeon when Solomon had heard the voice of God in a dream. If only more such dreamers would emerge today upon the world scene!

You see, encounters with God are no less real because they occur during a dream or a vision. Certainly we should not make more of dreams and visions than is right; but neither should we make less of them than we ought. For God *does* speak to man through these means. Some, however, question whether God still speaks through dreams and visions today. The Bible itself settles that dispute most emphatically:

> In the last days, God says, I will pour out my
> Spirit on all people. Your sons and daughters
> will prophesy, your young men will see visions, your old men will dream dreams (Acts
> 2:17).

On the day of Pentecost, Peter proclaimed that this ancient prophecy of Joel was now being fulfilled. It merits pointing out that *God* is the One who said this would happen. He alone has the authority and power to do a work of such awesome and global proportions.

Regardless of one's specific beliefs about the end times, we may all agree that we are surely in the last days. We have been since the day of Pentecost. The promised outpouring of the Holy Spirit is therefore as much for us today as it was for those who first heard of its arrival. Peter himself said, "The promise is for you and your children and for all who are far off — for all whom the Lord our God will call" (Acts 2:39). And with the outpouring of the Spirit comes prophetic revelation through dreams and visions. God Himself has said so and will see to it.

Dreams and Visions

There have been many occasions in my own life when the Lord has given significant insight to me through a dream or vision. These prophetic dreams deal sometimes with the church, with a nation or with leaders in the church. At other times the revelation is focused on a more personal level. It always results in an increased devotion to Jesus Christ and the Word of God! Here now, as specific illustration, are some examples of how God has spoken to me in dreams and visions.

The Vision of the Royal Doves

I had a clear and unforgettable vision from the Lord in the summer of 1986. As I closed my eyes for a moment of rest, it seemed as if I were suddenly transported to a spacious field of golden wheat. This wasn't in my mind or my imagination, nor was it an "out of the body" experience. It happened in the spirit, yet I was somehow truly there, and all of my senses were alerted to the sights, sounds and smells of the place.

The entire sky was blackened by an ominous storm in the distance. The storm billowed with thunderous power, threatening imminent and great destruction. Suddenly, I saw an immense shaft of golden light pierce through the dark cloud and shine upon the earth in stark contrast to the turbulent darkness of the storm.

Then I saw what looked like a mass of shimmering energy in the midst of the shaft of light, having the appearance of sparkles on the surface of moving water. It was the most vibrant, iridescent purple I had ever seen. There is no color on earth to compare with it. I was both fascinated and bewildered.

"What is that?" I asked aloud.

To my surprise, I was instantly caught up to see at close range what I had been viewing from the distance: hundreds of purple doves flying closely together. The rapid, spontaneous movement of their many wings is what gave them the appearance of dynamic power.

As I watched them, they flew together into a formation of one giant and powerful dove, moving from heaven toward the great field of wheat on the earth below. Then I distinctly heard the voice of the Lord say, "There is a great darkness coming upon the earth — such as the world has never known. There will be a great light that shines in the darkness — such as the world has never known. And there will be a great move of My Spirit in that light — such as the world has never known. Those whom I use in this coming move of My

Spirit will be characterized by royalty of character and unity of purpose as a great harvest of souls is gathered unto Me by the power of My Holy Spirit."

The vision ended. I opened my eyes and thought long about what I had seen. Was this from the Lord? What did it all mean? When would it take place? These and many other questions filled my mind for some time until I came upon an amazing passage of Scripture:

> Arise, shine, for your light has come, and the glory of the Lord rises upon you. See, darkness covers the earth and thick darkness is over the peoples, but the Lord rises upon you and his glory appears over you (Is. 60:1-2).

I could hardly believe my eyes. Here in the Bible was a striking description of the very thing I had seen in the vision: the great darkness, the great light. But what about the doves? As I continued to read this chapter of Isaiah, I came to verse 8: "Who are these that fly along like clouds, like doves to their nests?"

I hesitate to say how this made me feel because it could seem presumptuous; nevertheless, the thought entered my mind that the Lord had shown me in a vision what Isaiah himself had seen so long ago. I am not claiming that this is, in fact, the case. Rather I'm just describing how I felt. I can recall only a few occasions in my life when I have been rendered speechless — this was one of them. I *know* that the Lord God spoke to me in a vision about what is coming upon the earth. My conviction is founded not simply upon what I saw, but upon the sure Word of God, which so undeniably attests to the revelation He gave me.

Indeed, a great darkness is coming on the earth — such as the world has never known. A storm is menacing on the horizon. The thunderous clouds of political, economic and social chaos are pulsing with increasing tension. While men say, "Peace, peace," sudden destruction will come from every direction. The Bible says that all things that can be shaken will be shaken, and only the unshakable will remain. The astonishing upheavals that the world has recently witnessed in Eastern Europe and the former Soviet Union are but a small glimpse of the sweeping changes which will encompass the earth.

But, glory to God, in the midst of the chaos a great light will shine — such as the world has never known — and bring forth a mighty move of the Holy Spirit such as men have never seen! The Lord will be exalted above the nations and make His way known in the world, and the contrast to the ways of man will be stark. Though evil men increase in wickedness, the just will live by faith, and the righteous will shine like stars in heaven.

The Spirit of almighty God will unite Christians of every race into a holy nation, filling our hearts with the compassion of Jesus Christ and shaping our character to reflect His royal majesty. Our united movement of true brotherhood will manifest the love of God for those who are lost, and a great harvest of souls will be gathered before the throne of God by the power of the Holy Spirit. Amen! Let's join our hearts together in the Holy Spirit and cry to heaven: "Shine, Jesus, shine!"

The Light of Life

I dreamed I was literally inside the Lord. I had the ability to look through His eyes and to see what He was seeing — without being seen. He and I were in a large room filled with desperate, defeated men and women. Their faces were sullen and their skin gray. They all looked like victims in a concentration camp — beaten down, lifeless and hopeless, at the very point of death.

The Lord (and I through the Lord's eyes) fixed His gaze directly on one man. Sensing the Lord's unswerving attention, he slowly raised his head until he was looking straight into the eyes of Jesus. At that instant, the man was miraculously transformed! The ashen skin vanished, replaced by the golden glow of a body filled with radiant life — total restoration within seconds. The man looked at his arms and hands in utter astonishment, and as he looked back on the Lord Jesus, his eyes filled with tears in thankful adoration.

Jesus began to look around slowly, resting His eyes upon every person there, one by one, until He had completely circled the room. Each person experienced the same wonderful transformation. The room was filled with the glory of the Lord, as the brightness of His presence reflected back to Him from all He had turned from gray to golden. The Lord then said, "This is the light of life!"

I was awestruck.

The dream continued as I saw a woman lying unconscious on the floor. She was golden, like the others, but inert. She appeared to be comatose — possibly even dead.

Who is she? I thought. And how could she still be lying on the floor after what the Lord has done?

Jesus looked on her, reached out His hand and touched her. She was the only one He touched. Suddenly, as though she were electrified, the woman bolted to life and rose to her feet. Immediately she went about the room ministering to all those who were present. That's where the dream ended.

After I woke up, I recalled that "the light of life" was a biblical expression. Jesus spoke to the people:

> I am the light of the world. Whoever follows me will never walk in darkness, but will have the light of life (John 8:12).

His closest friend on earth, John the Beloved, wrote,

In him was life, and that life was the light of
men. The light shines in the darkness, but the
darkness has not understood it (John 1:4-5).

Further research into the Scripture led me to an impressive discovery in the book of Proverbs.

When a king's face brightens, it means life;
his favor is like a rain cloud in spring (Prov.
16:15).

Using Strong's concordance to define the key words
of this text, I arrived at the following paraphrase: "In
the radiance of the royal King's turning face, there is
freshness and strength; and His manifested delight, like
a spring rain, envelopes all those within His presence."
What a vivid picture this paints. What a wonderful
blessing this promises. This is why we say, May the
Lord bless you and make His face to shine upon you!

When God sent Jesus to earth, mankind was under
the power of darkness and was ruled by the oppressive
presence of evil (like prisoners in a concentration
camp). We were subject to the callous, indiscriminating
strike of death — unable to do anything for ourselves to
alter our grim situation. Jesus came and fulfilled the
ancient prophecy of Isaiah, "The people walking in
darkness have seen a great light; on those living in the
land of the shadow of death a light has dawned" (Is. 9:2;
Matt. 4:16). What I saw in the dream was a vivid example of this.

Another aspect of the dream that merits a closer look
is the idea of seeing through the eyes of Jesus. A few
years ago I had stopped at a traffic light when a man on
a motorcycle roared up beside me. His bike was cus-
tomized, his leather jacket was decked with various in-
signias, and his demeanor was fierce. As I looked at
him, the Holy Spirit asked me, "What do you see,

James?"

I answered matter-of-factly, "I see a biker." I then looked across the street and saw a man walking out of the bank. He was dressed in a pin-striped business suit and carried an expensive leather briefcase.

"What do you see there?" the Spirit asked me, and I answered, "I see a banker." Finally, I saw a man in the park emerging from the shrubs. He was dirty, unshaven and ill-clad. Evidently he had spent the night sleeping in the park and was waking up to yet another useless day.

Again I heard the question, "And what do you see there?" and I answered, "I see a bum."

All this happened within a few seconds, and as I answered aloud I heard my own words: "A biker, a banker and a bum."

The alliteration caught me off guard, and in that unsuspecting moment I heard the Spirit say, "That's the trouble with you, James. You've been touched once by Me and have just enough vision to be judgmental and opinionated. You see 'people as trees,' as things to be labeled and categorized. That is not how *I* see them. That 'biker,' that 'banker' and that 'bum' are men who each need My love — even as you do. I want to touch you again so that you can look clearly through My eyes and see 'people as people' " (see Mark 8:22-25). The Lord desires for each of us to be hidden in Him, not seeking our own glory or espousing our own opinions. He wants us to see the true needs of others through His eyes and to witness the power of selfless love in giving them the light of life! The Lord Jesus invites us to come along as He walks our city streets, passes through our neighborhoods and looks with compassion upon those who sit in darkness. His tender look, reflected in our eyes, will warm their hearts with hope and fill their lives with faith.

But who was the unconscious woman in the room? I believe she symbolizes the contemporary church, golden but comatose. Like the disciples of old "straining at the oars, because the wind was against them" (Mark 6:48), the church has grown weary in the absence of anointing. She needs another life-giving touch from the Master's hand so that she might recover from her slumber and arise to her calling. Be assured, she is about to get it. The Lord will surely touch the church with His power, and she will arise in the Spirit — selflessly serving those He brings to life and wholeness. This is the hope in my heart, the goal toward which I press. It is the aim of every sermon I preach, every dream I tell, every book I write and every deed I do.

The Reservoir Church

In another vision I saw a large ball hovering before me. A water bucket appeared and began to pour its contents upon the ball. The water splashed in every direction when it came into contact with the ball's surface.

Surprisingly, the image changed before me, and I saw a church sitting on top of a rounded hill. The Holy Spirit began to pour out of heaven like water from a vessel, falling directly toward the church. I knew that as soon as the Spirit came upon this church, God's presence would rush out in all directions, just as the water had when it fell upon the ball. Furthermore, I clearly understood that this was precisely what the Lord wanted to happen.

But the church people quickly built a high retaining wall around the perimeter of their property. When the Spirit fell upon the church, instead of going out in all directions, the presence of God was kept within the enclosed area — like water in a reservoir. The people from the church began to swim about and play in the water, splashing one another and having a merry time. They even went so far as to post a guard to walk along the top of the wall they had built, making sure no "trespassers" got in.

The Lord then appeared in the vision. He was standing on the *outside* of the wall, inspecting the dam the church had erected. He looked down in the valley at a dry and desolate village and then looked back at the dam withholding the great abundance of water. He kept looking back and forth, shaking His head in disapproval of what He was seeing. As the guard walked about the top of the wall, he came to a place where he was standing *above* the Lord, looking *down* upon Him. (I looked at the guard and thought, Oh, brother, are you ever gonna get it!)

With one hand Jesus pointed to the dry and desolate village off in the distance, and with the other He touched the dam the church had built. Then, looking directly at the guard, Jesus asked him this one devastating question: "Why do you damn those I have not damned?"

As I pondered this vision, the Holy Spirit reminded me of the time in the Bible when a terrible famine had devastated Samaria. The situation was made even more grim by the attack of an enemy army, besieging the city to plunder what resources were left. Slowly the events began to take their toll. The inhabitants of the city were in such dire straits that they disregarded the dietary and ceremonial laws of Leviticus and had begun eating donkeys' heads and doves' dung! Their digression into madness ultimately reached the point of cannibalism. A mother boiled her own child and ate him (2 Kin. 6:29)!

Inside the city the besieged citizens were living in a nightmare. Outside the city walls were four leprous men, rejected by the populace because of their dread disease. Day after day they sat near the gate of the city, waiting for death to end their misery. One of the lepers finally asked his companions, "Why stay here until we die?" (2 Kin. 7:3). Realizing that they had nothing to lose, they got up and walked toward the camp of the besieging army in hopes that they would be shown

mercy. If not, then they would surely die, which was
inevitable anyway.

But God intervened in a miraculous way. As the four
leprous men approached the camp, God caused the Ara-
mean soldiers to hear the thundering sound of an advancing army. It so terrified them that they fled the
camp, leaving everything behind. When the lepers arrived they found an abundance of food and water plus
many other spoils of war! They revelled in their discovery until a weight of conviction came on them. When
they thought of the people back in the city, they said to
each other, "We're not doing right. This is a day of good
news, and we are keeping it to ourselves. Let's go at
once and report this to the royal palace!" (v. 9). They
promptly did so, and God brought salvation to all the
people.

Can you see the application for us today? Hasn't
there been a terrible famine in the land, a famine of
hearing the voice of God (see Amos 8:11)? Aren't the
fair citizens of our cities plagued and devastated by the
absence of spiritual nourishment? Isn't there an enemy
army besieging the lives of men and women about us,
cutting them off from life itself? Do we not know that
people have now resorted to eating the "garbage" of
deceptive philosophy and vain imagination? And don't
we see them even biting and devouring one another?

Yet we who are Christians, like the leprous men who
were rejected from the city, are now enjoying the spoils
of victory. We worship God in freedom as we feast upon
the riches of His Word, the goodness of His Spirit and
the abundance of His house. Are we keeping it to ourselves? Have we built a dam around the perimeter of our
property, supposing that all these wonderful blessings
from God are just for us? Have we turned a deaf ear to
the groans of the prisoners and those condemned to die?
Don't we know that God wants His Spirit to flow from
our midst into the communities among whom we are to

shine as lights?

We are the salt of the earth, the light of the world; we have water to give to those who thirst; we have bread to give to those who hunger. If we withhold these things from those in need about us, it will be as though we ourselves wrote the death sentence against them — the very ones to whom we have been sent to give life. And the Lord asks us, "Why do you damn those I have not damned?"

The Barrier of Great Bitterness

One night in a dream I saw the islands of Great Britain. The entire coastland was completely barricaded by a great wall with the word *bitterness* scrawled on it like graffiti. Then I saw a fair maiden riding her bicycle on the wall. To my amazement, as the wheels of her bicycle turned, that portion of the wall on which the maiden was riding would literally vanish — leaving open borders behind her. After a while a policeman appeared and asked the maiden for her papers. He wanted to know on what authority she was doing this. The beautiful young lady smiled as she handed the officer a document. He looked it over thoroughly and noted that all was in order. Satisfied with her compliance to authority, the officer smiled courteously and handed the papers back to the maiden, ushering her on her way. She continued riding on the wall until it was completely gone. Britain's borders were again opened, and a great light shone from that land to the nations of the world. The dream ended, and I woke up.

As I sought for understanding in these things, the meaning of this dream became evident to me. From the early days of her history to the present, Great Britain has suffered the loss of many young and valiant men and women through war. She has laid down much to advance civilization in the world. The price she has paid has imposed a great burden of bitterness on the nation, causing the borders to become closed. This country, once a leader in evangelizing the world to Christ, has become burdened within its own borders by the anguish of a people bereft of those who were destined to be her great champions and leaders.

The fair maiden upon the bicycle represents the espoused bride of Christ, the church, overcoming the barrier of bitterness through the faithful and balanced declaration of the gospel of God's grace. Her authority comes from the commission given by the Lord Jesus Christ:

> All authority in heaven and on earth has been given to me. Therefore go and make disciples of all nations, baptizing them in the name of the Father and of the Son and of the Holy Spirit, and teaching them to obey everything I have commanded you. And surely I am with you always, to the very end of the age (Matt. 28:18-20).

The policeman represents the law, which always gives way to grace when "our papers are in order" — that is, when we submit our lives to the will of God.

I believe that the Lord will raise up the voices of the evangelists in America, men and women of faith who will tell the good news of salvation in Jesus Christ. Their lives will be characterized by modesty, chastity, submission and joy; and God's authority will be upon them as they share the gospel with the people throughout the country. The steady, straightforward witness of these servants will cause the wall of bitterness to come down. A visitation of God will light the flame of Christianity that once burned so brightly in America, and the light of the glory of God will shine forth from her coasts into the world once again. Amen. Come, Lord Jesus!

The Preacher's Last Sermon

In a dream I saw a preacher who had died and stood before the Lord. He was granted the unprecedented opportunity to return to earth and preach one more sermon from any subject of Scripture he desired, to any congregation he chose. He selected an auditorium filled with ministers as his congregation. For his text he chose Acts 20:20-27:

> You know that I have not hesitated to preach anything that would be helpful to you but have taught you publicly and from house to house. I have declared to both Jews and Greeks that they must turn to God in repentance and have faith in our Lord Jesus....Now I know that none of you among whom I have gone about preaching the kingdom will ever see me again. Therefore, I declare to you today that I am innocent of the blood of all men. For I have not hesitated to proclaim to you the whole will of God.

Having read these words, the preacher looked at the congregation of ministers and held up his hands for them to see; his fingers were stunted, stubby and dwarf-like. Then he passionately repeated one sentence over and over: "Whatever you withhold of the counsels of God from the people on the earth, it will be declared in the day of the Lord!" Each time the preacher said this piercing sentence, he would look directly into the eyes of a specific minister and wave his deformed hands before the man's face. It was the preacher's way of illustrating what he meant. He repeated this until he had preached to every single minister gathered in the great auditorium. With this, the dream ended.

While certain aspects of this dream were very clear, there were other parts that puzzled me — in particular,

the preacher's deformed hands and the way he waved
them as he repeated that single sentence. As I contem-
plated what this could mean, I recalled Paul's charge to
Timothy: "Take hold of the eternal life" (1 Tim. 6:12). I
realized that the preacher's stunted fingers symbolized
that he had *not* done this. By withholding from others
the Word of God while he was on earth, the preacher
had actually diminished his own ability to embrace the
full blessings awaiting him in heaven! This was the one
thing he wanted all other ministers to know: closing
one's heart to the words of God on earth will cripple
one's hands to the wonders of God in heaven.

Scripture teaches that our faithful service to the Lord
here on earth gains us an abundant entrance into the
kingdom of heaven.

> His master replied, "Well done, good and
> faithful servant! You have been faithful with
> a few things; I will put you in charge of many
> things. Come and share your master's happi-
> ness!" (Matt. 25:21).

The apostle Peter exhorts us,

> Therefore, my brothers, be all the more eager
> to make your calling and election sure. For if
> you do these things, you will never fall, and
> you will receive a rich welcome into the eter-
> nal kingdom of our Lord and Savior Jesus
> Christ (2 Pet. 1:10,11).

It must be stated emphatically that faithful service
does *not* secure the salvation of our souls, for the blood
of Jesus alone holds that power. It does, however, in
some way determine the scope of our blessings and our
participation in the eternal reign of the Lord Jesus
Christ. The angel of the Lord showed Daniel the future

glories of heaven:

> Those who are wise will shine like the bright-
> ness of the heavens, and those who lead
> many to righteousness, like the stars for ever
> and ever (Dan. 12:3).

Jesus said to the church of Ephesus,

> To him who overcomes, I will give the right
> to sit with me on my throne, just as I over-
> came and sat down with my Father on his
> throne (Rev. 3:21).

In the dream I observed, the preacher was speaking
with the passion of knowing these things to be true. As
I reflected on this dream, the Holy Spirit came upon me,
asking these probing questions: "Where have all the
preachers gone? Where are the champions of the Lord
who will stand and fearlessly proclaim the Word of God
with passionate authority? Why are the pulpits of your
land filled with those who merely echo the ideas of
others? Why do so many draw water from other men's
wells? Why do so many offer excuses for their weakness and succumb to the pressure of fear and self-
doubt? How is it that those who have been called to
preach the unsearchable riches of Christ can settle for
the mediocrity of dry and pointless sermons?"

Inspired by what I sensed to be the burden of the
Lord's heart, I wrote the following poem:

Where Have All the Preachers Gone?

> Gone are the Moodys, the Spurgeons, the
>   Wesleys;
> Gone are the Whitefields, the Champions of
>   yore.

Here to replace them — O heaven, please
     help us —
Philosophers, Doctors and Lawyers galore!

The timid and fearful ascend to the platform
to whisper their sermons to those who draw
     near.
The churches are empty, the pews long for-
     saken,
It's obvious to all that the Lord is not there.

Where is the fire that fell on our fathers
and gave them the tongue that spoke from
     above?
Where are the preachers who stand in the
     pulpit
and fearlessly tell us of Jesus' great love?

I have been led by the Lord occasionally to share this
dream and poem with several other ministers and have
witnessed the hand of the Lord touch and transform
many by the power of His Spirit as they have cried to
the Lord, "O God, I want to preach Your Word!" My
hope is that such a work is being effected even now as
people of God read these words. The Spirit says,

In the presence of God and of Christ Jesus,
who will judge the living and the dead, and in
view of his appearing and his kingdom, I
give you this charge: Preach the Word; be
prepared in season and out of season; correct,
rebuke and encourage — with great patience
and careful instruction (2 Tim. 4:1-2).

The Bible has issued the mandate. The Lord provides
the mantle. Where are the men and women?

The Car With No Brakes

One night I dreamed I was driving along the road when an oncoming car suddenly crossed into my lane. I quickly applied my brakes and discovered they were not working! I swerved and barely avoided a disastrous collision. Thinking I was out of danger, I relaxed to collect myself from the physical drain I felt. Then the road suddenly changed, and I soon found myself speeding down a steep hill, unable either to slow down or stop. A large concrete retaining wall ran alongside the road, and I ran my car into the embankment in an attempt to brake my speed. It did slow me down some, but it damaged my car in the process. Finally, I came to level ground where I was able to coast to a stop. Heavy traffic filled the road about a mile ahead, and I felt tremendous relief that I had been able to stop before rushing out of control into it.

A tow truck appeared and took me to a service station for repair. As I watched other cars speed along the highway, I became impatient waiting for service and decided to move my car into a more visible position. This presumptuous decision set off a chain reaction of ridiculous events, unfolding like a comedy of errors.

First, someone had leaned a guitar against my car, so as the car rolled backward, the guitar was crushed to pieces. Then I could not stop my car from rolling still farther, and it smashed into a window of an adjacent building. Pushing the car forward to get it out of the broken window, I carelessly ran over and destroyed the mechanic's tools which had been laid out on the driveway for the repair job on my car. I was exasperated!

Finally, with all this commotion, a policeman appeared and began writing me a citation. The dream ended as my car was impounded in a lot behind the service station, and night began to fall. When I woke up, these words resounded within my mind: Get your brakes fixed!

I knew this dream was a parable, so I asked the Lord what it meant. I remembered the verse in Mark's Gospel: "He did not say anything to them without using a parable. But when he was alone with his own disciples, he explained everything" (4:34).

This is what the Holy Spirit showed me. The brakes symbolize the discipline of self-control in our lives. The Lord wants us to walk in the Spirit, at all times avoiding presumptuous behavior and speech. Any time we overstep due boundaries, undertake a matter without clear justification or behave with daring audacity, we experience "brake failure." Impertinence, impatience and presumption: these are chief among the great human sins, and they are always reflected in how we act and talk. If our lives are characterized by "hurry" and "worry," it's a sure bet we are living in presumption and setting ourselves up for the unpleasant consequences.

The crazy events of my dream illustrate the seven consequences of presumptuous, impatient behavior. First, it jeopardizes our relationships with others. This was seen in the near-collision with oncoming traffic. Next it damages our ability to minister effectively (the car being damaged by the concrete wall). Then presumption quenches praise and worship; this was reflected in the crushed guitar.

Fourth, it will shatter your vision, resulting in the loss of ability to see clearly the things of God (the smashed window). Fifth, it hinders the work of restoration (the mechanic's broken tools). Sixth, presumption brings condemnation (the policeman writing the citation). And finally, persisting in presumptuous behavior and speech causes us to be set aside in darkness, like the car impounded behind the service station as night began to fall.

The psalmist cried out to God,

Who can discern his errors? Forgive my hid-

den faults. Keep your servant also from will-
ful sins; may they not rule over me. Then will
I be blameless, innocent of great transgression. May the words of my mouth and the
meditation of my heart be pleasing in your
sight, O Lord, my Rock and my Redeemer
(Ps. 19:12-14).

This prayer gives us insight into how we can "get our
brakes fixed." Ask these three things of God: Cleanse
me from secret faults; keep me from presumptuous sins;
and help me to please You in what I think and say.

One last important note from this dream: *There's
heavy traffic ahead!* More than ever, it is time for us to
"get our brakes fixed." God is calling us into greater
opportunity and accountability in ministry. The arena in
which He desires to use us requires a higher level of
trust and obedience than we have ever known. Those
who do not accept the discipline of the Holy Spirit in the
area of patience and self-control cannot be released into
the "greater works" Jesus promised we would do in His
name.

The Rhino in the Field

In another dream I saw a rhinoceros grazing in a
large field of grass. When I asked what this meant, a
voice answered, "What you are seeing is a religious
spirit." I woke up and pondered the puzzle which I had
seen. I had watched no National Geographic programs
lately, so there was no natural accounting for why I
would see a rhinoceros in my dreams. Also, I could
think of no reason whatsoever for associating a rhino
with a religious spirit. But then the Holy Spirit began to
speak to me.

I thought of the verse which says, "All flesh is as
grass, and all the glory of man as the flower of grass" (1
Pet. 1:24, KJV). I realized that the grassy field in the

dream represented the flesh — the carnal and independent heart of man — and that a religious spirit (represented by the rhino) feeds on this. Apart from God, people are most religious beings, preferring the predictable mechanics of lifeless ritual over the erratic fluctuations of spontaneous relationship and living faith. We are consumed with legalism, opinion, criticism, judgment and debate. We deem it more convenient to bow to an idol rather than to seek the face of God, especially when the idol is our own self-righteousness. Such is our glory, we suppose, and so we will fight to keep it. Thus *religion* makes war, but *relationship* makes peace. God has not called us to religion, but to relationship with Himself and with one another through Jesus Christ our Lord.

But why would the Lord use a rhinoceros to symbolize a religious spirit? That was the puzzling thing about my dream. I looked for the relevance of this riddle by reading the encyclopedia. To my amazement, I discovered several significant characteristics of the rhino which were remarkably parallel to people with religious attitudes.

First, the rhino has poor vision and will often attack what it does not recognize! Such could easily be said of religious folk whose opinions are so strong that they neither recognize nor tolerate anyone who differs from their narrow point of view.

Second, the predominant feature of the rhinoceros is its horn, which is located on the end of its nose. This is precisely why the rhino has such poor vision — his own horn blocks his view. In biblical symbolism, the horn represents power and authority. How interesting that religious people also usually cannot see past their own noses!

Third, the rhino uses intimidation as its principal means of attack. Have you ever noticed how self-righteous people intimidate others with critical words?

4   Fourth, the rhino is a very temperamental beast, subject to violent fits of unprovoked anger. It thrashes about wildly, making a loud, grunting noise and attacking any moving object. So it is with self-righteous people; one must exercise great caution, for one never knows what may set them off.

5   Finally, the rhino is called the "fire guard of the jungle" because he literally runs into a fire and stomps it out. Hasn't "religion" always tried to put out the fire of God? Wasn't it the Pharisees who demanded the crucifixion of Jesus? But the good news is that a small dagger in the hands of a skilled hunter can pierce the armor-like skin of the rhino; so also can the Word of God in the hands of a true believer cut through the pretense of the hypocrite and render him powerless.

The Angel and the Pot of Acid

In yet another dream I saw an angel standing with a large vat in his hands. The vat was filled with what appeared to be acid. A man came and stood before the angel, who then began to pour the acid upon the man's head!

"What are you doing?" I exclaimed.

The angel continued pouring as he looked at me and solemnly said, "These are the curses with which he has cursed others, now being poured out upon his own head!"

The sight was so riveting that I woke up and lay still in my bed, seized with bewilderment. I wondered first if *I* was the man and quickly started blessing everybody I could think of! Next I questioned if what I had seen in the dream could even be true, for it seemed so sinister and disturbing. And yet it also had a sobering sense of divine justice about it. I got up and began searching through the Scripture for an answer. My search was not fruitless.

He loved to pronounce a curse — may it
come on him; he found no pleasure in blessing — may it be far from him. He wore cursing as his garment; it entered into his body
like water, into his bones like oil (Ps.
109:17-18).

I clearly saw the lesson that the Lord was illustrating
through this dream: The man who curses others will
himself be cursed. Jesus said, "Do not judge, or you too
will be judged. For in the same way you judge others,
you will be judged, and with the measure you use, it will
be measured to you" (Matt. 7:1-2).

As it applies to cursing, so also does it apply to blessing. The man who blesses others will himself be
blessed. Whatever measure you mete out will be measured back to you. In yet another text Jesus said, "Bless
those who curse you" (Matt. 5:44, NKJV). Could it be
that the blessing we speak to those who are cursing us is
for the purpose of keeping us from ultimately cursing
ourselves? I think so.

How solemn to think that cursing another postures
you to receive that very curse upon yourself! But then
how wonderful to believe that by blessing another you
inevitably inherit the blessing yourself! Despite the be-
wildering images of this night vision, one thing is certain: Since having this dream I have been very careful
with my words. And if the dream served no other redemptive purpose than this, it is sufficient to be called a
dream from God.

Are All Dreams From God?

Any number of things can stimulate the mind to
dream. Some dreams are nothing more than the result of
diet or the day's activities. We are likely to dream about
whatever has dominated our thoughts throughout the

day. I recall one Christmas when I bought my children a video game. After I connected it to our television, I began to play it myself.

My kids voiced their disapproval. "C'mon, Dad, you bought it for us! Let us play."

Well, of course I was only playing it to make sure that it was working; how was I to know it would take a couple of hours? I finally did hand the control pads over to my kids. I had become so focused on that silly game that every time I closed my eyes all I could see were video characters bouncing around going "beep, beep, beep." You can just imagine what my dreams were like that night!

Other dreams come from the storehouse of personal history, the museum of memories. It's possible that both fond and painful experiences which are buried within our hearts may surface while we are unguarded in peaceful sleep. The Lord can use these times to bring healing to unresolved issues, but to say that the dream itself was from the Lord may be stretching the point.

And then some dreams are, in fact, a revelation of Satan's intentions against us or others. Nightmares, horror dreams and disturbing visions of the macabre and the awful fall into this category. We might fear that what we saw was an omen of impending disaster when actually it was an exposure of satanic schemes which can be thwarted by the prayer of faith. Knowing this is very helpful, for it ignites the heart of the warrior within our spirits to stand against the wiles of the devil. Rather than being filled with fear and anxiety by these dreadful images, we instead issue a bold and emphatic restraining order against the enemy: No! You may not do this evil thing!

So it cannot be said that all dreams are from God, but some most surely are. Keep in mind that our basic belief is that God will pour out His Spirit in the last days upon all people, that our sons and daughters will prophesy and that young men will see visions and old men will dream dreams. Ultimately it is the duty of every dreamer to learn how to make the distinction between the precious and the vile; we must develop the ability to distinguish what is of God and what is not so that we can interpret our dreams and become "spokesmen" for the Lord (see Jer. 15:19).

Perhaps you are wondering if God will speak to you in dreams. You have every reason to believe that He will. Here are two essential things you can do to prepare yourself to receive dreams from God. First, ask the Lord to speak to you while you sleep and expect Him to do so.

> So I say to you: Ask and it will be given to you; seek and you will find; knock and the door will be opened to you. For everyone who asks receives; he who seeks finds; and to him who knocks, the door will be opened. Which of you fathers, if your son asks for a fish, will give him a snake instead? Or if he asks for an egg, will give him a scorpion? If you then, though you are evil, know how to give good gifts to your children, how much more will your Father in heaven give the Holy Spirit to those who ask him! (Luke 11:9-13).

Second, be ready to wake up and write down the things the Lord reveals to you. In the past I've often awakened from a vivid dream in the middle of the night thinking that I would remember it when the morning came. Falling back to sleep, I would rise at dawn to only vague recollections of what the Lord had shown me in the night — sometimes not even remembering it at all.

This has happened enough times to motivate me to capture the sight while it is fresh in my mind by keeping

a pen and notepad at my bedside to write down those
things I see and hear in the night visions. I also make
note of my thoughts about it at the time. When I awaken
the following morning, I am able to recall it clearly and
study it through to its interpretation. Also, I have found
that the very act of doing this causes me to become even
more sensitive to hearing and receiving from the Lord
while I sleep, which in turn enables Him to speak more
frequently to me in this way.

> I sleep, but my heart is awake; listening for
> the voice of my Beloved (Song 5:2, para-
> phrased).

Briefly touching on the matter of dream interpretation, I suggest these four basics: relationship, research,
relevance and respect. First, a personal relationship
with Jesus Christ is vital to developing interpretive
abilities. You simply must know the Lord in order to
understand what He is saying through dreams and
visions. The more vital your relationship with Jesus, the
more adept you become at discerning His voice through
the otherwise obscure meanings of dreams and visions.

Second, you must be committed to researching the
symbols and sayings of the revelations given. The Bible, the encyclopedia, a dictionary and access to the
library — all these are helpful tools which must be util-
ized for digging the pearl out of the oyster.

One of the most helpful things another older brother
in the Lord ever did for me was to stop interpreting my
dreams for me. As David told Solomon,

> My son, if you accept my words and store up
> my commands within you, turning your ear
> to wisdom and applying your heart to under-
> standing, and if you call out for insight and
> cry aloud for understanding, and if you look

for it as for silver and search for it as for
hidden treasure, then you will understand the
fear of the Lord and find the knowledge of
God (Prov. 2:1-5).

Third, be sensible in interpreting what you have seen.
Ask the Lord to show you its relevance to you or others.
Don't ever force an interpretation, trying to make it fit a
predetermined opinion or desire. And, finally, respect
others when you share what you have seen. They may,
in fact, hold the interpretive key, supplying you with
knowledge which you otherwise would not have. Submit what you have seen and what you think it means to
others who can help you arrive at a truthful and objec-
tive interpretation.

May the Spirit of God awaken your heart in the night
to show you great and wonderful things. May He impart
to you the wisdom to interpret and explain them to others. And may all your dreams from God come true! ✤

Chapter 7

God Speaks Through the Natural Realm

J esus said, "God is spirit, and his worshipers must worship in spirit and in truth" (John 4:24). In another place the Bible states, "No one has ever seen God, but God the One and Only, who is at the Father's side, has made him known" (John 1:18).

When He became a man, Jesus Christ gave us the definitive revelation of the Father. After He rose from the dead and ascended on high, Jesus received from His Father the gift of the Holy Spirit, which He poured forth upon the church and by whom He continues to reveal God to us today. Therefore, the more yielded we become to the Holy Spirit, the more we perceive the things of God.

The Bible says that "the invisible things of him from the creation of the world are clearly seen, being understood by the things that are made, even his eternal power and Godhead" (Rom. 1:20, KJV). A popular expression derived from this text asserts that "the natural things speak of the invisible." That is to say, we may understand spiritual things about God by looking at the natural things He has created. Since God is Spirit, He is therefore invisible, but the Bible says that the invisible things of God are *clearly* seen.

How is this possible? How can we *see* what is *invisible*? The answer is simple. In the old Hollywood movie *The Invisible Man* we were able to see the man only because he wore *clothes!* In a similar way God wears the garments of the natural world, and He can be seen, figuratively speaking, in all of life's circumstances.

> In the beginning you laid the foundations of the earth, and the heavens are the work of your hands. They will perish, but you remain; they will all wear out like a garment. Like clothing you will change them and they will be discarded. But you remain the same, and your years will never end (Ps. 102:25-27).

As a shadow gives some indication of what casts it, so creation reflects something of the Creator. The omnipotence of God can be seen in the vast expanse of the glorious heavens, His faithfulness in the unfailing orbit of planets. The bounty of earth's resources shows His thoughtful care toward us — as the songwriter said, "All I have needed, Thy hand hath provided!"[1] The animal kingdom fascinates us with God's ingenious wisdom and humor, while every human face and fingerprint show the immeasurable variety of God's creativity.

The majesty of the great mountains, the brilliance of

the noonday sun, the fragrance of a rose, the antics of a monkey, the sparkle of the stars and the industry of an ant — we need only look to see that all creation joins in glad adoration of God, each part revealing some aspect of the unfathomable depth of His personality and preferences. In this way it may be said that the natural things themselves are speaking to us something of the Lord. However, they can in no way express adequately the surpassing greatness of God Himself.

When walking through the Alps, Charles Spurgeon felt that the Lord was infinitely greater than all His grandest works and so wrote the following words.

Yet in all these how great soe'er they be, we see not Him. The glass is all too dense and dark, or else our earthborn eyes too dim. Yon Alps, that lift their heads above the clouds and hold familiar converse with the stars, are dust, at which the balance trembleth not compared with His divine immensity. The snow-crowned summits fail to set Him forth, Who dwelleth in eternity and bears alone the name of High and Lofty One. Depths unfathomed are too shallow to express the wisdom and knowledge of the Lord. The mirror of the creatures has no space to bear the image of the Infinite. 'Tis true the Lord hath fairly writ His name, and set His seal upon creation's brow. But as the skilful potter much excels the vessel which he fashions upon the wheel, even so, but in proportion greater far, Jehovah's self transcends His noblest works. Earth's ponderous wheels would break, her axles snap, if freighted with the load of Deity. Space is too narrow for the Eternal's rest and time too short a footstool for His throne. Even avalanche and thunder lack a voice to

utter the full volume of His praise. How then
can I declare Him? Where are words with
which my glowing tongue may speak His
name? Silent I bow, and humbly I adore.[2]

Many times throughout Scripture God chose to speak
through things in the natural realm, giving us some
memorable "pictures."

First, we see the innocent lamb slain as a sacrifice for
the guilty sinner, pointing to the time when the sinless
Son of God would be crucified so that man might be
saved (Gen. 22:8; John 1:29).

Then there was the dramatic exodus of the children
of Israel out of slavery in Egypt, foretelling the great
deliverance God now gives to those He frees from
bondage to sin (Ex. 13–15).

The tabernacle in the wilderness, filled with many
symbolic witnesses, testifies to the time when God's
presence would dwell among us despite our unbelief
and barrenness (Ex. 25:22; John 1:14). The manna,
which was given fresh every morning, foretold the
Bread of Life sent down from heaven to renew us daily
(John 6:31-35).

The brass serpent lifted up by Moses was an unmistakable portrait of the crucified Christ (John 3:14-16).
He who knew no sin was made sin for us that we, by
looking unto Him, might be healed of the fiery serpent's
poisonous bite. The promised land, filled with abundant
fruit and great challenges, shows us what it means to
live in the fullness and power of the Holy Spirit (Heb.
3:18–4:2).

And God continues to speak to us *today* through
natural things, vesting them with revelation rich in symbolism. The literal becomes symbolic; the natural becomes spiritual and takes on the distinctive
characteristics of a parable — revealing truth in an unforgettable way. The key is the *association* we make

between what we see and what God is doing or saying. For example, if you were to see a *dove* fly into a church through an open window and hover above the congregation during a worship service, you would *naturally* take it as a sign that the Holy Spirit was present. You see? God speaks by *association*. He knows what we will think, so He shows us something that triggers our thoughts that way.

But someone may ask, Why doesn't He just say it plainly? Because a picture is worth a thousand words! We are moved more by vision than by sound, and we are less likely to forget what we see than what we hear. Thus, God will often use an everyday, natural occurrence as a "picture" that shows us what He is saying or doing in our lives — and beyond.

The Communion Table

During a time of worship at the church I felt strongly impressed to go to the communion table for a moment of private confession and devotion. I stood before the bread and wine, gazing upon the famous painting of the Lord's Last Supper hanging on the wall above the table. I sensed the Holy Spirit ask me, "James, which disciple are you most like?"

I thought for a moment and realized that there are times when I am like each one of them. It is the truth. Looking at that painting, my eyes were opened by the Lord to see things in myself I could not deny.

Sometimes I am like John, reposing with my head near Jesus' heart. At other times I am like Peter, impetuous and outspoken. I was converted as dramatically as Matthew, the former tax collector. Yet there are times when the doubts of Thomas take a distant second to my own, making him appear a great man of faith. Like Andrew, I have brought others to Jesus, and, on the other hand, like James and John, the Sons of Thunder, I've

wanted to call down fire from heaven upon those who
reject the Lord. I, like Nathaniel, have often questioned
those who have spoken the word of the Lord to me, and
many times I've completely missed the point of what
He was saying, just like Philip. I have known the obscurity of Simon, James the lesser, Thaddaeus and
Bartholomew. And, yes, I have been a Judas on more
than one occasion — denying the Lord and betraying
Him before His enemies.

Humility swept over my soul as I stood before the
communion table. The one I wanted most to be like was
Jesus, and yet I was so much like all the others. The
Lord said, "That is why I have invited you to drink of
My cup."

A few months later, I was in England for a meeting
with church leaders hosted at Holy Trinity Church,
Brompton, in London. During one of the breaks, I
strolled downstairs to the "catacombs" for refreshment.
I noticed something in the corner of a storage area and
took a closer look. It was an elaborate wood carving of
the Last Supper dating from the eighteenth century.
However, parts of it were broken, and holding it gave
me mixed feelings — a sense of reverence at how old it
was, a sense of regret over how damaged it had become
and a sense of intrigue over the strange appearance
caused by the missing pieces.

First and most obvious, the Lord was not there! A
haunting gap existed in the center of the table where one
expected to see Jesus. This created an interesting image
— two groupings of disciples, huddled together and
talking apart from the other group. Finally, the two figures on opposite ends of the table completed the strange
sight: Both were missing their heads!

I was fascinated with this broken work of art, but
even more so after the Holy Spirit said to me, "When
the Lord is not present, the disciples become divided
and lose their heads. That's when I place them in stor-

age to become covered with dust!"

There was a time when I would have passed over this broken carving without a second thought, or maybe at most I would have expressed dismay at someone's negligence for breaking it. But the Holy Spirit used it to catch my eye, and when I looked I heard the voice of God! Do you see how a simple occasion of life can become an opportunity to have a conversation with God? I was merely wandering about in a church when I came upon a "conversation piece" that the Holy Spirit wanted to talk about!

Even though God speaks this way to all of us, some people never hear the message. Preoccupied with the cares of life, pierced through with the deceitfulness of fleeting riches and carnal pleasures, they have eyes but do not see; ears but do not hear or understand. They "cannot see the forest for the trees."

Therefore Jesus said:

> This is why I speak to them in parables: "Though seeing, they do not see; though hearing, they do not hear or understand." In them is fulfilled the prophecy of Isaiah: "You will be ever hearing but never understanding; you will be ever seeing but never perceiving. For this people's heart has become calloused; they hardly hear with their ears, and they have closed their eyes. Otherwise they might see with their eyes, hear with their ears, understand with their hearts and turn, and I would heal them" (Matt. 13:13-15).

Jesus expressed His bewilderment with Nicodemus over this very matter, "I have spoken to you of earthly things and you do not believe; how then will you believe if I speak of heavenly things?" (John 3:12). Perhaps we are like Nicodemus, looking to heaven for the secrets of life while dismissing the ordinary things of earth that speak those secrets to us every day.

All I Saw Was Dust

There is a marvelous story about a little girl who entertained herself by playing with a beam of sunlight shining through her bedroom window. "Look, Mommy," she said, "Isn't it beautiful?" She then began explaining all the things she saw as she played with the sunbeam. "It's like an angel's gown and I'm fixing the hem," she said. "Now it's like a film projector, and I can make actors appear on the wall." With childlike excitement she continued, "Now I'm pretending it's a magic slide! See how my hand glides down the surface?"

On and on the little girl went, telling her mother all the delightful things she saw in the sunbeam. Finally, as the little girl went out to play with a friend, the mother stood alone in thoughtful silence looking at the sunbeam. And to think, she then said to herself, a moment ago all I saw was dust.[3]

Perhaps in a rather simple way, this story illustrates how much can be seen in the natural things all around us every day. Like the little girl, we need only look past the dust to see the light. Jesus said, "I tell you the truth, unless you change and become like little children, you will never enter the kingdom of heaven" (Matt. 18:3). And again in another place Jesus said, "I tell you the truth, no one can see the kingdom of God unless he is born again" (John 3:3). Childlike faith is a fundamental requirement for "seeing" the things of God, and such faith is fostered only by a vital relationship with Jesus Christ.

I was casually browsing through a magazine one day when an advertisement caught my eye. The picture was of a bottle filled with pure oil, bathed in a golden light that made it appear almost invisible. The label had been removed from the bottle and set off to the side, allowing the light to shine through the oil. Here is what the ad said:

> In this age of televangelists who sin, politicians who lie, athletes who cheat, billionaires who evade taxes, movie stars who assault policemen, baseball managers who gamble, and teen idols who make home movies...it is nice to know there's still one thing that's completely pure!

The Holy Spirit began speaking to me as I looked at that curious advertisement. The unlabeled bottle filled with pure oil is like the church as well as individual believers. We are to be full of the Holy Spirit, radiant with the light of the Lord. Let's set our labels off to the side, eliminate the impurities in our lives, yield to the Holy Spirit and reflect the presence of Jesus to those who look our way. That is what it will take to answer the spirit of the age that has contaminated much of Western contemporary Christianity.

On another occasion, I was reading a newspaper as I flew to Canada for a seminar. The headline of the news article said, "Canada's Warning System Far From Alert." Accompanying the story was a large photograph of an unusual-looking air-raid siren mounted on the top of a telephone pole. The article claimed that these sirens were essentially out of order because of a number of peculiar reasons.

Swarms of bees had made honey in some of them, plugging the mechanisms and rendering them useless. In other sirens, squirrels had found an excellent dry place for storing their nuts — thereby obstructing the siren. Also, hunters frequently used the sirens for target practice, adding to the damage already imposed by nature. Evidence even showed that some of the sirens had failed because mice had eaten through the insulation and electrical wiring systems. The article pointed out that the sirens were so weak that their sound would not even penetrate most modern flats. It concluded by calling for a new and powerful system that would reach the population in all areas. I found the story informative, interesting and humorous because of its oddity.

I was greeted at the airport by my host who drove me directly to the church where the seminar was to be held. As we approached the facility I saw, to my amazement, one of the very air-raid sirens I had just read about, mounted on a post near the corner of the church! The Holy Spirit then impressed in me that the newspaper article I had read was a "parable" of the church's condition in Canada. With that in mind I read the article again and received significant insight from the Lord.

The "siren" represents the church's voice to an endangered world. But "if the trumpet does not sound a clear call, who will get ready for battle?" (1 Cor. 14:8). The malfunction of the siren was caused by four things: bees, squirrels, hunters and mice. The bees represent Christians who want to keep the "honey" for themselves and will sting any outsider who reaches into the hive. The squirrels represent those who have turned the church into a "nut house." The hunters are those who drive past the church and fire critical words at it. ("Did you hear what the pastor did with his secretary?" or "Did you hear what the bishop did with all the money?") And, finally, the mice who cut off the power represent the creeping things of the demonic realm that find access into our midst through unconfessed sin.

All these things have robbed the church of her voice for this generation. In this predicament we no longer can penetrate into the hearts of men. We must, then, even as the news article stated, bring forth a "new and effective means of reaching the population in all areas!"

How amazing are the ways of the Lord! I was simply

reading a newspaper to pass time during the flight. But God knew that the church I was bound for had one of those sirens on its property, so He caught my eye with the photo and article to speak a word to my heart! The Bible says, "To the pure, all things are pure" (Titus 1:15). Jesus said, "Blessed are the pure in heart, for they will see God" (Matt. 5:8). God looks for those with discerning hearts, those who are learning how to extract the precious from the worthless, so that He might speak to them and send them out as His messengers.

What About Forced Interpretations?

Perhaps a word of caution is in order here. It is possible to get carried away with flights of imagination and begin to read something spiritual into everything that happens. That reminds me of the man who desperately needed direction from the Lord for his life. As he was driving his car he prayed for God to speak to him through a sign along the roadway. He then looked up at a road sign and read these words, "Clean Restrooms Ahead" — so he cleaned the next twenty!

Some have been almost this absurd in pursuit of revelation. Consider for instance: On his way to church one Sunday morning, a man who thought himself a prophet saw a black cat cross the street in front of him. At the same moment, a pumpkin fell off a produce truck passing by, and the song playing on his radio was "Don't Sit Under the Apple Tree With Anyone Else But Me," followed by "Swing Low, Sweet Chariot."

Naturally, the ambitious prophet concluded that all those wearing orange clothes to church that day were about to be attacked with depression by the devil because they had been unfruitful in serving the Lord.

To prevent the attack each church member would have to eat twenty-three apples, because the twenty-third psalm says that the Lord is our shepherd, and He makes us lie down in green pastures. As we all know, green pastures are where apple trees grow! Besides, the Bible says that we are the apples of His eye, and eating that many apples shows our great hunger for God and our desire for Him to lead us by the still waters into the paths of righteousness for His name's sake.

Finally, because *chariot* sounds like *charity* — which doesn't mean love anymore, but giving money to needy causes — the Lord wants everybody in the church to give money to the "prophet" who gave them this revelation because it kept the bad things from happening to them; they are supposed to share material things with those who give them spiritual things! Somebody say amen! If any of this makes sense to you, then you could be one of the very people I'm talking about!

Such foolish interpretation is fostered by an inordinate appetite for spiritual revelation and for the admiration it may bring among others seeking after God. Those given to forced interpretation are often characterized by mystical mannerisms and a subtle, or sometimes blatant, desire for acceptance of their authority in spiritual matters. At the heart of this faulty approach is the personal need to control situations and people. Such behavior is obviously unacceptable, for it only promotes the assumed spirituality of the offender, while it repels those who would otherwise give an ear to a genuine word from the Lord.

A personal, thriving relationship with Jesus is a sure antidote for such nonsense. This should be the primary quest of all aspiring prophets, for He alone can be trusted to discipline us in the way of righteousness as He leads us into all the truth. Additionally, keeping our focus on the Scripture serves as an excellent deterrent to becoming preoccupied with the absurd excesses of mystical spiritualism.

I have hidden your word in my heart that I

might not sin against you (Ps. 119:11).

Finally, a willingness to submit to others the things we believe to be revelations from the Lord is a sure way to keep our souls from presumption. Having offered these important cautions for avoiding silly and negative extremes, we can continue our examination into some of the ways God often speaks through the natural realm.

Prophets and Parables

The holy prophets of Scripture are venerated as the undisputed spokesmen of the Lord. Any lingering question over how God speaks today can be settled quickly by a close examination of just how He spoke to and through the prophets in the past.

The Lord Himself declared through Hosea, "I spoke to the prophets, gave them many visions and told parables through them" (Hos. 12:10). The psalmist said, "I will open my mouth in parables, I will utter hidden things, things from of old" (Ps. 78:2). "Hidden things" means mysteries, puzzles and enigmas.

We see, then, that God sometimes speaks today through parables, riddles, allegories, puzzles and mysteries, often using natural things as the material for His script.

"The Scribe With the Sacred Pen"

The kind of moral failure displayed in the lives of David and Bathsheba seems to be a recurring problem that has caused the downfall of many prominent ministers of God. In our own day, many notable leaders have fallen prey to the power of lust. I asked the Lord to speak to me about this, and He answered with a parable:

A scribe stood before a great king, who

placed into his hands a sacred pen filled with golden ink. He gave the scribe authority to write in the king's name with the pen. Whatever he wrote on with this pen would be inscribed with golden ink and would become the exclusive treasure of the king. He then sent the scribe out with one warning: "Write only upon that which is lawful to be written upon." Humbled by the grace of his king and filled with a deep sense of wonder, the scribe went out with the sacred pen and its golden ink.

Shortly thereafter, he came upon a brokenhearted man who was bowed under a great burden. The scribe took the pen and wrote the king's name on the man. As the golden ink traced the broken man's features, the burden suddenly rolled away, and the man leaped to his feet, proclaiming his allegiance to the king. There was much joy and celebration among all the man's friends at his recovery. The citizens were greatly pleased with their gracious king and held a great banquet in his name.

Then the scribe went on his way again. Everywhere the scribe went, he found many in need of the king's inscription, and so he would write on them with the sacred pen. The results were always the same: freedom, joy, peace and allegiance to the king for his kindness and love.

Men began to seek out the scribe, begging him to come and write on them with the sacred pen. The scribe would always hurry to help, so his fame began to spread. Many asked him for counsel and direction, which he gladly gave. Others asked for his help in matters for which he was not suited, yet he would respond, and people would boast of his wisdom.

His fame continued to grow to legendary heights. Everyone talked about the scribe and his wisdom, shared his counsel with one another and gave banquets in his honor. Soon the scribe became so accustomed to the attention he was receiving and the ease of what he was asked to do that he lost the awe which marked the early days when he was first given the sacred pen. And he forgot the king's warning to "write only upon that which is lawful to be written upon."

So it happened one day that a beautiful woman came to him for help. She was fairer than the lily and more lovely than the rose. Her beauty captured his heart, and her innocent need stirred his natural desires. He wanted her for himself, but she was another man's wife.

The scribe was deeply troubled and pondered what could be done. He reasoned with himself that he could write on the woman with the king's pen, but in his own name — then she would be his. And so he did this. But the golden ink turned into mud, and the inscription he wrote on the woman covered her with shame and darkness. In desperation, the scribe wrote yet again and again to cover his mistake, but it only made matters worse. The more he wrote, the greater the darkness and the deeper the shame.

Suddenly, the door of his room burst open! Standing before him with their weapons fully drawn were the king's royal soldiers. They arrested the scribe and took away the sacred pen and the golden ink, placing him in the prison of disgrace to await the king's judgment. The dear woman was given to the king's physicians to be cleansed and cured of the evil done to her.

Great sorrow swept through the kingdom as people heard the report of the scribe's arrest. Alas, yet another of the king's servants had been seduced by the power of darkness. Still, there was some hope that the king's mercy would yet again triumph over judgment, as it had on many other occasions.

Meanwhile, in the royal palace, another scribe stood before the great king. The king placed in his hands a sacred pen filled with golden ink, saying, "Write only upon that which is lawful to be written upon." So the scribe went forth, humbled by the grace of his king and filled with a deep sense of wonder.

Did you notice how you were drawn into the story as you were reading and how you awaited its outcome? Did you see the images in your mind as you read it? Did you sense the impending fall of the scribe when men began to exalt him? Could you feel the anxiety of the scribe as he tried to fix his mistake? Did you empathize with the woman who was abused by one who was supposed to minister to her? Did you consider what the king must have been thinking and feeling? What does this parable teach us today? Perhaps you can now see why the Lord so often uses the story form of communication; it captures our attention as few other things can.

The prophet Ezekiel said, "The word of the Lord came to me: 'Son of man, set forth an allegory and tell the house of Israel a parable' " (Ezek. 17:1-2). Webster's dictionary defines an allegory as "the expression by means of symbolic fictional figures and actions of truths or generalizations about human existence." The Collins English Dictionary defines an allegory as "a poem, play, picture, and so forth, in which the apparent meaning of the characters and events is used to symbolize a deeper moral or spiritual meaning." Taking a closer look into the lives of the prophets reveals that God often required them to do things in the material realm which were clearly meant to portray a spiritual reality. For example, Isaiah walked barefoot and naked for three years as a prophetic witness of the impending captivity and shame of Egypt and Ethiopia (see Is. 20:2-4). Any volunteers for *that* ministry?

Jeremiah said,

> This is the word that came to Jeremiah from the Lord: "Go down to the potter's house, and there I will give you my message." So I went down to the potter's house, and I saw him working at the wheel. But the pot he was shaping from the clay was marred in his hands; so the potter formed it into another pot, shaping it as seemed best to him.
>
> Then the word of the Lord came to me: "O house of Israel, can I not do with you as this potter does?" declares the Lord. "Like clay in the hand of the potter, so are you in my hand, O house of Israel" (Jer. 18:1-6).

It would have been easy for the Lord just to *say* this to Jeremiah or even to *show* it to him in a vision or a dream. Instead, the Lord instructed him to make the trip to the potter's house to receive a word from Him. Imagine how the potter must have felt when this holy, awesome, totally anointed, incredibly intimidating, nationally renowned prophet of almighty God walked into his humble workshop and said, "The Lord told me to come here because He wants to speak to me about something." My personal opinion is that the clay was "marred in the potter's hands" because the man was a nervous wreck with Jeremiah sitting there watching his work!

The prophet Hosea may top the list on tough assignments. He was told to marry a *prostitute* who would serve as a sign from God of Israel's unfaithfulness to the covenant.

> When the Lord began to speak through Hosea, the Lord said to him, "Go, take to yourself an adulterous wife and children of unfaithfulness, because the land is guilty of the vilest adultery in departing from the Lord" (Hos. 1:2).

Notice also that this was his *first* word from the Lord —"when the Lord *began* to speak through Hosea." Hosea was some kind of a man to be trusted with such a heavy word at the outset of his ministry. It is also worth pointing out that his faithfulness inaugurated a prophetic ministry that spanned the reigns of five kings (see Hos. 1:1).

How about Ezekiel? God required him to do many things that served as symbolic words from the Lord. He drew a picture of Jerusalem on a clay tablet and then, like a child in a sandbox, acted out a small scale battle against the city — complete with enemy encampments, ramps and battering rams. The Lord said,

> Take an iron pan, place it as an iron wall between you and the city and turn your face toward it. It will be under siege, and you shall besiege it. This will be a sign to the house of Israel (Ezek. 4:3).

Ezekiel lior left side 390

right side. 40 dy

After the sandbox battle, God told Ezekiel to lie on his left side for 390 days to symbolize the number of years that Israel had been in sin. Then he was to turn onto his right side and lie there for another forty days to symbolize the sin of Judah (see Ezek. 4:4-8).

Undoubtedly, the most burdensome "prophetic symbol" imposed on Ezekiel was when he had to bake a barley cake using human excrement as fuel for the fire! His conversation with God in Ezekiel 4 went like this:

The Lord said, "In this way the people of Israel will eat defiled food among the nations where I will drive them" (v. 13).

Ezekiel appealed, "Not so, Sovereign Lord! I have never defiled myself. From my youth until now I have never eaten anything found dead or torn by wild animals. No unclean meat has ever entered my mouth" (v. 14).

Ezekiel's argument was acceptable with the Lord, so He responded, "Very well, I will let you bake your bread over cow manure instead of human excrement" (v. 15). What a bargain! I wonder if Ezekiel ever wanted to change places with Isaiah?

This method of symbolic revelation continued even in the New Testament. The prophet Agabus took Paul's belt and tied his own hands and feet with it and said, "The Holy Spirit says, 'In this way the Jews of Jerusalem will bind the owner of this belt and will hand him over to the Gentiles' " (Acts 21:11). Why not just *say* it? Why go through the dramatic gestures of tying his own hands with Paul's belt? *Because a picture is worth a thousand words!*

Each of these prophecies was "staged." That is to say, the Lord directed the prophets to do these things so that they might serve as allegories and signs to the people. Sometimes, however, an incidental circumstance became *co*incidental with a word from God and thereby served as a prophetic message from the Lord — just as

these others that had been deliberately set up and carefully acted out.

Consider, for example, the time when Israel asked for
a king so that the nation could be like other nations
around it (see 1 Sam. 8:5). The Bible says that Samuel
was greatly displeased with the request, so he prayed to
the Lord for an answer. The Lord said to Samuel, "Listen to all that the people are saying to you; it is not you
they have rejected, but they have rejected me as their
king" (1 Sam. 8:7). This was indeed serious; the people
assumed they were merely dismissing an old prophet
and getting in step with the contemporary world about
them. But this seemingly innocent request betrayed a
deeper and far graver act. They were rejecting God and
seeking to replace Him with a man as their king! What
manner of king would be suitable for such a stubborn
and stiff-necked people as this? What man could God
place on the throne to rule such an obstinate empire?

How truly appropriate that Saul, the son of Kish,
should be chosen for the job. For on the very day of his
anointing he was out in the hills chasing runaway donkeys (1 Sam. 9:3). God gave the rebellious people of
Israel a king who was experienced in dealing with way-
ward jackasses! What a *coincidence!* Is it possible that
God was saying something by this to the people of Israel? I think so.

By stark contrast, consider the circumstances when
David was chosen to replace Saul as king. David was
tending sheep in his father's pasture (1 Sam. 16:11).
How remarkable is the comparison of these two kings.
The people's choice was a donkey-chaser; God's choice
was a shepherd! Can't we see in this the heart of God
for ourselves? Surely He longs for us to be sheep, not as
mules.

I will instruct you and teach you in the way
you should go; I will counsel you and watch

over you. Do not be like the horse or the mule, which have no understanding but must be controlled by bit and bridle or they will not come to you (Ps. 32:8-9).

By self-rule (like Saul) we make asses of ourselves. But God's rule over our lives (like David, who represents Christ) makes us like sheep now "returned to the Shepherd and Overseer of our souls" (see 1 Pet. 2:25).

Another noteworthy incident from Saul's life must be included, for it illustrates perfectly how God speaks through what appears to be incidental. It came about on the day when Saul was being reprimanded by Samuel for his disobedience. Samuel said:

> You acted foolishly....You have not kept the command the Lord your God gave you; if you had, he would have established your kingdom over Israel for all time. But now your kingdom will not endure; the Lord has sought out a man after his own heart and appointed him leader of his people, because you have not kept the Lord's command (1 Sam. 13:13-14).

After this Saul continued to deteriorate and mishandle his authority. His disobedience became increasingly blatant and intolerable. Samuel rebuked Saul at length in the strongest of words,

> For rebellion is like the sin of divination, and arrogance like the evil of idolatry. Because you have rejected the word of the Lord, he has rejected you as king (1 Sam. 15:23).

The Bible says that as Samuel turned to go away, Saul took hold of the edge of his mantle so that it

ripped. Suddenly, an accidental ripping of a mantle became an unforgettable word from the Lord. Samuel said
to Saul, "The Lord has torn the kingdom of Israel from
you today and has given it to one of your neighbors —
to one better than you" (1 Sam. 15:28)! With those
words the truth was burned into Saul's heart. From that
day forward he would never be able to shake the visual
imagery of the ripped mantle which he had held in his
dirtied hands that day.

Let's now compare an incident which occurred years
later in Saul's life. While hiding in a cave to escape the
wrath of Saul, David was surprisingly faced with an
excellent opportunity to kill Saul and so end his problems. But remember, David was a man after God's
heart, a man more righteous than Saul. Such an act was
unbefitting of a king, and David saw the occasion as a
test of his character. Despite the urging of his soldiers to
kill Saul, David instead merely cut off a piece of Saul's
mantle that he might show it as the evidence of his
goodwill to the king of Israel. We now pick up the story
as it is told in the Bible.

> [David] said to Saul, "Why do you listen
> when men say, 'David is bent on harming
> you'? This day you have seen with your own
> eyes how the Lord delivered you into my
> hands in the cave. Some urged me to kill you,
> but I spared you; I said, 'I will not lift my
> hand against my master, because he is the
> Lord's anointed.' See, my father, look at this
> piece of your robe in my hand! I cut off the
> corner of your robe but did not kill you. Now
> understand and recognize that I am not guilty
> of wrongdoing or rebellion. I have not
> wronged you, but you are hunting me down
> to take my life. May the Lord judge between
> you and me. And may the Lord avenge the

wrongs you have done to me, but my hand
will not touch you" (1 Sam. 24:9-12).

After David had finished speaking, Saul cried out,
"You are more righteous than I....You have treated me
well, but I have treated you badly" (1 Sam. 24:17).
Surely, as Saul saw David at the opening of the cave
holding the cut piece of the mantle in his hand, his mind
must have flashed back to those piercing words spoken
by the prophet Samuel so long ago. Thus, in the painful
realization that those words were being fulfilled right
before his eyes, Saul declared to David, "You are more
righteous than I!" What volumes God had spoken
through a simple piece of cloth! Samuel saw it as a word
from the Lord; Saul would never forget it; and David
innocently fulfilled it.

There was another time when the ripping of a garment had great significance. Jesus stood before the high
priest of Israel the night He was betrayed and saw him
rip the priestly robes in a fit of religious anger (see
Matt. 26:65). Surely Jesus saw this as a reassuring token
from His Father that the old priesthood was ending and
the eternal priesthood of Christ was being established.
The coincidental and supernatural ripping of the temple
veil "from top to bottom" (Matt. 27:51) was nothing
less than the witness of God Himself to this glorious
fact. The holy of holies is now open to mankind through
Jesus Christ, our High Priest before God!

In yet another parallel, note that the soldiers at His
crucifixion did *not* rip the robe of Jesus — it will forever be *one piece*! Men of war may cast lots to see who
lays claim to it, but His kingdom will never be torn from
Him! What volumes God did indeed speak through a
few simple pieces of cloth!

These are but a few of the many "pictures" God has
given us in the Bible. Make no mistake about it — these
things all happened. They were literal, actual, *natural*

events which happened in the lives of those living at the time. But, as the New Testament says, "These things happened to them as examples and were written down as warnings for us, on whom the fulfillment of the ages has come" (1 Cor. 10:11). The word *example* means something that strikes and leaves a lasting impression. *Warning* means something that makes us alert through a timely reprimand. Simply stated, it is the Lord's will that we be impacted and quickened by things that occur in the natural realm when they reveal something of Him to us.

The Prison My Father Built

In the first chapter I described at length how it came about that I went to prison as a young man. I also told of my encounters with the Lord on several occasions, how He would speak to me out of the Scripture and bring healing into the depths of my being. I concluded that part of my testimony by telling how the Lord spoke to me that I was to go home to my friends and tell them the great things the Lord had done for me; how He had compassion on me and saved me (see Mark 5:19). Now I would like to tell you an amazing incident that occurred a few years after I was released from the penitentiary.

About a year after my release, I married Belinda, and we began to raise a family. After the birth of our third child, I felt a strong need to contact my estranged father, to get to know him and talk to him about what had happened when I was a child. I wanted to know why he was sent to prison when I was two years old and what had happened to him during the years that I was growing up without a father. I also wanted him to see his grandchildren. And I wanted him to be proud of the man I had become.

He was living in Houston, Texas, at the time, so we

drove the several hundred miles from Colorado to spend two weeks visiting him. We arrived safely and were welcomed with opened arms. The absence of a shared history made for shallow conversation at first, but we kept at it. We slowly worked our way through the awkward feelings of being intimate strangers, connected only by genetics, and we began having dialogue of depth and substance.

One night the conversation turned to our memories of prison, since we both had been there at separate times. Out of curiosity, my dad asked me which prison I had been in (for there are several prisons in the state of Texas).

When I told him, his faced flushed, and his mouth dropped open. "Dear God, son," he said, "I was on the labor crew that built that prison."

That's when *my* face flushed, and *my* mouth dropped open! My dad literally built the prison that I was held captive in fifteen years later. He welded the very bars of my prison cell when he was in prison himself. What an astonishing "coincidence"!

In that unforgettable moment the Lord used this natural event to speak this supernatural word to my heart. "James," He said, "just as I have freed you from the prison which your father built, so now I send you to set others free from the prisons which their fathers have built!"

Over the years I have met many sons and daughters who themselves are in prisons which their fathers have built — prisons of prejudice and hatred, anger and abuse, abandonment and loneliness, fear and anxiety, lust and shame. And I have shared with them the truth of forgiveness and deliverance in Jesus Christ, watching them walk out of captivity into freedom and life. This indeed has been my principal engagement for the past twenty years, as the Lord foretold, and I can now by faith extend that same hope to you. Perhaps you are in a

prison *your* father built, and you fear there is no way out
for you. That is not true. In the same way that God set
me free, He will also set you free. I know this is the
truth because He said so, and I have witnessed Him do
it hundreds of times in many places.

Three vivid memories come to mind as I reflect on
the day when I walked out of prison. There was "the
gauntlet of the catcalls" when all the other inmates
rained insults upon me as I was walking out of the cell
block. There was the anxiety of administrative process-
ing. As I stood in the prison offices waiting to be offi-
cially released, I feared they might find some reason to
keep me locked up longer. And there was the impact of
personal responsibility the moment I stood outside the
prison walls. I suddenly realized I would have to take
care of myself from then on. What about you as you
walk out of the bondage of your own prison?

First, you must ignore the mockery of the enemy as
you run the gauntlet of the catcalls. Satan will accuse
you, lie to you, belittle you — anything to make you
think prison is where you belong. Ignore him and keep
walking into freedom!

Second, make sure there is nothing in you that would
give opportunity to the devil. Things like unforgiveness,
hidden sin and other unresolved issues will give Satan
the license he needs to delay your release and keep you
locked in the prison. Confess your sins and forgive others who have sinned against you.

Finally, accept the fact that you are responsible for
yourself! Walking out of prison means walking into personal responsibility. Some get so accustomed to having
others care for them that they would rather live within
the confinements of dependency than face the challenges of life. Like the infirm man who had been sick
for thirty-eight years, they must be asked by the Lord,
"Do you *want* to get well?" (John 5:6). If you truly want
to be freed from the prison that your father built, you

must firmly resolve to walk into the freedom of the Lord and begin a new chapter in your life as a responsible adult.

Having said these things, I now extend to you this blessing in the name of Jesus Christ, and I trust the Holy Spirit to endorse these words with supernatural power in your life right now. May the Lord Jesus Christ quicken you with faith to accept your freedom from the prison that has held you captive and give you courage to accept the personal responsibility to walk in newness of life. May He grant you His Spirit so that you might extend forgiveness to your own father and to others, even as Christ has forgiven you. May you feel the exhilaration of liberty as you walk away from the past and into the future which God has ordained for you.

> Then you will know the truth, and the truth will set you free (John 8:32).

And,

> If the Son sets you free, you will be free indeed (John 8:36).

"A New and Better Hearing Aid"

During a pastor's conference held in Chicago in the summer of 1988, a close friend, known widely for his prophetic gifting, approached me with a peculiar prophecy heralding an increase in the clarity of my prophetic ministry. "I see the Lord giving you a new and better hearing aid!" he said.

I chuckled as he said this to me, thanked him and then went on with my day, not thinking much about the word at the time.

Some months later I began experiencing a marked increase of revelation during ministry times. By the

Spirit of the Lord, I was able to look at people and know things about them. And when I shared these revelations with the people concerned, it brought tremendous expressions of faith and joy into their lives. There was definite improvement in the effectiveness of my ministry. However, I made no connection between these experiences and the prophetic word my friend had given me.

Then one day I arrived at a church to be the guest minister for the Sunday morning worship. The church met in a building on the main street of the town. I turned into the one available parking space in front of the building, only to discover it was reserved for handicapped drivers. Dutifully I backed out of the space and looked for another spot to park my car. Noticing a space in front of a shop across the street, I maneuvered my car into it. As I turned the engine off, I glanced up at the store sign now directly over my car. It read, "A New and Better Hearing Aid Company"! At that moment I remembered the word which my friend had spoken to me months earlier.

As I crossed the street to the church, I sensed the Holy Spirit say, "James, I have moved your ministry from the 'handicap' zone to the 'new and better hearing' zone!" I paused in amazement to absorb all this. That was truly (and literally!) a "sign" from the Lord, and it blessed me with a special sense of His personal involvement in my life. I laughed out loud and looked around for someone to share this moment with. Then I realized no one would be much impressed with a stranger stopping him on the street saying, "God is speaking to me through that sign!" So I quietly cherished it in my own heart. I share it now because it serves as another illustration of how God speaks to us through natural things.

Fit to Be Tied!

I have the privilege of serving as the volunteer chaplain for our university football team, the Colorado Buffaloes. Coach Bill McCartney and his family attend our church, and our relationship has developed into a close friendship. In his book *From Ashes to Glory*, Bill wrote openly of the anguish of his private battle with anger and the distress it caused him as a Christian. On many occasions he and I have prayed specifically about this need in his life, and we have seen the Lord effect significant changes.

One particular instance when God spoke to us about Bill's anger was during a football game at the start of the 1990 college football season. The Buffaloes were playing the University of Tennessee at Anaheim. The game had been hard fought in the blistering heat of Southern California, and with only five minutes left in the contest, the Buffaloes led 31 to 17. Our team had the victory well in hand — or so we thought.

Suddenly, my attention was captured by the sight of Coach Mac losing his temper. An assistant coach had made a costly mistake at a critical point in the closing moments of the game. As a result Coach Mac erupted with anger, and his rage fell on this man. The air filled with the tension created by his sudden outburst. What made matters worse was that Bill wouldn't stop. He continued speaking his mind to this other coach, getting angrier with each word. And as all this was unfolding, the University of Tennessee abruptly scored a touchdown! The score was now 31 to 24. Of course, that did nothing to ease the situation.

As Mac confronted the embarrassed assistant coach with intensified vigor, our opponents scored again, making the game a tie at 31 to 31. (This all happened in the space of five minutes.) The Buffaloes then stalled on yet another drive. Tennessee took possession of the ball with explosive momentum and began what threatened to be the winning march down the field. Fortunately for us, time expired, and the game ended with the final score tied at 31.

As everyone walked off the field to the locker rooms, we felt sickened and bewildered by the game's closing moments. I was also troubled for my friend over his undeniable transgression. Then the Holy Spirit spoke these words to me: "Tell Mac that he was fit to be tied — so I 'tied him up'! I allowed the score to serve as a sign to him. Tell him I am taking him to a higher level of accountability in his Christian witness; that the eyes of the nation will be upon him; and that he cannot indulge in such outbursts of anger any longer."

I swallowed hard at the prospects of delivering this confrontive message. (But at least the Lord hadn't asked me to take my clothes off, as He had Isaiah!) I shared the message with Bill, and he humbly accepted the word of the Lord. We prayed together for forgiveness and restoration, and God answered us. He also gave us practical wisdom on how to win the battle against anger in the inevitably tense, heated moments of athletic competition. The remainder of the season provided many opportunities to test the validity of Bill's faith and obedience. Each game was filled with intensity and struggle as the Buffaloes faced worthy opponents determined to stifle our aspirations of a national championship. Yet through it all, Bill displayed the fruit of the Spirit as listed by the apostle Paul — "love, joy, peace, patience, kindness, goodness, faithfulness, gentleness and self-control" (Gal. 5:22-23).

Coach McCartney's steady composure in the face of trying circumstances was truly a tribute to the power of God's Spirit in the life of a yielded servant.

One final noteworthy fact: Our football team finished first in the nation that year, and the Buffaloes were crowned as the national champions after our dramatic victory over Notre Dame University in the Orange Bowl on New Year's Day, 1991. Truly, the eyes of the nation were upon us. Coach McCartney's Christian poise throughout the season had exemplified his integrity as a man of God. Our victorious season was made even sweeter by the events of the previous year. Let me elaborate.

The Buffaloes' Broken Horn

On August 22, 1989, I dreamed our football team was huddled together under an oppressive, dark cloud. The hand of God pushed the cloud aside, and a rainbow appeared over the players. The black jerseys and gold helmets of the tightly grouped men made them appear like a pot of gold at the end of the rainbow. Something like an energy field then encircled the team and filled them with power. Their gold helmets began to glow in the light. Then I heard a voice that said, "This will be their golden season!" That's when I awoke.

Later that day I shared this dream with Coach McCartney, and he graciously accepted my enthusiastic interpretation. "God is going to remove the oppression which has plagued the team for the past few years," I told him. "The Lord will now fulfill promises which He has made to you by empowering the players with His Spirit. This will be the golden season!"

I prayed for a sign from the Lord to confirm this word; it came the day after our first game of the season. When we defeated the University of Texas by a commanding margin of victory, the front page headlines of the newspaper read, "Colorado Buffaloes Have Golden Season Debut." I was astonished when I saw the very words which God had spoken to me in a dream two weeks earlier!

We went on that year to a perfect record, the only undefeated team in college football. At the season's end, the newspapers printed a special, twelve-page supplement documenting each game. Bold letters on its front page proclaimed: "The Golden Season!"

Our success brought us to the 1990 post-season Orange Bowl game against mighty Notre Dame. I felt certain that we would win and be crowned the national champions of college football — we were already firmly locked in the number one position in the polls. I was *sure* that we would win; my confidence was unshakable! But then I saw something that hit me like a ton of bricks.

Fifteen minutes before the game was to start, I walked toward the playing field through the players' tunnel. As I passed by our team mascot, a one-ton female buffalo nicknamed Ralphie, I saw that her right horn was broken off, leaving only a bloody stump on her head. Her trainer informed me that her horn had broken when she snagged it on a gate as she ran into the pen. Remembering that the horn was a biblical symbol for power and authority, I sensed the Lord saying, "The buffalo's horn is broken; the Buffaloes' power is gone!" That was not good news, and I didn't accept it. After all, I had already made up my mind that we were going to win.

But Notre Dame won that night, 21 to 6. It was the only game we lost that year. As I stood in the stadium, completely stumped by the outcome, I felt that the Holy Spirit told me to read Isaiah 21:6: "This is what the Lord says to me: 'Go, post a lookout and have him report what he sees.' " I knew then that these events had been orchestrated by the Lord for a purpose. My curiosity was awakened. First of all, I wanted to know why we had lost the game. The Lord showed me that it was because of pride. When I asked why He hadn't told me about it, He reminded me that He had spoken to me through the broken horn, but I had dismissed the insight because of my personal desires. Finally, I asked the

Lord what the next year's football season was going to be like. The Holy Spirit reminded me of a scripture, "In that day the Lord will reach out his hand a second time..." (Is. 11:11). I was certain this meant the Lord would bless us again.

Perhaps now you can see how amazing it was that we played Notre Dame exactly one year later, at the same bowl game, for the same prize: the national championship. Only this time we won! And, yes, before the game began I did check to see how Ralphie's horns were — they were fine! Coincidentally, our final season win-loss-tie record was 11-1-1, exactly matching the chapter and verse numbers of Isaiah 11:11. The Lord indeed stretched forth His hand a second time!

It may sound preposterous to some when I suggest that God spoke to me through the events of a football game and the numbers on a scoreboard. Why would almighty God concern Himself with such carnal and mundane affairs? Remember that God wants to communicate with us at all times; He will often use what already has our attention to reach us. Sports play a major role in the lives of millions of men, women and children all around the world. Don't think for a moment that God would pass up an audience like that. Even Scripture uses sports analogies to inspire us toward life's greater realities: "Fight the good fight of the faith" (1 Tim. 6:12); "Let us run with endurance the race that is set before us" (Heb. 12:1, NKJV); and "Run in such a way as to get the prize" (1 Cor. 9:24) — to mention a few.

Learning to Take a Closer Look

It is a healthy thing for Christians always to be thinking about the Lord, no matter what they are doing. David said, "I am always thinking of the Lord; and because he is so near, I never need to stumble or to fall" (Ps. 16:8, TLB). If we all did this, everything in which we involved ourselves would offer us the opportunity to discover something new about God. With this in mind, the Lord is teaching me to pay attention to the things that catch my eye, to look for the things He wants to show me. He said to me once, "James, pay attention when something causes you to do a double take, for I will be speaking to you."

I may have also heard Him add, "This applies for everywhere *except* the beach! If you do a double take *there*, then I *will* be speaking to you!" To which my wife says, "Amen, brother!"

Stop for a moment and look around. What catches *your* eye? Ask the Holy Spirit to show you what you can learn about God by seeing that as something He has made. What was He thinking when He made it? How does He feel right now as you look it over? What was God thinking when He made *you?* Do you suppose He thinks of you in the same endearing ways that you think of those you love?

Let's take this to broader applications. In what ways can your occupation serve as an allegory to the things of God? What "parables" can you tell from the activities that engage your time and attention? What can you see about God in the events of life happening around you? How do the world's main news events indicate His involvement in human affairs? The more questions like this you ask and answer, the more you will see of the Lord in the otherwise ordinary occasions of daily life.

The clearest case for God's speaking to people through the natural circumstances of life can be made from the life of Jesus Himself. The natural world, in fact, provided the basis for His teaching style. He regularly spoke in parables as a preferred method of revealing truth about His Father.

> Jesus spoke all these things to the crowd in
> parables; he did not say anything to them

without using a parable (Matt. 13:34).

Consider, for example, the parable of the sower (see Matt. 13:3-9). Jesus used an agricultural illustration to convey truth to a people whose principal industry was farming. When Jesus talked to farmers about God, He used farming stories. When He talked to fishermen about God, He used fishing stories. When Jesus talked to merchants about God, He used stories that illustrated the wisdom of wise investments. The Lord uses the language of those to whom He is speaking and reveals to them the wonders of His Father through symbols familiar to them. This way they are sure to remember what He says to them when they are at work.

This again validates the effectiveness of parables as one of God's principal means for communicating spiritual truth. Often a message couched in symbolic language affects us far more than if it were analytically spelled out. God wants us to be impacted by His Word, so He is more likely to wrap it in an enigma to arouse our curiosity, stimulate our imaginations and startle our minds as we unravel the mystery, piece together the puzzle and solve the riddle.

> It is the glory of God to conceal a matter; to search out a matter is the glory of kings (Prov. 25:2).

Each of us should consider it a noble occupation to search out the spiritual matters of life which God has concealed in the packages of daily occurrences.

With this in mind, we should respond to the Lord in the words of blind Bartimeus, made famous by the Gospel accounts of his encounter with the Son of God.

> Jesus asked him, "What do you want me to do for you?" "Lord, I want to see," he re-

plied. Jesus said to him, "Receive your sight;
your faith has healed you." Immediately he
received his sight and followed Jesus, praising God (Luke 18:41-43).

May it be even so with us! May the Lord Himself
pronounce upon us the great blessing of revelation,

Blessed are your eyes because they see, and
your ears because they hear (Matt. 13:16).

Ears that hear and eyes that see — the Lord
has made them both (Prov. 20:12).

O Lord, make our ears to hear and our eyes to see!
Then shall the prayer of Moses, the man of God, be
fulfilled,

I wish that all the Lord's people were prophets and that the Lord would put his Spirit on
them! (Num. 11:29).

Amen! ❧

Chapter 8

God Speaks Through the Supernatural

As we explore some of the many ways through which God speaks, it is essential that we not overlook the spiritual dimension of the supernatural realm. By this I mean the things that are outside the rational, concrete, logical world of facts and figures. The dictionary defines supernatural as "existing or occurring through some agency beyond the known forces of nature, and outside the natural order; relating to an order of existence beyond the visible, observable universe; transcending the laws of nature."

This definition in itself testifies to the existence of the supernatural realm. Why else would anyone even bother to define it? Yet, though it is defined and experienced, nonetheless it is not easily understood. The audible voice of God, sublime spiritual experiences, angelic visitations — such things wreak havoc with the Western mind simply because they cannot be explained. And for many people, the mental anxiety generated by the perplexing mysteries of the spiritual dimension is placated by blatant denial: It doesn't make *sense*, therefore it is not *real*. But just because we may not understand a thing is no reason to dismiss it as nonexistent.

When God made man in His image, He created each one of us as a trinity: spirit, soul and body. The Scripture says,

> May God himself, the God of peace, sanctify you through and through. May your whole spirit, soul and body be kept blameless at the coming of our Lord Jesus Christ (1 Thess. 5:23).

God fashioned us as physical beings so that we might relate to a physical world. He made us with souls so that we might relate to one another. And the Lord breathed into man the breath of life, the Spirit, so that we might relate to the spiritual world. We are only complete when all three portions are balanced and functioning as God intended. To deny the spiritual (and supernatural) dimension of life is to reject a substantial measure of our very selves.

Before venturing any further, I want to make it perfectly clear that by the use of the word *supernatural* I do not — and this is stated emphatically — I do *not* mean the hocus-pocus of the occult. Our world is preoccupied with an inordinate appetite for the phenomenal and the sensational. Few places are exempt from bizarre cults and unconventional doctrines. The persuasive, seductive power of deception has swayed many to open themselves to things God has strictly forbidden. Here I refer to fortune-telling, ouija boards, tarot cards, palm reading, seances, crystals, crystal balls, channeling, false religions, divining and any other practice that supposes a "revelation from God" can be had apart from Jesus Christ.

Make no mistake: God has spoken finally and completely in His Son.

> In the past God spoke to our forefathers through the prophets at many times and in various ways, but in these last days he has spoken to us by his Son, whom he appointed heir of all things, and through whom he made the universe. The Son is the radiance of God's glory and the exact representation of his being, sustaining all things by his powerful word (Heb. 1:1-3).

There is *no* true revelation apart from Jesus Christ, nor will God say anything that leads man away from Him! Anyone claiming otherwise is deceived by Satan and hastening to his own ruin. Tragically, in many cases, the deceived are also taking others down with them.

Men and women from every walk of life, with little or no concern for how dangerous it is or how foolish it appears, pursue the occult as though it offered legitimate forms of revelation and spiritual guidance for their lives. While much has been done in the name of tolerance to lend respectability and credibility to these counterfeits, the fact remains that they are fraudulent and extremely detrimental. We must clearly understand that God neither sanctions nor speaks through any of these means. Rather He forthrightly condemns them all as wicked and destructive:

> When you enter the land the Lord your God
> is giving you, do not learn to imitate the de-
> testable ways of the nations there. Let no one
> be found among you who sacrifices his son
> or daughter in the fire, who practices divina-
> tion or sorcery, interprets omens, engages in
> witchcraft, or casts spells, or who is a me-
> dium or spiritist or who consults the dead.
> Anyone who does these things is detestable
> to the Lord, and because of these detestable
> practices the Lord your God will drive out
> those nations before you. You must be blame-
> less before the Lord your God. The nations
> you will dispossess listen to those who prac-
> tice sorcery or divination. But as for you, the
> Lord your God has not permitted you to do so
> (Deut. 18:9-14).

In yet another passage God says, "I will set my face
against the person who turns to mediums and spiritists
to prostitute himself by following them, and I will cut
him off from his people." (Lev. 20:6). We can see how
serious God was about this in past history, but does He
still feel this way today? Consider His own answer, "I
the Lord do not change" (Mal. 3:6). It is therefore un-
imaginable that God would sanction now what He so
thoroughly denounced then. He did not speak through
these perverted forms of false revelation in the past, and
He does not speak through them today. Thus I say without hesitation, in the words of Scripture, that "those
who practice such things will not inherit the kingdom of
God" (Gal. 5:21, NKJV)!

Counterfeits aside, God is a supernatural being and
surely speaks through supernatural means. I refer to the
audible voice of God, divine manifestations of His presence, angelic encounters and similar phenomena which
can occur when God reveals Himself.

The Audible Voice

This form of revelation probably stands as the most assumed, yet least experienced, way that God expresses Himself. Most of us naturally imagine that when God speaks we should hear the classic "booming voice" of Hollywood films. Our assumption is aided by the fact that God did, on rare occasion, speak in this way to certain men. The most awesome example was when the nation of Israel literally *heard* the voice of God thunder from the top of Mount Sinai.

> When the people saw the thunder and light-
> ning and heard the trumpet and saw the
> mountain in smoke, they trembled with fear.
> They stayed at a distance and said to Moses,
> "Speak to us yourself and we will listen. But
> do not have God speak to us or we will die"
> (Ex. 20:18-19).

Nobody bothered to ask, "Is that You, Lord?" God's voice was audible and awesome. The people were terrified — and thankful not to hear Him again! Maybe this supplies us with a clue as to why God doesn't speak to us this way more often.

Centuries later on the mount of transfiguration the audible voice of God spoke to the disciples with the same unsettling effect.

> While he was still speaking, a bright cloud
> enveloped them, and a voice from the cloud
> said, "This is my Son, whom I love; with him
> I am well pleased. Listen to him!" When the
> disciples heard this, they fell facedown to the
> ground, terrified (Matt. 17:5-6).

This was an unforgettable experience for these men.

Peter wrote of it many years later in his letter to the dispersed Christians:

> We did not follow cleverly invented stories when we told you about the power and coming of our Lord Jesus Christ, but we were eyewitnesses of his majesty. For he received honor and glory from God the Father when the voice came to him from the Majestic Glory, saying, "This is my Son, whom I love; with him I am well pleased." We ourselves heard this voice that came from heaven when we were with him on the sacred mountain (2 Pet. 1:16-18).

There was no question in his mind that God had spoken to them. Though decades separated him from that ageless moment on the mountain, Peter's heart still trembled with awe at the memory of the holy experience he shared there with his Lord.

Sometimes, however (and this is baffling), when God spoke audibly it was not always so awesome. Neither was it that obvious or life-changing for those who were present when it happened. Consider the baptism of Jesus.

> When all the people were being baptized, Jesus was baptized too. And as he was praying, heaven was opened and the Holy Spirit descended on him in bodily form like a dove. And a voice came from heaven: "You are my Son, whom I love; with you I am well pleased" (Luke 3:21-22).

There is no hint whatsoever in any of the Gospel accounts that the baptism of Jesus was considered out of the ordinary by the people who witnessed it, even though it certainly was. What this means is that the great crowd there did *not* hear God's voice on this occasion, even though it was audible. The voice was for Jesus alone. To the crowd, Jesus was just another Jew being baptized!

John the Baptist said of this event,

> I saw the Spirit come down from heaven as a dove and remain on him. I would not have known him, except that the one who sent me to baptize with water told me, "The man on whom you see the Spirit come down and remain is he who will baptize with the Holy Spirit." I have seen and I testify that this is the Son of God (John 1:32-34).

Notice that John makes no reference whatsoever to the voice speaking to Jesus from heaven because he himself did not hear it. But John did *see* the Spirit, because it was the sign from God to him that Jesus was the One sent to be the Savior of the world.

On another occasion Jesus looked up and prayed, "Father, glorify your name!" The Bible continues, "Then a voice came from heaven, 'I have glorified it, and will glorify it again' " (see John 12:28). Clearly this was the voice of the Father, for it is the direct answer — in the first person — to the request Jesus had just made to Him. But now here is the astonishing thing:

> The crowd that was there and heard it said it had thundered; others said an angel had spoken to him (John 12:29).

Almighty God spoke *audibly* to Jesus Christ, yet only a few actually heard and understood His voice. The others, though they heard, completely missed what was happening and said that an *angel* was talking. Still others saw *nothing at all* supernatural in the incident. To them it was only thunder which they had heard countless times before, and so they went on about their day completely unaffected by this transcendent event! How strange that God could speak and some people not perceive it. Yet it happens, even today.

Still another puzzling example occurred at the dramatic conversion of the apostle Paul. Acts 9:7 records, "And the men who journeyed with him stood speechless, hearing a voice but seeing no one" (NKJV). But then, as Paul tells this story later, he says, "Now those who were with me indeed saw the light and were afraid, but they did not hear the voice of Him who spoke to me" (Acts 22:9, NKJV). One verse says they heard the voice but saw no one; the other says that they saw the light but did not hear the voice. Well, which was it? Clearly it was *both*, for some of the men saw but did not hear, while the others heard but did not see.

Now here is the point: evidently there are degrees of volume in the audible voice of God. Sometimes it is terrifying in its unfurled majesty, while at other times it is indistinct and veiled. Yet it is always discernible to those who have ears to hear. I know this is true because I myself have heard "a voice behind [me], saying, 'This is the way; walk in it' " (Is. 30:21). I hasten to add that, to date, I have *not* heard God speak as though from Mt. Sinai, nor as on the holy mount of the transfiguration. But I surely have *heard* His voice, not only in my dreams but in my waking hours as well.

As I related at the beginning of this book, I heard the voice of the Lord speak to me as a young boy running away from the orphanage. Those who were with me heard nothing, however; nor did they even notice that I had stopped in the field to converse with the One who had spoken to me. The voice was inside me, yet I looked up to see from where it came. Admittedly, this is an enigma, a difficult thing to explain. Nevertheless, it happened just as I have told it. I remember that incident so vividly today because it was not the simple fantasy of an adventurous youth; it was an actual experience that had a dramatic effect on the shaping of my character.

In more recent years, I found myself in desperate need of a clear, indisputable "word from God." I was faced with the major decision of whether or not to move our church congregation to a new location and to undertake the challenge of raising hundreds of thousands of dollars to that end. This was a time of intense pressure as I was stretched beyond all limits of my faith and ability to lead. The tension existed because the Spirit of God had surely given me several Scripture portions which clearly prompted me to do this, yet at the same time there were many in the church whose insight and counsel I highly esteemed who were adamant in their disagreement with me.

Frankly, several factors made such a move seem ill-advised. First, four previous churches had tried to succeed at the particular location to which we would be moving, and each had experienced dismal failure. We would be the fifth congregation attempting to prosper at this site. And the location itself was another solid reason for *not* doing this. The empty church facility sat in the middle of a forty-acre weed patch away from all surrounding communities. Would it be wise to plant a church in such a barren place?

The church elders, the deacons and most of the congregation all felt strongly that this proposal was not what God wanted us to do. Some even declared that the idea was nothing more than my own vanity and ambition. Whatever counsel I sought, whether from within or from outside the church, was either flatly against the move or neutral toward it. No one was able or willing to encourage me to seize this opportunity — except, of course, those who wanted to sell us the property!

Another major factor that added to the arguments

against the proposed move was the great cost it would entail. The challenge of multiplying our financial obligations by ten times the amount we were already struggling to give seemed impossible. Some went so far as to say it was absurd. I truly respected what others were saying, and I saw the sense of their arguments. But I simply could not shake off what I felt to be a word from the Lord leading us to do this crazy thing.

The gap between what I truly sensed the Lord was telling me to do and the public opinion within the church grew wider and wider, and the pressure increased with each passing day. The final blow, which almost knocked me out, came late in the evening on the night before I was to announce the official decision to the congregation. I poured my heart out to Belinda about these things and asked, "What is the Lord saying to you?"

"I don't know about this, James. I'm not so sure it's the Lord's will." Suddenly I felt totally alone in this decision. In retrospect, I can see that this was precisely what the Lord was seeking to accomplish. He was bringing me to the place where I would have to stand alone, for I had grown up dependent upon the opinions of others.

All my life had been spent trusting that others would make the tough decisions. I would always defer to them in some clever or convenient way, thereby avoiding the pressure of personal responsibility. I was a man-pleaser. I never intentionally did anything that would incur the disapproval and rejection of those around me. Whatever the crowd wanted was usually what I would do. But now, in this matter of pastoring and leading the church, God was holding me under divine constraint to persist on a course directly against the popular voice! This was to be my unsought baptism into leadership.

That moment of crisis was designed by God not simply to move the church from one place to another, but to move *me* from one place to another! It was an unavoidable transition from childhood into manhood, and my rite of passage necessitated the awful anguish of a lonely and unpopular decision. I once heard someone say, "Maturity does not come with age; it begins with the acceptance of personal responsibility." God was now bringing me into a new level of maturity, and I discovered in the process that every form of birth is attended with great pain.

That evening, after Belinda had expressed her honest misgivings, I left my house and began walking around the neighborhood crying out to God. Tears streamed down my face as the pressure, the anxiety, the fear and the confusion mounted against my soul. I specifically asked the Lord to speak to me audibly, for I felt I couldn't trust anything else. As I wandered aimlessly late into the night, I heard His voice. It was as before — inside of me, yet causing me to look up from where it came. All He did was ask me three simple questions, but in those moments God gave me what I needed.

The first question was abrupt and direct, stopping me in my tracks: "Why are you *crying?*"

"I'm crying because of all the bothersome things others are saying about this decision."

Then the Spirit of the Lord asked me the second question: "And what is it that makes you *happy?*"

I replied, "The things that *You* are saying about all of this."

There was but a moment's pause before this final inquiry from the Lord. "So, then, *whom* are you going to listen to?"

I cannot adequately explain all that happened in me as I stood there, but, to say the least, unshakable faith filled me. "Why, of course," I said, "I'm going to listen to *You!*" That settled it. All doubt was removed, and joy filled my heart.

The Holy Spirit highlighted a timely passage of

Scripture to me the next morning:

> Now, my son, the Lord be with you, and may
> you have success and build the house of the
> Lord your God, as he said you would. May
> the Lord give you discretion and under-
> standing when he puts you in command over
> Israel [His people], so that you may keep the
> law of the Lord your God. Then you will
> have success if you are careful to observe the
> decrees and laws that the Lord gave Moses
> for Israel. Be strong and courageous. Do not
> be afraid or discouraged.
>
> I have taken great pains to provide for the
> temple of the Lord a hundred thousand tal-
> ents of gold, a million talents of silver, quan-
> tities of bronze and iron too great to be
> weighed, and wood and stone. And you may
> add to them. You have many workmen:
> stonecutters, masons and carpenters, as well
> as men skilled in every kind of work in gold
> and silver, bronze and iron — craftsmen be-
> yond number. Now begin the work, and the
> Lord be with you! (1 Chron. 22:11-16).

I resolved to do what I believed the Lord had been
saying all along: to move the church and take on the
challenge. The hearts of many people changed as they
suddenly caught the vision of what God was doing, and
in the following months we began to experience a dramatic turnaround in the church. Each passing season has
brought us deeper and deeper into the faithfulness of
God. Now everybody celebrates our move to the new
location as a wise decision, for we are sitting right in the
middle of an area booming with growth. God has
blessed us with staggering success, multiplying our
church over ten-fold in its size since we moved — and it

continues to grow! Our initial fears of incurring great
financial debt have been superceded by God's faithfulness to His Word:

> "Bring the whole tithe into the storehouse,
> that there may be food in my house. Test me
> in this," says the Lord Almighty, "and see if I
> will not throw open the floodgates of heaven
> and pour out so much blessing that you will
> not have room enough for it" (Mal. 3:10).

Our church now stands among the many who bear
witness to the truth of the Holy Spirit's encouraging
promise: "God is able to make all grace abound to you,
so that in all things at all times, having all that you need,
you will abound in every good work" (2 Cor. 9:8).
Praise the Lord! All the glory belongs to God, and this
story illustrates again the dramatic impact of hearing
the voice of the Lord — and the happy consequences of
obeying Him.

The "conversation" God had with me as I walked that
night was not audible in any *awesome* way; nor would
anyone else have heard His voice or seen His form.
Nevertheless, I *surely* heard the Lord ask those three
questions. It could not have been clearer or more certain
even had it been discernible to my natural ears. And the
effects are lasting to this very day, for the word of the
Lord has come to pass as He gave me hope to believe it
would that night when He heard my cry. There is absolutely no doubt in my mind that God still speaks audibly
to His people today. My prayer is that you will hear His
voice for yourself; that will be proof enough.

Divine Manifestations of God

There are many times in the Bible when God actually
appeared to His people. Sometimes He came to them in

dreams and visions (as we have already observed), while at other times He came in different forms. But always the encounters were tangible.

> The Lord appeared to Abraham near the great trees of Mamre while he was sitting at the entrance to his tent in the heat of the day. Abraham looked up and saw three men standing nearby. When he saw them, he hurried from the entrance of his tent to meet them and bowed low to the ground. He said, "If I have found favor in your eyes, my lord, do not pass your servant by" (Gen. 18:1-3).

Abraham knew one of these men was the Lord because he had seen Him before (Gen. 12:7; 15:1-6). The other two "men" standing with the Lord were the angels that would later be sent to judge Sodom and Gomorrah. Evidently this was a stopover visit on their way.

Abraham's meeting with the Lord here was *real*. It was a supernatural event in natural circumstances. The Lord actually appeared in the discernible form of a man and spoke with Abraham, and He even ate a dinner Sarah had cooked (see Gen. 18:8)!

Nor was this the last time the Lord visited Abraham. Take, for example, the mysterious Melchizedek who met Abraham as he was returning from battle. Who was he? His description in the book of Hebrews indicates that he was none other than the Lord Jesus Christ in a pre-incarnate form!

> This Melchizedek was king of Salem and priest of God Most High. He met Abraham returning from the defeat of the kings and blessed him, and Abraham gave him a tenth of everything. First, his name means "king of righteousness"; then also, "king of Salem"

means "king of peace." Without father or
mother, without genealogy, without beginning of days or end of life, like the Son of
God he remains a priest forever. Just think
how great he was: Even the patriarch Abraham gave him a tenth of the plunder! (Heb.
7:1-4).

In yet another time and place the Lord appeared as a
military officer to Joshua.

Now when Joshua was near Jericho, he
looked up and saw a man standing in front of
him with a drawn sword in his hand. Joshua
went up to him and asked, "Are you for us or
for our enemies?"

"Neither," he replied, "but as commander
of the army of the Lord I have now come."
Then Joshua fell facedown to the ground in
reverence, and asked him, "What message
does my Lord have for his servant?"

The commander of the Lord's army replied, "Take off your sandals, for the place
where you are standing is holy." And Joshua
did so (Josh. 5:13-15).

The story begins with a man standing before Joshua,
but it ends with Joshua bowing before the Lord! And
there is absolutely no doubt that it was the Lord who
was speaking to Joshua, for those words echo the Lord's
words to Moses as he approached the burning bush that
did not burn up (Ex. 3:1-5).

The fire that Moses saw in the midst of the bush was
a *supernatural* manifestation of the presence of the
Lord. It was something beyond the rational, concrete,
logical world of facts and figures: glowing flames in a
bush that was not consumed. This is remarkably similar

to what is referred to as "the glory of the Lord," that
resplendent cloud of light that appeared on special occasions throughout the Bible.

> Then the cloud covered the Tent of Meeting,
> and the glory of the Lord filled the taberna-
> cle. Moses could not enter the Tent of Meet-
> ing because the cloud had settled upon it, and
> the glory of the Lord filled the tabernacle
> (Ex. 40:34-35).

This unique manifestation of God served as a divine
imprimatur on the tabernacle Moses had erected in obedience to the word of the Lord.

The people of Israel *knew* what this cloud of glory
meant, for they had seen it themselves in an earlier dramatic encounter with God:

> Moses and Aaron, Nadab and Abihu, and the
> seventy elders of Israel went up and saw the
> God of Israel. Under his feet was something
> like a pavement made of sapphire, clear as
> the sky itself. But God did not raise his
> hand against these leaders of the Israelites;
> they saw God, and they ate and drank (Ex.
> 24:9-11).

As the people of Israel waited on the plains below
with their eyes fixed upon the mountain, they saw the
glory of the Lord settle on Mount Sinai. For six days the
cloud covered the mountain, and on the seventh day the
Lord called to Moses from within the cloud.

> To the Israelites the glory of the Lord looked
> like a consuming fire on top of the mountain
> (Ex. 24:17).

Several hundred years later, at the dedication of the temple in Jerusalem, this glorious cloud appeared yet again when the priests brought the ark of God into the holy of holies.

> When the priests withdrew from the Holy Place, the cloud filled the temple of the Lord. And the priests could not perform their service because of the cloud, for the glory of the Lord filled his temple (1 Kin. 8:10-11).

Each time this cloud of God's glory appeared, all who saw it were awestruck and filled with unspeakable joy. The most wonderful example of all time happened on the night that Jesus was born in Bethlehem.

> An angel of the Lord appeared to them, and the glory of the Lord shone around them, and they were terrified (Luke 2:9).

How fitting that this cloud of light should attend His birth, seeing it had also been present at every other time He appeared. Though to the eyes of man, Jesus was but a baby in a manger, the *glory of God* bore witness of His birth, and the angelic host loudly proclaimed that the true Ark of God had now come into the temple of the Lord!

I believe that God is pleased to bless us with this phenomenon today. Jesus prayed in the upper room:

> Father...I have given them the glory that you gave me, that they may be one as we are one: I in them and you in me. May they be brought to complete unity to let the world know that you sent me and have loved them even as you have loved me. Father, I want those you have given me to be with me where I am, and to

see my glory, the glory you have given me
because you loved me before the creation of
the world (John 17:21-24).

Though it defies explanation, I know for certain that
I have, from time to time, seen a *measure* of the appearance of the likeness of the glory of the Lord (Ezek.
1:27-28) during church meetings and other Christian
assemblies. It appeared as a cloud of light, a brilliant
mist, giving the entire room a glow that would not otherwise be there. A sense of wonder filled the air as we
worshipped God and loved one another. And to a measure, for those brief moments when heaven touched the
earth, Jesus' prayer that we might see His glory was
answered!

We have seen that God appeared to men on earth.
Now let's look at the few times when He actually took
men up into heaven through supernatural experiences in
the spirit.

The prophet Isaiah comes to mind as a great example.
He didn't simply wake up one day and decide that he
would make a career move and become a prophet. No,
God initiated the work in Isaiah by a sovereign invitation and commissioning. Here is Isaiah's testimony of
that sublime encounter.

In the year that King Uzziah died, I saw the
Lord seated on a throne, high and exalted,
and the train of his robe filled the temple.
Above him were seraphs, each with six
wings: With two wings they covered their
faces, with two they covered their feet, and
with two they were flying. And they were
calling to one another: "Holy, holy, holy is
the Lord Almighty; the whole earth is full of
his glory." At the sound of their voices the
doorposts and thresholds shook and the tem-

ple was filled with smoke. "Woe to me!" I
cried. "I am ruined! For I am a man of unclean lips, and I live among a people of unclean lips, and my eyes have seen the King,
the Lord Almighty."

Then one of the seraphs flew to me with a
live coal in his hand, which he had taken with
tongs from the altar. With it he touched my
mouth and said, "See, this has touched your
lips; your guilt is taken away and your sin
atoned for." Then I heard the voice of the
Lord saying, "Whom shall I send? And who
will go for us?" And I said, "Here am I. Send
me!" (Is. 6:1-8).

The reality of Isaiah's experience is validated by the
fact that to this day we know his name, heed his sayings
and worship his God. What other wandering poet of 700
B.C. can boast as much?

The prophet Ezekiel is yet another witness whose
supernatural encounters with the Lord cannot be overlooked. His initial meeting with God was so overwhelming that he would forever remember exactly
when and where it happened.

In the thirtieth year, in the fourth month on
the fifth day, while I was among the exiles by
the Kebar River, the heavens were opened
and I saw visions of God (Ezek. 1:1).

He then proceeds to describe, as best he can, exactly
what he saw.

I saw that from what appeared to be his waist
up he looked like glowing metal, as if full of
fire, and that from there down he looked like
fire; and brilliant light surrounded him. Like

> the appearance of a rainbow in the clouds on
> a rainy day, so was the radiance around him.
> This was the appearance of the likeness of
> the glory of the Lord. When I saw it, I fell
> facedown, and I heard the voice of one
> speaking (Ezek. 1:27-28).

I respect Ezekiel's qualified description and the pru-
dence of his well-chosen words. "Hey, Ezekiel, did you
see the Lord?"

"Well, no, I didn't actually see the *Lord.* What I saw
was the *glory* of the Lord. No, wait a minute — it
wasn't the glory of the Lord that I saw; it was the *likeness* of the glory of the Lord. No, no, no, that's not it
either; what I saw was the *appearance* of the likeness of
the glory of the Lord. Yes, that's it. That's what I saw!"
In the first chapter alone Ezekiel uses words such as *like*
and *appearance* at least eighteen times. It's virtually
impossible to describe the indescribable.

Ezekiel's first visitation led to many others:

> Then the Spirit lifted me up, and I heard be-
> hind me a loud rumbling sound — May the
> glory of the Lord be praised in his dwelling
> place! — the sound of the wings of the living
> creatures brushing against each other and the
> sound of the wheels beside them, a loud rum-
> bling sound. The Spirit then lifted me up and
> took me away, and I went in bitterness and in
> the anger of my spirit, with the strong hand
> of the Lord upon me (Ezek. 3:12-14).

And yet another time Ezekiel says:

> In the sixth year, in the sixth month on the
> fifth day, while I was sitting in my house and
> the elders of Judah were sitting before me,

the hand of the Sovereign Lord came upon
me there. I looked, and I saw a figure like
that of a man. From what appeared to be his
waist down he was like fire, and from there
up his appearance was as bright as glowing
metal. He stretched out what looked like a
hand and took me by the hair of my head. The
Spirit lifted me up between earth and heaven
and in visions of God he took me to Jerusalem, to the entrance to the north gate of the
inner court, where the idol that provokes to
jealousy stood. And there before me was the
glory of the God of Israel, as in the vision I
had seen in the plain (Ezek. 8:1-4).

Each visitation had a purpose. The Lord spoke to
Ezekiel during these experiences and showed him what
he was to say and do.

I make no apology for admitting that at this point I
am only able to draw upon the examples recorded in the
Bible for this kind of visitation. I have *never* been
picked up by the hair and taken anywhere by the Spirit!
What this must have been like for Ezekiel can only be a
matter for speculation within our hearts — until the
Lord visits us in similar ways. (But, rest in peace; modern scholarship has assured us that God doesn't *do*
things like this anymore!)

The apostle Paul testifies in the New Testament that
God's use of supernatural phenomena as a means of
guidance was *not* exclusive to the days of old. He wrote
to the Christians in Corinth and told them of visions and
revelations he had received from the Lord:

I know a man in Christ who fourteen years
ago was caught up to the third heaven.
Whether it was in the body or out of the body
I do not know — God knows. And I know

that this man — whether in the body or apart
from the body I do not know, but God knows
— was caught up to paradise. He heard inexpressible things, things that man is not permitted to tell (2 Cor. 12:2-4).

We know that Paul is speaking about himself in this
cryptic passage because he writes later in the same
chapter, "To keep me from becoming conceited because
of these surpassingly great revelations, there was given
me a thorn in my flesh, a messenger of Satan, to torment
me" (v. 7). His personal testimony supplies us with wisdom when it comes to discussing these kinds of things
today. First, notice the simultaneous clarity *and* perplexity of a supernatural experience. "I know a man in
Christ who fourteen years ago was caught up to the third
heaven." That much is clear to him, but then he adds:
"Whether it was in the body or out of the body I do not
know — God knows." There's the perplexity. He *knows*
that it happened, he just can't figure out *how* it happened.

Another lesson we learn from Paul is the importance
of exercising great discretion when talking about spiritual matters of this sort. He says that this man "heard
inexpressible things, things that man is not permitted to
tell." Though Paul is speaking of himself, he veils it in
language that does not draw attention to himself but
leads us to think it was someone else. Also, he doesn't
give much detail of what he saw when he was "caught
up to the third heaven." He simply says that it happened
and leaves it at that. Paul's experience was undeniable
and mysterious, and he handled it with wisdom.

The "tongues of fire" that appeared upon the disciples on the day of Pentecost were yet *another* visible
and supernatural sign of the presence of the Lord, as
was the miraculous power evident in their midst. The
intoxicating joy of this experience was so divine as to

be unmistakably from the Lord.

> Then Peter stood up with the Eleven, raised
> his voice and addressed the crowd: "Fellow
> Jews and all of you who live in Jerusalem, let
> me explain this to you; listen carefully to
> what I say. These men are not drunk, as you
> suppose. It's only nine in the morning! No,
> this is what was spoken by the prophet Joel:
> 'In the last days, God says, I will pour out my
> Spirit on all people. Your sons and daughters
> will prophesy, your young men will see vi-
> sions, your old men will dream dreams. Even
> on my servants, both men and women, I will
> pour out my Spirit in those days, and they
> will prophesy. I will show wonders in the
> heaven above and signs on the earth below,
> blood and fire and billows of smoke. The sun
> will be turned to darkness and the moon to
> blood before the coming of the great and glo-
> rious day of the Lord. And everyone who
> calls on the name of the Lord will be saved' "
> (Acts 2:14-21).

Later, Peter saw this happen again in the house of
Cornelius, and he was quick to acknowledge that it was
the Lord visiting the Gentiles. This was unprecedented
and totally unexpected.

> The circumcised believers who had come
> with Peter were astonished that the gift of the
> Holy Spirit had been poured out even on the
> Gentiles....Then Peter said, "Can anyone
> keep these people from being baptized with
> water? They have received the Holy Spirit
> just as we have" (Acts 10:45-47).

A few months later, when the brothers in Jerusalem challenged Peter about his unbelievable episode with Gentiles, Peter answered, "As I began to speak, the Holy Spirit came on them as he had come on us at the beginning" (Acts 11:15). Having silenced them with the facts, Peter closes his defense with a convincing argument, "So if God gave them the same gift as he gave us, who believed in the Lord Jesus Christ, who was I to think that I could oppose God?" (Acts 11:17). The point is that God gave Peter an assurance that this experience was of the Lord by a manifestation of the Holy Spirit with which he was familiar.

The apostle Paul wrote, "Now to each one the manifestation of the Spirit is given for the common good" (1 Cor. 12:7). The word translated as *manifestation* means "exhibition, expression, a bestowment; to touch with the hand." I once heard a preacher refer to the moving of the Holy Spirit upon a congregation as "the festive hand of God." This is rich imagery, for it portrays the Lord in the midst of His church touching His people in random, joyful expressions of the Spirit's presence. These "visits" are to be taken for all they are worth. Many times the Lord has guided me by nothing more than "His hand upon me." This gave me assurance of anointing and favor, but by no means relieved me of the personal responsibility to believe and obey.

Angels

God also makes Himself known to us through the visitation and ministry of angels. Many such instances are given to us in the Bible. The prophet Daniel tops the list when it comes to encounters with angelic beings. The angel Gabriel, noted throughout Scripture as a special envoy of the Lord, appeared to Daniel on more than one occasion:

> While I was speaking and praying, confessing my sin and the sin of my people Israel and making my request to the Lord my God for his holy hill — while I was still in prayer, Gabriel, the man I had seen in the earlier vision, came to me in swift flight about the time of the evening sacrifice. He instructed me and said to me, "Daniel, I have now come to give you insight and understanding. As soon as you began to pray, an answer was given, which I have come to tell you, for you are highly esteemed. Therefore, consider the message and understand the vision (Dan. 9:20-23).

Gabriel went on to explain to Daniel the meaning of what he had seen in a vision. Reading through this account makes angelic visitations seem rather matter-of-fact. But not all of Daniel's experiences were so serene.

> On the twenty-fourth day of the first month, as I was standing on the bank of the great river, the Tigris, I looked up and there before me was a man dressed in linen, with a belt of the finest gold around his waist. His body was like chrysolite, his face like lightning, his eyes like flaming torches, his arms and legs like the gleam of burnished bronze, and his voice like the sound of a multitude. I, Daniel, was the only one who saw the vision; the men with me did not see it, but such terror overwhelmed them that they fled and hid themselves. So I was left alone, gazing at this great vision; I had no strength left, my face turned deathly pale and I was helpless. Then I heard him speaking, and as I listened to him, I fell into a deep sleep, my face to the ground.

> A hand touched me and set me trembling
> on my hands and knees. He said, "Daniel,
> you who are highly esteemed, consider care-
> fully the words I am about to speak to you,
> and stand up, for I have now been sent to
> you" (Dan. 10:4-11).

Daniel's account of this visitation is very informative. He clearly remembers where he was and what he
was doing when it happened. He was able to give a
detailed description of how the angel looked. He knew
distinctly that he was seeing things which others were
not able to see, and he somehow managed to compose
himself in the presence of what terrified the others. (It is
noteworthy that on most occasions when angels appear
to people, the angels' first words are "Fear not!") The
experience ultimately proved to be so overwhelming
that he passed out, for the angel was not merely visible,
but tangible as well, *touching* Daniel with his hand. And
finally, there was purpose in the visit: The angel spoke a
message from the Lord.

My point in highlighting these facts is to show that a
person can be levelheaded in the midst of a supernatural
experience. We are not talking about some hokey nitwit
with a palm-reading sign set up in his front window on
the seedy side of town. Daniel was an astute, highly
educated man who was well suited for conversation in
the presence of kings and lords.

> The king talked with them, and he found
> none equal to Daniel, Hananiah, Mishael and
> Azariah; so they entered the king's service.
> In every matter of wisdom and understanding
> about which the king questioned them, he
> found them ten times better than all the magi-
> cians and enchanters in his whole kingdom
> (Dan. 1:19-20).

Daniel's experiences show that one can be *both* intelligent and metaphysical at the same time. Some people are so heavenly minded that they are no earthly good, while others are just the opposite. But God wants us to be balanced men and women, our feet firmly on the ground while our hearts are fixed on heaven.

Job's friend shared an encounter similar to Daniel's with another supernatural visitor.

> A word was secretly brought to me, my ears caught a whisper of it. Amid disquieting dreams in the night, when deep sleep falls on men, fear and trembling seized me and made all my bones shake. A spirit glided past my face, and the hair on my body stood on end. It stopped, but I could not tell what it was. A form stood before my eyes, and I heard a hushed voice: "Can a mortal be more righteous than God? Can a man be more pure than his Maker?" (Job 4:12-17).

This text not only gives another example of a supernatural encounter in which a man receives a word from God, but it also shows some of the physical and emotional "overload" that occurs when a mortal meets with a being from eternity.

Note the secrecy of it, coming as a whisper. At first it is something that could almost be missed, unnoticed. But mark the disturbance it brings amid disquieting dreams of the night and troubled thoughts. Fear and trembling are then added to the experience, shaking the man to the core of his being as his hair stands on end. Finally, with his own eyes he sees a spirit, yet, in his own words, he "could not tell what it was." However, when the words were spoken, he knew he was hearing a message from God — delivered no doubt by an angel.

Are all angels this obvious and terrifying? The answer is no. The Bible says, "Do not forget to entertain strangers, for by so doing some people have entertained angels without knowing it" (Heb. 13:2). How many angels do you suppose *you* have actually seen without realizing it? This is not a ridiculous question. The Scripture does say, "In speaking of the angels he says, 'He makes his angels winds, his servants flames of fire' " (Heb. 1:7). And again, "Are not all angels ministering spirits sent to serve those who will inherit salvation?" (Heb. 1:14). The Lord is pleased to send them on their missions of mercy, and we for our part should welcome their service.

Jesus Himself was visited by angels at different times. After His grueling temptation in the wilderness, God sent angels to comfort Him (Matt. 4:11). During His unspeakable agony in Gethsemane "an angel from heaven appeared to him and strengthened him" (Luke 22:43). And as He hung on the cross there were more than twelve thousand mighty angels at His disposal, waiting for His call (Matt. 26:53)! Two angels dressed in white stood at the portal of His empty tomb on the morning of His resurrection (Luke 24:4). (What a happy assignment that must have been!)

After Jesus ascended, two angels again appeared and asked the disciples, "Men of Galilee...why do you stand here looking into the sky? This same Jesus, who has been taken from you into heaven, will come back in the same way you have seen him go into heaven" (Acts 1:11). Now that Jesus sits enthroned in heaven, and the angels fly about Him crying, "Holy, holy, holy is the Lord Almighty; the whole earth is full of his glory!" (Is. 6:3). Finally, when the Lord returns to the earth as the King of kings, the Bible says His coming will be attended with thousands upon thousands of holy angels! (See 2 Thess. 1:7; Jude 14.)

The first disciples had their own encounters with angels and received significant guidance from God through their intervention. Jesus prophesied to Nathaniel that he would "see heaven open, and the angels of God ascending and descending on the Son of Man" (John 1:51). While we have no biblical account of this happening later, we know, in fact, that it did. Philip was told by an angel to leave a citywide revival meeting for an isolated rendezvous with a man in the desert (Acts 8:26). He obeyed and saw the dramatic conversion of an Ethiopian dignitary and then experienced a supernatural transportation to another city miles away (Acts 8:40).

Cornelius, a commander of Italian soldiers, was a just man who feared God and loved His people. An angel from the Lord appeared to him and gave him specific instructions about securing the evangelistic services of a man named Peter. (Why didn't the angel just preach the gospel to him right then? Because angels have not been entrusted with that privilege — *we* have!) Cornelius followed the instructions and saw his whole household converted as Peter shared the story of Jesus Christ (see Acts 10). Peter himself was let out of prison by an angel (Acts 12:7-11), and Paul was given assurance of salvation during a storm on the high seas (Acts 27:23). Finally, I need only allude to the many angelic encounters John the Beloved had while exiled on the dreadful Isle of Patmos.

In the summer of 1989, Belinda and I were attending a conference on prophecy at the Anaheim Vineyard in California. Early one morning I woke up and saw an angel of the Lord standing at my bedside in the hotel. He looked like a soldier standing at attention. He was resolute with a sense of duty and actually held his hand above his forehead in a military salute — as if acknowledging a senior officer. His form resembled a tornado, narrow at the bottom and broad at the top. He stood taller than the room, but somehow I could see through the ceiling to his full height!

I shuddered with fear and jumped out of my bed to my feet. The appearance lasted for a few short seconds, and as my eyes finally adjusted to the darkness of my room, I concluded that all I had seen were shadows on the curtain or perhaps the effects of filtered light showing through the window.

I calmed my racing heart with a few deep breaths and climbed back into my bed. After repeatedly opening my eyes every few moments (just to make sure), I warily drifted off to sleep. I probably would have dismissed and forgotten the incident altogether if it were not for the dream I then had.

In my dream it was the next morning. I was dressed and putting on my shoes when a friend walked into our hotel room.

"Hi, James," he said, and I returned his greeting. He then looked directly at me and asked, "Did you see the angel last night?"

I was shocked. "So that *was* an angel! What did he want?" I asked.

My friend replied, "He has been assigned to you by the Lord to oppose you any time you do *not* do what the Lord wants you to do!"

That is *not* good news, I thought, knowing how often I falter in my obedience to the Lord.

But then my friend concluded, "However, he will *also* oppose those who stand against you when you *are* doing what the Lord wants!" That changed my view considerably.

I awoke from the dream, sobered by a sense of responsibility. Many times since then I have thought about that night, and the memory of it always motivates me to walk faithfully before the Lord — and before the guardian angel! Believe me, I realize how bizarre all this might sound, but I would be less than honest if I denied that it had happened.

More recently I was again visited by an angel in a

dream. He came and stood before me, saying nothing. I gathered by his silence that he was waiting for me to initiate conversation, so I asked, "What are you doing here?"

The angel looked at me and answered, "I have been sent from the Father to ask you a question."

"All right," I responded, "what's the question?"

Then the angel said, "The Father wants to know, 'Are you going to go the distance?' "

I was speechless. The first thought that struck my mind was, You mean He doesn't *know*? Then I remembered a lesson I had learned some time before: When God asks a question it is not because He needs to know the answer. Rather it is His way of letting us hear the answer that we give, so that *we* can see what that reveals about us. With this in mind I said to the angel, "Let the Father know that I said, '*Yes!* Yes, I am going to go the distance!' "

As I spoke, I suddenly felt something lift from me — a weight I did not know I had been carrying.

"What was that?" I asked the angel.

"That was the spirit of indecision," he replied. "It is the one thing that keeps so many of God's servants from going the distance. They are afraid of being presumptuous and ambitious, so they surrender to indecision and inactivity. Afraid to believe, they hesitate to be decisive in faithfulness and obedience. The reason it fell off you is that your faith broke its power when you answered decisively."

What about you? Are *you* going to go the distance?

Chapter 9

Discerning
the Voice
of the Lord

I s that *You*, Lord?" Who among us has never asked this question? Perhaps many times we have dreamed or have seen an unusual event and pondered its meaning. Maybe we have had an inner impression as we talked with another person, or even looked at a Scripture verse that seemed to address an immediate need in our lives — wondering all the while if the Lord was *really* speaking to us through these things. We know that He does speak to us — now one way, now another — but we also understand that we have a responsibility to *discern* whether or not what we are seeing or hearing is truly from the Lord.

Are all dreams from God? Are all angels from God? Are all revelations from God? Are all quotations from the Bible to be taken as the Lord speaking to me now? Certainly not. Dreams can be triggered by many things other than God. As for angels, "Satan himself masquerades as an angel of light" (2 Cor. 11:14). And one should not take every quotation from the Bible as a personal word from the Lord. The devil settled that for us when *he* quoted Scripture to Jesus, tempting Him to jump from the pinnacle of the temple.

Then how can I *know* that the Lord is truly the One who is speaking to me? How can I know that I am not making things up to assert my own opinions or to suit my own desires? Or, worse yet, how can I be sure I am not actually being *deceived* with false revelation from some sinister spirit? Every earnest seeker of God asks these legitimate questions. Is there, then, a true standard of judgment to which we may submit all revelation and settle questions authoritatively? *Yes!*

Before looking into how we can discern the ways God speaks, now is a good time to address the nagging questions in some of our minds. Why does God make it so difficult to hear His voice? If the Lord really desires to speak to us, why doesn't He just part the skies every day and tell us what He wants us to do? Why hide it in all these riddles? Why is God's voice something we must discern? Why must we dig through mountains to find the gold? Why must we dive for oysters to find a pearl? There are at least two reasons why the Lord speaks in the ways that He does: *memory* and *motivation*.

Memory

God speaks in vivid pictures which forever etch themselves within our minds — like paintings hanging on the walls of a museum — because a picture is worth a thousand words. He often teases our minds with baffling riddles, knowing full well that we will never forget their meaning once He unfolds them to us. Nothing is so impacting as the long-awaited solution to a puzzle. Think back over your life with the Lord and see how true this is. Aren't your clearest memories the ones when the Lord turned on the lights in a darkened room? When a revelation from the Lord actually causes your mouth to drop open in astonishment, you are not likely to forget that moment.

Consider the playful way in which He spoke to the youthful Jeremiah.

> The word of the Lord came to me: "What do you see, Jeremiah?" "I see the branch of an almond tree," I replied. The Lord said to me, "You have seen correctly, for I am watching to see that my word is fulfilled" (Jer. 1:11-12).

What in the world is the Lord talking about? An almond branch means God is watching? I just don't get it. I have read this verse many times from several translations, and it simply does not make any sense to me.

The answer to this riddle is found in the Hebrew words which were used in the text. When Jeremiah saw the branch of an *almond* tree, he used the Hebrew word, *shaqed* (pronounced shaw-kade′), which means the almond tree when it is earliest in bloom. And when the Lord said, "I am *watching* My word," the word He used was *shaqad* (pronounced shaw-kad′), which means to be alert and sleepless; on the lookout.

This prophetic revelation came to Jeremiah from the Lord, and it was a *pun!* What a laugh (or moan) Jeremiah must've had. I can just see him rolling his eyes and saying, "Oh, brother." Whether this is how Jeremiah responded or not I really can't say, but this much I do know: He would never again look at an almond tree in the same way. Every time he saw one, he would remember that God was *watching* over His Word to see that it was performed. In the cold of winter, when all else lay dormant beneath the chilled earth, the early bloom of the almond tree was there to remind him of God's faithfulness to His promises! This undoubtedly brought much encouragement to Jeremiah on many occasions throughout his life.

Motivation

> It is the glory of God to conceal a matter; to search out a matter is the glory of kings (Prov. 25:2).

The dark and mysterious sayings of God in no way indicate an unwillingness on His part to grant us revelation. Rather these things are to be taken as invitations to an adventure! The whole point of seeking God for a solution to a mystery is not simply that we may have the answer but that we might develop a relationship with Him. The Lord wants to spend time with us; "hide and seek" is one way He does this.

The Lord often presents us with an enigma to see how serious we are about seeking His face. Often He catches our ear with just a whisper to see how desperate we are to hear His voice. The inconvenience of "dark sayings" separates the halfhearted from the diligent — the commoners from the kings. In other words God often "hides" what He wants us to know to test our motives. He is seeing if we will stir ourselves to pursue Him or merely settle for the notion that God's ways are past finding out. "You will seek me and find me when you seek me with all your heart" (Jer. 29:13).

As we seek to hear and discern the voice of God, we are not that different from His people of old when they entered the promised land. God said,

> I will send the hornet ahead of you to drive
> the Hivites, Canaanites and Hittites out of
> your way. But I will not drive them out in a
> single year, because the land would become
> desolate and the wild animals too numerous
> for you. Little by little I will drive them out
> before you, until you have increased enough
> to take possession of the land (Ex. 23:28-30).

Later we find that the Lord left some nations to test
those Israelites who had not experienced any of the
wars in Canaan. The writer of Judges says, "He did this
only to teach warfare to the descendants of the Israelites
who had not had previous battle experience" (Judg.
3:2). God wants us to hear and understand His voice,
but at the same time He leaves some obstacles between
us and Him in order to teach us how to fight through the
cloud of spiritual opposition.

God also hides the treasure from us as a means of
fostering His own values in our hearts. If He were to set
before us the full portion of all He would have us know,
we would surely take it for granted and eventually set it
aside. One of life's lessons is that we devalue things that
are obtained too easily. On the other hand, the more
complicated the hunt, the more cherished the prize; the
fiercer the battle, the sweeter the victory.

Maturity

When we are newborn Christians, we require the
"milk" of the Word. That is, we need someone to feed us
with the elementary truths of the Christian life and show
us right from wrong. As we grow spiritually, we must
begin to develop our own ability to hear and discern
God's Word to us — moving from milk to solid food.

Hebrews 5:14 states, "Solid food is for the mature, who by constant use have trained themselves to distinguish good from evil." God uses progressively challenging ways to help us mature and develop our spiritual insight and understanding of how He communicates with us personally. When He gives us a riddle to solve, He is expanding our diet.

> And if you extract the precious from the worthless, you will become My spokesman (Jer. 15:19, NAS).

Our Helper, the Holy Spirit

Jesus promised that we would never be left to fend for ourselves without His help and guidance:

> I will ask the Father, and he will give you another Counselor to be with you forever — the Spirit of truth. The world cannot accept him, because it neither sees him nor knows him. But you know him, for he lives with you and will be in you. I will not leave you as orphans; I will come to you (John 14:16-18).

The apostle Paul wrote:

> For who among men knows the thoughts of a man except the man's spirit within him? In the same way no one knows the thoughts of God except the Spirit of God. We have not received the spirit of the world but the Spirit who is from God, that we may understand what God has freely given us. This is what we speak, not in words taught us by human wisdom but in words taught by the Spirit, expressing spiritual truths in spiritual words.

The man without the Spirit does not accept
the things that come from the Spirit of God,
for they are foolishness to him, and he cannot
understand them, because they are spiritually
discerned. The spiritual man makes judgments about all things, but he himself is not
subject to any man's judgment: "For who has
known the mind of the Lord that he may instruct him?" But we have the mind of Christ
(1 Cor. 2:11-16).

The logic of Paul's argument is brilliant and irrefutable. He begins by saying that the Holy Spirit alone
knows the thoughts of God. Have you ever had someone
try to put words in your mouth or tell you what you were
thinking — when they were completely wrong?

"Wait just a minute!" you answer. "That's not at all
what I'm thinking!"

We don't like others making assumptions about us,
yet how often have *we* done this very thing to the Lord?

The Lord's response to us is as equally direct as our
response is to others: Don't put *your* words in *My*
mouth, and don't try to tell *Me* what I am thinking!

"For *I know* the plans I have for you," de-
clares the Lord, "plans to prosper you and not
to harm you, plans to give you hope and a
future" (Jer. 29:11, italics added).

The first fact Paul sets before us is: No one knows
what God is thinking but God Himself.

The second point of Paul's argument is that God has
filled us with His Holy Spirit, "that we may understand
what God has freely given us!" The Holy Spirit turns
our hearts away from sinfulness and selfishness (the
two major barriers to hearing His voice) and gives us
spiritual minds by teaching us spiritual truths. There-

fore, the more we develop in our relationship with the Holy Spirit, the greater our capacity becomes for discerning what God is saying and doing.

> Do not conform any longer to the pattern of this world, but be transformed by the renewing of your mind. Then you will be able to test and approve what God's will is — his good, pleasing and perfect will (Rom. 12:2).

Paul's third point is that the natural mind cannot receive the truth of God, for such truth seems utterly ridiculous when viewed through the lens of practical reasoning. Imagine, for example, what would happen if a junior executive of a successful corporation announced at a board meeting of national stockholders that an angel appeared to him in a dream saying that the proposed merger with another company was a bad deal. Or consider a shop assistant suggesting that a customer, money in hand, should return home and first pray about the purchase he or she was about to make.

And while we're on the subject of money, try this some time: Waltz into any business and tell the people that God will prosper them if they give ten percent of their profits to a local church! The proprietor might give you an incredulous stare as he roared, "Are you completely out of your mind?"

The things of the Spirit appear foolish to our own reasoning. By contrast, Paul assures us that *spiritual* people are able to judge all things because God has given them "the mind of Christ" by the indwelling of the Holy Spirit. But the assurance that we *can* discern the things of God doesn't explain *how* to do it. The question still before us is simple and direct: How do we discern the voice of the Lord?

The Threefold Test for All
"Words From God"

To make this as pragmatic as possible, let me list
three specific ways the Holy Spirit has taught me to test
every word claiming to be from God. When I receive
insight about anything, I always ask: Does it honor the
lordship of Jesus Christ? Does it align with the Scriptures? Does it produce the fruit of the Spirit? These are
the indisputable means of discerning every verse,
dream, vision, prophecy, impression or spiritual experience we encounter.

The Lordship of Jesus Christ

> In the past God spoke to our forefathers
> through the prophets at many times and in
> various ways, but in these last days he has
> spoken to us by his Son, whom he appointed
> heir of all things, and through whom he made
> the universe. The Son is the radiance of
> God's glory and the exact representation of
> his being, sustaining all things by his power-
> ful word. After he had provided purification
> for sins, he sat down at the right hand of the
> Majesty in heaven. So he became as much
> superior to the angels as the name he has in-
> herited is superior to theirs (Heb. 1:1-4).

The supreme test of all words from God is how they
affirm the glory and lordship of Jesus Christ, for this is
the ultimate purpose of all revelation.

While exiled on the Isle of Patmos, John was overwhelmed by the splendor of a heavenly visitor.

> At this I fell at his feet to worship him. But he
> said to me, "Do not do it! I am a fellow ser-

vant with you and with your brothers who hold to the testimony of Jesus. Worship God! For the testimony of Jesus is the spirit of prophecy" (Rev. 19:10).

All prophecy which comes from God will bear witness to the person and work of Jesus Christ, and it will always direct men to worship Him exclusively.

While the *words* of the message may address any number of subjects, the *spirit* of the message will always testify to the lordship of Jesus Christ, the Alpha and Omega!

> Therefore God exalted him to the highest place and gave him the name that is above every name, that at the name of Jesus every knee should bow, in heaven and on earth and under the earth, and every tongue confess that Jesus Christ is Lord, to the glory of God the Father (Phil. 2:9-11).

This is the fundamental, essential truth we must lay hold of before we pursue prophetic revelation. When God speaks, He always, *always*, ALWAYS glorifies His Son, Jesus Christ the Lord.

The Father loves Jesus! Everything that God the Father thinks, determines, says or does will have as its ultimate purpose the absolute and peerless exaltation of His beloved Son. He wants the entire realm of all creation to know just how glorious Jesus is! Furthermore, the Holy Spirit has been sent *specifically* to bear witness to the Son of God.

> When he, the Spirit of truth, comes, he will guide you into all truth. He will not speak on his own; he will speak only what he hears, and he will tell you what is yet to come. He

will bring glory to me by taking from what is
mine and making it known to you. All that
belongs to the Father is mine. That is why I
said the Spirit will take from what is mine
and make it known to you (John 16:13-15).

This is why the Bible also says, "Therefore I tell you
that no one who is speaking by the Spirit of God says,
'Jesus be cursed,' and no one can say, 'Jesus is Lord,'
except by the Holy Spirit" (1 Cor. 12:3).

Even Scripture itself must submit to this standard of
judgment. We know how easily certain people twist the
Word of God, quoting portions of it to lend credibility to
what otherwise is totally false. Any teaching which de-
tracts from, or in any way diminishes or adds to the
work and person of Jesus Christ, is *false*, even if it uses
the Bible as the basis for its authority. The apostle Peter
wrote:

Above all, you must understand that no
prophecy of Scripture came about by the
prophet's own interpretation. For prophecy
never had its origin in the will of man, but
men spoke from God as they were carried
along by the Holy Spirit.
But there were also false prophets among
the people, just as there will be false teachers
among you. They will secretly introduce destructive heresies, even denying the Sovereign Lord who bought them — bringing
swift destruction on themselves. Many will
follow their shameful ways and will bring the
way of truth into disrepute (2 Pet. 1:20–2:2).

John the Beloved, one of the closest disciples to
Jesus, wrote in his letter to the churches,

> Who is the liar? It is the man who denies that
> Jesus is the Christ. Such a man is the anti-
> christ — he denies the Father and the Son.
> No one who denies the Son has the Father;
> whoever acknowledges the Son has the Fa-
> ther also (1 John 2:22-23).

Feeling the need to bring correction to an emerging
error, John cautioned the early believers with these lasting words of wisdom:

> Dear friends, do not believe every spirit, but
> test the spirits to see whether they are from
> God, because many false prophets have gone
> out into the world. This is how you can rec-
> ognize the Spirit of God: Every spirit that
> acknowledges that Jesus Christ has come in
> the flesh is from God, but every spirit that
> does not acknowledge Jesus is not from God.
> This is the spirit of the antichrist, which you
> have heard is coming and even now is al-
> ready in the world (1 John 4:1-3).

Any prophet from God will always bring the testimony of Jesus (see Rev. 19:10); he will bear record of
what God has said about His Son. If he is speaking by
the Holy Spirit, he will surely honor the Son. This, then,
is the first and foremost test of all prophetic words. Do
they lead me to Christ, or do they direct me somewhere
else? Do they exalt Jesus in all of His glory and majesty? Do they make me fall more in love with Him than
I thought possible? Or do they take me away from the
simplicity of single-hearted devotion to Jesus Christ?

The Bible
The second way to test prophetic words is by the
Bible, the Word of God. When the Lord speaks to you,

the word will concur with biblical truth, in no way con-
tradicting what the Bible teaches. As we saw earlier,
Scripture alone stands as the final authority on all revelation; it is our highest court of appeals on all matters of
faith and doctrine. "To the law and to the testimony!"
Isaiah cried, "If they speak not according to this word, it
is because there is no light in them" (Is. 8:20, NKJV).

The same Holy Spirit who inspired the Scripture will
also be our personal Teacher when we study it. He will
educate us in the ways of the Lord — teaching, rebuking, correcting and training us in righteousness — and
thereby equipping us for "every good work" (2 Tim.
3:16-17). But this does not happen by *osmosis*. We cannot place a Bible under our pillows at night expecting to
wake up the following morning with Bible verses filling
our minds. We simply must devote ourselves to the ar-
duous discipline of study in order to know Scripture
well enough to employ it as a means of discerning
God's voice. It is a small price to pay for the treasures
we will attain.

> The law of the Lord is perfect, reviving the
> soul. The statutes of the Lord are trustworthy,
> making wise the simple. The precepts of the
> Lord are right, giving joy to the heart. The
> commands of the Lord are radiant, giving
> light to the eyes. The fear of the Lord is pure,
> enduring forever. The ordinances of the Lord
> are sure and altogether righteous. They are
> more precious than gold, than much pure
> gold; they are sweeter than honey, than
> honey from the comb. By them is your ser-
> vant *warned;* in keeping them there is *great
> reward* (Ps. 19:7-11, italics added).

Let's take the Bible off the bookshelf. Let's take its
words from the pages and cherish them in our hearts.

Let's each regard the words of Paul to Timothy as though the Holy Spirit had spoken them directly to us:

> Do your best to present yourself to God as one approved, a workman who does not need to be ashamed and who correctly handles the word of truth (2 Tim. 2:15).

The Fruit of the Spirit

We can rest assured that the Holy Spirit is speaking to us when the revelation attests to the lordship of Jesus and aligns itself with the Word of God. There is yet one more means of discernment: What *fruit* does it produce? Jesus said,

> Watch out for false prophets. They come to you in sheep's clothing, but inwardly they are ferocious wolves. By their fruit you will recognize them. Do people pick grapes from thornbushes, or figs from thistles? Likewise every good tree bears good fruit, but a bad tree bears bad fruit. A good tree cannot bear bad fruit, and a bad tree cannot bear good fruit (Matt. 7:15-18).

We can know that the Holy Spirit is speaking to us when the revelation bears the fruit of the Spirit: "love, joy, peace, patience, kindness, goodness, faithfulness, gentleness and self-control" (Gal. 5:22-23).

The Scripture says that "the fruit of righteousness will be peace; the effect of righteousness will be quietness and confidence forever" (Is. 32:17). We can be certain that the Lord would never speak or act in any way that would produce effects other than those we are taught by Scripture to expect. This does not mean we are putting God in a box. Rather it shows Him to be faithful to what He has given us to believe in as a standard of sound judgment. Jesus said we would know a tree by its fruit — the outward manifestation of an inward nature, the visible effects of vitality. The following are some of the effects of a word from God.

Conviction and Repentance

> For the word of God is living and active. Sharper than any double-edged sword, it penetrates even to dividing soul and spirit, joints and marrow; it judges the thoughts and attitudes of the heart (Heb. 4:12).

Peter, filled with the Holy Spirit, stood before a great crowd on the day of Pentecost and said,

> "God has raised this Jesus to life....Exalted to the right hand of God....God has made this Jesus, whom you crucified, both Lord and Christ." When the people heard this, they were cut to the heart and said to Peter and the other apostles, "Brothers, what shall we do?" (Acts 2:32-37).

Peter preached his first sermon, and three thousand people were saved! The Holy Spirit fell upon them, piercing them with conviction and turning their hearts to the Lord. This penetrating work of the Spirit often accompanies the preaching of the gospel.

As Peter was preaching on another occasion, a similar outpouring of the Spirit reaped an even greater harvest. Peter said, "Repent, then, and turn to God, so that your sins may be wiped out, that times of refreshing may come from the Lord" (Acts 3:19). The Bible tells us, "Many who heard the message believed, and the number of men grew to about five thousand" (Acts 4:4). The apostle Paul repeatedly witnessed the same thing as he advanced Christianity among the Gentiles. Writing to the church he had planted in Thessalonica, Paul said,

> We know, brothers loved by God, that he has chosen you, because our gospel came to you not simply with words, but also with power, with the Holy Spirit and with deep conviction (1 Thess. 1:4-5).

The conviction was so deep it turned them away from idols to serve the true and living God. And in his letter Paul commended them for the dramatic influence their repentance had upon others throughout the entire region.

> And so you became a model to all the believers in Macedonia and Achaia. The Lord's message rang out from you not only in Macedonia and Achaia — your faith in God has become known everywhere (1 Thess. 1:7-8).

When God speaks, His word penetrates us with conviction and leads us to repentance. He brings to light things that are hidden and shows us things as they really are.

> You have set our iniquities before you, our secret sins in the light of your presence (Ps. 90:8).

Some time ago at the conclusion of a teaching, John Wimber began to list randomly the sins God had shown him were in some of the pastors who were present, including me. When John named my secret sin, I thought every person in the audience knew for sure that he was talking about me! I felt my heart jump, and I gasped as he spoke with such direct authority. I *knew* it was the Lord. And the conviction so penetrated me that I happily have never given myself to that sin again!

Sometimes conviction comes like a piercing stab of conscience. At other times it is like a great heaviness weighing on you. King David experienced this after his adultery with Bathsheba and the murder of her husband, Uriah.

> Blessed is he whose transgressions are forgiven, whose sins are covered. Blessed is the man whose sin the Lord does not count against him and in whose spirit is no deceit. When I kept silent, my bones wasted away through my groaning all day long. For day and night your hand was heavy upon me; my strength was sapped as in the heat of summer. Then I acknowledged my sin to you and did not cover up my iniquity. I said, "I will confess my transgressions to the Lord" — and you forgave the guilt of my sin (Ps. 32:1-5).

There is a clear distinction to be made between conviction and condemnation. God convicts us; Satan condemns us. Condemnation makes you feel bad and *leaves* you that way. Conviction might make you feel bad, but it also shows you the way to *recovery*.

The Pharisees brought before Jesus a woman they had caught in adultery. "They made her stand before the group and said to Jesus, 'Teacher, this woman was caught in the act of adultery. In the Law Moses commanded us to stone such women. Now what do you say?' " (John 8:4-5). They were using this question as a trap, to accuse Him, but Jesus didn't react as they expected. Instead He bent down and started to write on the ground with His finger.

When they kept on questioning Him, He straightened

up and said to them, "If any one of you is without sin, let him be the first to throw a stone at her" (8:7). Jesus again stooped down and began writing on the ground, leaving them to decide who among them was without sin:

> Those who heard began to go away one at a time, the older ones first, until only Jesus was left, with the woman still standing there. Jesus straightened up and asked her, "Woman, where are they? Has no one condemned you?" "No one, sir," she said. "Then neither do I condemn you," Jesus declared. "Go now and leave your life of sin" (John 8:9-11).

The power of Jesus' words to this woman so convinced her of His love that she not only left her life of sin, but devoted herself to Him unendingly! She is the one who washed His feet with her tears and wiped them with her hair. It was she who anointed Him with the costly perfume shortly before He was crucified. And today, as Jesus said, "wherever this gospel is preached throughout the world, what she has done will also be told, in memory of her" (Matt. 26:13). The Lord's word bears the fruit of conviction and repentance.

Faith, Boldness and Power

> Faith comes by hearing and hearing by the word of God" (Rom. 10:17, NKJV).

Belief is a choice we make based upon the evidence we have heard. *Faith*, on the other hand, is *not* a choice. Rather it is the inevitable consequence of *hearing* the voice of God. When God speaks, man is infused with a living faith — the God-given ability to rise above the limits of mere thought and belief, actually to *know* a thing, whether or not it can be proven.

> Now faith is being sure of what we hope for and certain of what we do not see (Heb. 11:1).

Abraham is set forth in Scripture as an exemplary man of faith. God spoke to Abraham one night as he looked at the stars: "So shall your offspring be" (Gen. 15:5). God promised Abraham a son, and through him many descendants, yet he was old, and his wife was barren. The Bible says,

> Against all hope, Abraham in hope believed and so became the father of many nations, just as it had been said to him, "So shall your offspring be." Without weakening in his faith, he faced the fact that his body was as good as dead — since he was about a hundred years old — and that Sarah's womb was also dead. Yet he did not waver through unbelief regarding the promise of God, but was strengthened in his faith and gave glory to God, being fully persuaded that God had power to do what he had promised (Rom. 4:18-21).

Abraham was "fully persuaded." This implies the prevailing influence of an outside source. Faith is not mere self-talk or positive thinking. It is *persuaded* thinking, and God is the One who does the persuading.

One day Belinda and I went to lunch in a downtown restaurant called "Deluxe Diner #3." We are now convinced the owners named it that to make people think there were two more somewhere else! It was a very tiny building, dwarfed by the towering skyscrapers all around it. Inside, it was cramped, crowded and completely void of ambiance, and eating there required much patience and cooperation from everybody present.

As we sat at the counter eating our lunch, an older gentleman sitting next to us struck up a conversation. We were happily making small talk when the Holy Spirit unexpectedly said to me, "This man is going to buy your lunch." His voice was clear as a bell, and I immediately *knew* this was going to happen. I felt somewhat awkward as we continued chatting with the old gentleman not knowing if *he* knew it yet. It became increasingly difficult for me to keep from laughing, so I excused myself tactfully — pretending preoccupation with "important papers" while Belinda carried the conversation.

At last the man finished his meal, said good-bye politely and made his way to the cashier. Though he had said nothing to us about paying for our lunch, I was *fully persuaded* that he was doing so as he stood at the cash register. The thought then occurred to me that the cashier might be dishonest, perhaps charging us for the meal as well. I started praying, "Lord, I know this man is buying our lunch. But what am I to do if the cashier tries to charge double for the meal by saying that he *didn't* pay for us?"

As I thought this, the old gentleman walked back to us, tapped me on my shoulder and said, "Sonny, I just paid for your meal, so don't let them pull any tricks on you when you leave." That amazed me even more than the fact that he bought our lunch!

> Before they call I will answer; while they are
> still speaking I will hear (Is. 65:24).

While I was asking the question, the Lord prompted him to give me the answer that put my anxious heart at ease — even though it almost made me choke on my hamburger!

Faith not only makes us certain of what God has said; it also produces boldness and power in our lives. Fear and indecision are sure indications that we lack faith. For when we *know* the will of God, we are empowered to act decisively and courageously.

> The people who know their God shall be strong, and carry out great exploits (Dan. 11:32, NKJV).

We need only look at a sampling of the faith hall of fame in the book of Hebrews to see how true this is:

> By faith Noah, when warned about things not yet seen, in holy fear built an ark to save his family....By faith Abraham, when called to go to a place he would later receive as his inheritance, obeyed and went, even though he did not know where he was going....
>
> By faith Moses' parents hid him for three months after he was born, because they saw he was no ordinary child, and they were not afraid of the king's edict. By faith Moses, when he had grown up, refused to be known as the son of Pharaoh's daughter. He chose to be mistreated along with the people of God rather than to enjoy the pleasures of sin for a short time. He regarded disgrace for the sake of Christ as of greater value than the treasures of Egypt, because he was looking ahead to his reward. By faith he left Egypt, not fearing the king's anger; he persevered because he saw him who is invisible....
>
> By faith the people passed through the Red Sea as on dry land; but when the Egyptians

tried to do so, they were drowned. By faith
the walls of Jericho fell, after the people had
marched around them for seven days (Heb.
11:7-8, 23-27, 29-30).

Peter and John were summoned before the religious
council to stand trial for believing in Jesus Christ. The
rulers of that austere and venerated assembly held the
power of life and death when they decided about these
men, yet Peter and John proclaimed their faith boldly.
When asked, "By what power or what name did you do
this?" (Acts 4:7), Peter answered with undaunted courage.

Rulers and elders of the people! If we are
being called to account today for an act of
kindness shown to a cripple and are asked
how he was healed, then know this, you and
all the people of Israel: It is by the name of
Jesus Christ of Nazareth, whom you crucified but whom God raised from the dead, that
this man stands before you healed. He is "the
stone you builders rejected, which has become the capstone." Salvation is found in no
one else, for there is no other name under
heaven given to men by which we must be
saved (Acts 4:8-12).

No one had ever dared speak to the rulers so forthrightly. Sheer intimidation alone had caused lesser men
to cower before this feared tribunal. It was not so with
Peter and John. Their composure before the court was
an undeniable tribute to their relationship with Jesus
Christ.

When they saw the courage of Peter and John
and realized that they were unschooled, ordi-

nary men, they were astonished and they took note that these men had been with Jesus (Acts 4:13).

Luke then records that they sent them on their way with nothing more than a warning to stop preaching in the name of Jesus. But the warning held no influence over men whose hearts had become emboldened by the Word of God.

Peter and John replied, "Judge for yourselves whether it is right in God's sight to obey you rather than God. For we cannot help speaking about what we have seen and heard" (Acts 4:19-20).

Paul exhibited legendary courage on the high seas as a direct result of hearing a word from God.

After the men had gone a long time without food, Paul stood up before them and said: "Men, you should have taken my advice not to sail from Crete; then you would have spared yourselves this damage and loss. But now I urge you to keep up your courage, because not one of you will be lost; only the ship will be destroyed. Last night an angel of the God whose I am and whom I serve stood beside me and said, 'Do not be afraid, Paul. You must stand trial before Caesar; and God has graciously given you the lives of all who sail with you.' So keep up your courage, men, for I have faith in God that it will happen just as he told me. Nevertheless, we must run aground on some island" (Acts 27:21-26).

When God speaks, it inspires our hearts with unshakable courage and irrefutable wisdom. Furthermore, what He says *happens*. Paul and his shipmates were indeed saved, and Paul made it to Rome where he stood before Caesar. This is one sure way to test a word from God. Is power released when it is spoken, and does it come to pass?

Several years ago the church where Belinda and I had worshipped as young Christians hosted a national conference on revival. We had been to a number of these conferences in other cities, so I was not keen on setting aside time to go to yet another — even though it was in our own church. After all, I thought, the sermons were always the same, as were the people who attended. In fact, I was so familiar with the messages that I could almost recite them point by point along with the speakers. Besides, I was feeling disillusioned with much of what I saw in the church, and I just didn't see the sense of "playing the game" any longer.

Somehow, Belinda talked me into going to the opening session on Sunday morning. I reluctantly entered the church and quickly found a place to sit so nobody would bother me with all that "happy Christian stuff." As the service began I sat in the pew with my arms folded, my legs crossed and my heart closed. Everything about me was sending an unmistakable message: Go ahead; just try to reach me.

To my surprise the Lord spoke to me. There was a distinct sense of sport in what He said. "Well, well, here you are again, James, at another conference on revival!"

Inside I was thinking, Ha, ha, ha! Very funny.

My attitude was deplorable, but the Spirit of the Lord continued: "Now didn't I bless you at the conference in Denver?" I agreed that indeed He had. "And what about the conference in Texas; now I'm sure I blessed you there. Is that right?" Again I acknowledged that He had blessed me. "And, James, I *know* I blessed you deeply at the conference in the South — now, didn't I?"

"Yes, Lord, You did," I said, wondering why He was saying these things.

He paused for a moment and then added, "Well, I'm *not* going to bless you at this conference."

I was startled, "What do you mean, You're not going to bless me? You can't do that!"

Then He said these words, "No, I'm not going to bless you this time. At this conference, James, I'm going to *change* you!"

The power of His words struck my spirit with such authority that my entire demeanor changed in an instant. Nothing else needed to happen for the word of the Lord had already done the deed. I did attend the remainder of the conference and received much from the Lord during that week, but I was changed from the moment He spoke those words. The word of the Lord bears the fruit of faith, boldness and power. What He says will happen!

Righteousness, Peace and Joy

> For the kingdom of God is not a matter of eating and drinking, but of righteousness, peace and joy in the Holy Spirit, because anyone who serves Christ in this way is pleasing to God and approved by men (Rom. 14:17-18).

The primary desire of God is that we love Him and one another. This is the essence of true righteousness; it is the sum of all the commandments. God speaks to us to bring about the righteousness which gives us peace, which in turn results in joy. Any word from God will bear this as its fruit.

The Word of God is *truth* and therefore makes us truthful in our relationship with Him, with ourselves and with others.

But whoever lives by the truth comes into the
light, so that it may be seen plainly that what
he has done has been done through God
(John 3:21).

If a person says God has spoken to him and then
becomes secretive and separate, whispering in corners
of the church away from the eyes and ears of the leadership, that person is not speaking by the Holy Spirit;
what he is doing is unrighteous, divisive and burdensome. It is a sure sign that he is deceived and seeking to
deceive others.

The word of God is *liberating*, setting us free.

Now the Lord is the Spirit, and where the
Spirit of the Lord is, there is freedom. And
we, who with unveiled faces all reflect the
Lord's glory, are being transformed into his
likeness with ever-increasing glory, which
comes from the Lord, who is the Spirit (2
Cor. 3:17-18).

Jesus told His disciples in the upper room, "You are
already clean because of the word I have spoken to you"
(John 15:3). When the Lord speaks a word to you, it will
cleanse you from sin and set you free to serve the Lord
with gladness and transparency.

On the other hand, *religion* imposes great burdens of
guilt and obligation on broken worshippers of God. This
is not pleasing to the Lord.

Jesus replied, "And you experts in the law,
woe to you, because you load people down
with burdens they can hardly carry, and you
yourselves will not lift one finger to help
them" (Luke 11:46).

To those oppressed by self-righteous judges, Jesus says,

> Come to me, all you who are weary and bur-
> dened, and I will give you rest. Take my yoke
> upon you and learn from me, for I am gentle
> and humble in heart, and you will find rest
> for your souls. For my yoke is easy and my
> burden is light (Matt. 11:28-30).

The Word of God is *wholesome*, and it therefore fills us with peace. Jesus said, "I have told you these things, so that in me you may have peace. In this world you will have trouble. But take heart! I have overcome the world" (John 16:33). After His resurrection, each time Jesus appeared to His disciples, the first words He said were "Peace be with you!" (John 20:19) The peace of God is a great barometer for discerning a word from the Lord.

> Do not be anxious about anything, but in
> everything, by prayer and petition, with
> thanksgiving, present your requests to God.
> And the peace of God, which transcends all
> understanding, will guard your hearts and
> your minds in Christ Jesus (Phil. 4:6-7).

We can trust the Holy Spirit to keep our hearts and minds filled with peace when He is speaking to us be- cause "God is not the author of confusion, but of peace" (1 Cor. 14:33, NKJV). The more confusing a revelation is, the less likely it is from God.

The word of God is *wonderful*, and it fills us with joy.

> The disciples were overjoyed when they saw
> the Lord (John 20:20).

Jeremiah said, "When your words came, I ate them; they were my joy and my heart's delight, for I bear your name, O Lord God Almighty" (Jer. 15:16). The sweet psalmist of Israel sang, "I rejoice in your promise like one who finds great spoil" (Ps. 119:162). And the apostle Paul prayed, "May the God of hope fill you with all joy and peace as you trust in him, so that you may overflow with hope by the power of the Holy Spirit" (Rom. 15:13).

Conviction, repentance, faith, boldness, power, righteousness, peace and joy — these are some of the results when God speaks, some of the fruit produced by a word from God. I am sure there are more, but these seem sufficient to get you started in your own search.

Again, the three primary means by which you can discern a "word from God" are 1) how it measures up to the testimony of Jesus Christ as Lord; 2) how it measures up to the Scripture; and 3) how it measures up to the fruit of the Spirit. Does it stir you with devotion and obedience to the Lord Jesus Christ? Does it turn you from sin and selfish ambition? Does it fill you with faith and resolve to strengthen and encourage others? If so, you have heard the voice of God!

God never diminishes the glory and power of the Lord Jesus Christ; nor will He ever contradict the teaching of Scripture; nor will He bring forth bad fruit. With these facts firmly in our minds, we are free to explore the depths of revelation with the Holy Spirit. It is my heart's desire that the Lord will accelerate your growth and launch you into the discovery, discernment and delight of hearing the voice of God. Happy hunting! ❦

Chapter 10

Sharing With Others What God Has Shown You

Follow the way of love and eagerly desire
spiritual gifts, especially the gift of prophecy
(1 Cor. 14:1).

We are instructed specifically by the Word of
God to set our hearts upon developing and
exercising the gift of prophecy. The reason is
given clearly: "Everyone who prophesies speaks to men
for their strengthening, encouragement and comfort" (1
Cor. 14:3). What a glorious day it will be when all
within the household of faith obey this text. How truly
wonderful to be a part of a church where *everybody*

speaks to one another for their mutual strengthening, encouragement and comfort! Moses must have foreseen such a day when he prayed: "I wish that all the Lord's people were prophets and that the Lord would put his Spirit on them!" (Num. 11:29).

But some may ask, Not *all* are prophets, are they? Of course not (see 1 Cor. 12:28). Why then are we told to desire earnestly that we may all prophesy? Because it is a gift which builds up the church. Prophesying does not make one a prophet any more than sharing one's faith makes one an evangelist. We should all prophesy, just as we should all teach the Bible, exercise pastoral care for others, preach the gospel and advance the church, because these things are what believers do. Paul said, "Since you are eager to have spiritual gifts, try to excel in gifts that build up the church" (1 Cor. 14:12).

It has helped me to think of prophecy in four phases: the role, the gift, the ministry and the office. Every believer is to pursue being used by God in the *role* of "prophet," though only some will display a true *gift* for prophesying. Still others who have developed their gifting through use will have an unmistakable prophetic *ministry*. Finally, there are those who will no doubt hold the *office* of prophet in keeping with Ephesians 4:11:

> It was he who gave some to be apostles, some to be prophets, some to be evangelists, and some to be pastors and teachers....

Start walking, and you will find just how far God will take you!

What does it mean, then, to prophesy? Prophecy expresses the heart of God through the words of man to a person (or a group) in any given situation for the purpose of building them up in faith and love. Any believer can, and should, do this. The Lord is speaking to us almost constantly. We need to learn how to listen to His

voice and to pass it on to others. Paul's advice to the
Christians in Rome is equally applicable to us today:

> God has given each of us the ability to do
> certain things well. So if God has given you
> the ability to prophesy, then prophesy when-
> ever you can — as often as your faith is
> strong enough to receive a message from
> God (Rom. 12:6, TLB).

> Do not put out the Spirit's fire (1 Thess.
> 5:19).

There is a warmth and a glow about the presence of
the Spirit that we must not extinguish. The fact that we
are able to "put out the Spirit's fire" means that we must
be careful to guard against that possibility. But how?
Paul answers the question himself: "Do not treat
prophecies with contempt" (v. 20). The nature of prophecy is such that we generally *do* treat it with contempt
— probably not with open antagonism, but rather in the
passive sense. We typically consider prophetic utterances as something not worth our consideration, unless,
of course, the person speaking is highly esteemed. Then
we are very attentive — perhaps overly so. When we go
to the extreme of either overlooking or overestimating
the prophetic word, we put out the Spirit's fire, and our
fellowship with one another becomes cold and dark.

Are we to take *every* prophecy as a word from God?
Paul again provides the answer. "Test everything. Hold
on to the good" (v. 21). Rather than scorning prophetic
utterances, we are to *test* them. This tells us that not
every prophecy is going to be correct. No one is going
to be 100 percent accurate all of the time. In this regard
New Testament prophets differ considerably from their
Old Testament counterparts. The Old Testament prophets spoke what was to be recorded as the very word of

God and therefore could not falter at all. If the words they spoke proved to be untrue to any degree, they were to be executed. But the New Testament era provides greater flexibility, primarily because *the* Word of God in Scripture has already been given. When we prophesy today, we are basically conveying in our own words what we believe to be the thoughts and feelings of God about a person or event. We have been given ample space to learn in the process.

This is one reason why Paul said, "Follow the way of love" (1 Cor. 14:1), when he told us to seek spiritual gifts earnestly. When a church commits itself to pursue love, that releases freedom to fail in the learning process.

> Above all, love each other deeply, because love covers over a multitude of sins. Offer hospitality to one another without grumbling. Each one should use whatever gift he has received to serve others, faithfully administering God's grace in its various forms (1 Pet. 4:8-10).

The fledgling "prophet" must be secure in the atmosphere of love in order to spread his or her wings and soar like an eagle. The initial "take-offs" are going to look more like those of a turkey than an eagle, but given time, this same prophet will sing, "Love lifted me!"

Finally, we must keep in mind the prophecy of Joel that has been so central to the discussion:

> I will pour out my Spirit on all people. Your sons and daughters will prophesy, your old men will dream dreams, your young men will see visions (Joel 2:28).

We know that this prophecy was initially fulfilled on

the day of Pentecost. The world is still reeling from that time when God poured His Spirit upon the believers in Jerusalem at nine o'clock in the morning! But we are *still* in the last days and therefore have reason to hope for God to do this again — in even greater measure. Those few believers in Jerusalem are but the firstfruits of what God will do with His sons and daughters in all the earth!

What is the starting point in giving a prophecy? To speak a word *for* God, we must first hear a word *from* God. How does a word from God come to us? We have addressed this theme in detail already, so a brief summary will suffice here.

Generally speaking, I have discovered that God speaks to us prophetically, intuitively and rationally. The *prophetic* pertains to that which is written, spoken, seen, heard or experienced. The *intuitive* pertains to that which is felt and sensed though perhaps is indefinable. And the *rational* pertains to that which is thought and remembered or simply known through common sense. The prophetic touches our senses, the intuitive touches our spirits, and the rational touches our minds. All three are equally valid and vital to our hearing a word from God.

Once we believe God has spoken to us, we must take the next step and speak the word to those to whom He directs us. One thing that often causes us to hesitate is our fear of being wrong. It's not simply that we are afraid of appearing foolish; rather we are genuinely concerned about misleading another individual. Or perhaps we are anxious that we might even misrepresent the Lord. These fears could immobilize us indefinitely.

When I first began to prophesy to others, I asked the Lord, "What if I'm wrong?"

"As long as love is your motive," He told me, "and building them up is your goal, you can't miss."

It is the truth. "Love does no harm to its neighbor"

(Rom. 13:10). When you are motivated by love, you will seek only the good of those to whom you are prophesying; you will speak only to build them up in the faith.

Love is the principal issue in prophetic ministry.

> If I have the gift of prophecy and can fathom
> all mysteries and all knowledge, and if I have
> a faith that can move mountains, but have not
> love, I am nothing (1 Cor. 13:2).

Take inventory in the life of anyone whom God is using in prophetic ministry, and you will find at least these four things: a personal relationship of intimacy with Jesus, a love for all people, a devotion to Scripture and a willingness to take risks for the sake of helping others.

A relationship with Jesus is imperative, for you cannot speak a word from the Lord if you do not know Him. Love for people causes you to handle them with care. Knowledge of the Scripture keeps you in line with God's will. And a willingness to take risks launches you forth in faith. Prophetic ministry will not develop as a wholesome dimension of Christian practice apart from these things.

> Then I was the craftsman at his side. I was
> filled with delight day after day, rejoicing al-
> ways in his presence, rejoicing in his whole
> world and delighting in mankind (Prov.
> 8:30-31).

These words express the heart of every true prophet from God.

Tips for Giving a Prophetic Word

Seek Earnestly to Prophesy

You will never give a prophetic word to anyone until you first *desire* to do so. God will only use you as you yield yourself to Him as an instrument of righteousness. If you seek to hear God's voice, if you listen intently, if you search with your eyes, then you will see God's heart and be given the words and the opportunity to communicate it to others. Begin to pray for your family and friends, your church and your pastor, your city and your nation — asking God to tell you what is on His heart for them. Pray for insight that is relevant, revealing and redemptive.

> Call to me and I will answer you and tell you great and unsearchable things you do not know (Jer. 33:3).

Seize the Opportunities the Lord Provides

When the Lord gives you a word, He will also give you the opportunity to share it with others. Be alert for the opportunity. If God speaks to you about someone you have been praying for and you then meet him or her unexpectedly as you go about your day, that's a good indication He wants you to share the word He has given you. Or perhaps the Lord has shown you something that concerns your church. I recommend you talk to the pastor about it first. Then, if he agrees with what you have said and makes provision for sharing the prophetic word publicly as part of the worship service, be prepared to do so. Be alert to what the Spirit of the Lord is doing in the church when you come together. Wait for an opportunity to speak so as not to disrupt the worship or distract from what God may be doing. Love works no ill toward its neighbor.

Safeguard the Spirit of the Moment

If you are speaking to an individual, be sensitive to where you are and what is going on all about you. Don't say or do anything that might embarrass your friends or make them feel uncomfortable. Don't detract from their work or disrupt their private plans for the sake of your convenience in giving them the message. Exercise understanding and sensitivity. This certainly applies to the congregational setting also. Be sure that what you are going to say and how you say it suits the moment. Be alert and sensible. Remember, God gives words which are *relevant*. He is not the author of confusion, but of peace.

Say Only What the Lord Shows You

Speak forth what you have seen.

> This is what the Sovereign Lord showed me: a basket of ripe fruit. "What do you see, Amos?" he asked. "A basket of ripe fruit," I answered (Amos 8:1-2).

Amos saw it first, then he said exactly what he saw. It is interesting to note that the *interpretation* came only after he said what he saw:

> *Then* the Lord said to me, "The time is ripe for my people Israel; I will spare them no longer" (Amos 8:2, italics added).

We may indeed *see* something from the Lord and yet not *know* what it means. Often we see only a poor reflection, as in a mirror, and it is up to us to describe the foggy images the best we can.

> For we know in part and we prophesy in part... (1 Cor. 13:9).

We are to say only what the Lord shows us, trusting that He will expound on the revelation as we go. Speak what you know to be true; prophesy according to your measure of faith.

Speak Clearly and Loudly Enough to Be Heard

> Even in the case of lifeless things that make sounds, such as the flute or harp, how will anyone know what tune is being played unless there is a distinction in the notes? Again, if the trumpet does not sound a clear call, who will get ready for battle? So it is with you. Unless you speak intelligible words with your tongue, how will anyone know what you are saying? You will just be speaking into the air (1 Cor. 14:7-9).

The whole point of prophesying is for the message to be heard and received by those to whom it is given. See to it, then, that you speak so as to be heard and understood.

Don't Be Theatrical or Pretentious

The sweeping gestures and swelling tones of melodrama are unnecessary in true prophetic ministry; more than unnecessary, they are unwanted. "Thus saith the Lord, 'One needeth not to speaketh in ye olde King James language, yea verily, to be speaking forth a word from God to whomsoever believeth. Amen.'" This style of prophesying comes from an outdated ministry model and is exclusive and irrelevant. While it may sound spiritual, it is nevertheless lacking in any real substance.

> If I speak in the tongues of men and of angels, but have not love, I am only a resounding gong or a clanging cymbal (1 Cor. 13:1).

Unpretentious honesty is the best policy for advancing prophetic ministry. It is well within the bounds of propriety to preface your remarks with something as simple as this: "I'm really nervous right now, and my heart is beating so fast I can hardly catch my breath, but during worship I received a scripture (or an impression, a vision) that I think the Lord wants me to share with you." Then share your word; it's as simple as that.

Stay Within the Guidelines of Scripture

The apostle Paul gave specific instructions for prophetic ministry when the church gathers to worship:

> Two or three prophets should speak, and the others should weigh carefully what is said. And if a revelation comes to someone who is sitting down, the first speaker should stop (1 Cor. 14:29-30).

This reflects common sense. If you have too many people prophesying, you lose track of what God was trying to say. The clamor of many voices drowns out the only Voice you really wanted to hear!

> For you can all prophesy in turn so that everyone may be instructed and encouraged (v. 31).

As we have seen, prophecy is for the express purpose of giving strength, encouragement and comfort to the people of God. Nowhere is it a permit for correction or rebuke. When rebuke or correction is necessary, it should happen through means other than the prophet and prophetic ministry. Typically, it is the pastor's responsibility. God may under certain circumstances send a prophet to perform such a task, but even then it will be done in a pastoral way with love and wisdom and in

privacy. Someone wisely said, "Prophets are known on
earth by what they say. They are known in heaven by
what they *don't* say."

> The spirits of prophets are subject to the con-
> trol of prophets. For God is not a God of
> disorder but of peace (vv. 32-33).

The prophetic ministry does not displace levelheaded
intelligence and self-control. Our eyes do not glaze
over, nor do we drift on the wings of the wind into a
never-never land. We are responsible to behave ourselves in the discharge of the ministry. Paul said,
"Everything should be done in a fitting and orderly
way" (1 Cor. 14:40). If the prophecy doesn't fit, or if it
will cause disorder, don't give it — because it is not
from the Lord.

Stop When You Are Supposed To
Nervous energy can carry beginners beyond the
boundary of their faith into presumption and exaggeration. Let your words be true and few. For some people,
giving a prophetic word is like diving off the ninety-
meter platform in an Olympic competition; it takes all
their courage to open their mouths and speak. But sometimes these are the very ones who find it equally difficult to know when to stop! They started with a true
word, but somewhere between "Thus says the Lord"
and "Yea, I also say to you," they lost the anointing —
and everybody knows it except them.

> When words are many, sin is not absent, but
> he who holds his tongue is wise (Prov.
> 10:19).

Submit Your Word to the Person or to the Church
Let them have the final say on how fitting it was —

or wasn't. One of the greatest errors of new "prophets" is their inability to submit themselves to others. They tend to feel separate from the rest of the church and on an inside track with the Holy Spirit, knowing things that others do not know. For the most part, this is completely unintentional; but it must be corrected, or it will ultimately disqualify a person from being used by God in ministry. There are no "Lone Rangers" in this business. We are all members one of another, equally accountable to one another for the things we say and do.

There is an old saying, "If you can't play by the rules, then you can't play." *Submission* is one of the rules of prophetic ministry. We do not lord it over others nor seek in anyway to control them with prophecy. To do so would be to practice witchcraft. True prophetic utterances have no strings attached. The recipients will be left to determine how they are to respond to the message they have heard.

Survey the Results of Sharing the Word

See what God did or did not do and learn from it. Apply what you learn to the next time you step out and prophesy. Debriefing with pastors and other leaders as well as getting feedback from individuals to whom you gave prophetic words is an invaluable means for fine-tuning the prophetic gift and ministry.

I trust these tips will be helpful as you continue learning how to use the prophetic gifts for the glory of God and the good of the church. ✵

Chapter 11

The Hippo
in the
Garden

In the autumn of 1989, I dreamed I was standing in my house looking at an English garden in my backyard. Warm sunshine bathed the wide assortment of flowers, while a gentle breeze wafted through the garden, carrying the fragrance of each blossom into the neighborhood — noticeably pleasing all my neighbors. Beyond the garden, I observed the children's swing set, the sandbox, assorted toys, lawn chairs and a hammock. Everything was in its place, even the idle lawnmower that beckoned me to cut the grass. I felt like a king surveying his domain: a peaceful, tranquil scene, a happy little kingdom. Little did I realize that the Lord was about to change things considerably.

A sudden movement to the right of the garden caught my eye, and I turned to see a man enter it uninvited. I was somewhat affronted by his presumptuous intrusion, but when I saw what followed after him I became flabbergasted! Trailing behind the man like a domestic pet was a huge hippopotamus! The man was leading it along with reins he held firmly in his hand. I collected myself from the shock of the outrageous sight of the hippo in my garden and called to the man, "What is that? What are you doing there?" At that precise moment I woke up. The oddity of the dream had jarred me from my sleep.

I lay awake in my bed in the early morning hours contemplating the curious and unsettling sight. I asked, "Lord, what was the meaning of that?" I was surprised by His answer.

"I am about to do a strange, new thing in My church," He said. "It will be like a man bringing a hippopotamus into his garden. Think about that."

"What is the strange thing You will do?" I asked.

He answered, "I will surely pour out a vast prophetic anointing upon My church and release My people as a prophetic voice into the earth. It will seem so strange and out of place — like a hippo in a garden — but this is what I will do."

The "hippo in the garden" is a fulfillment of Joel's ancient prophecy (that is, Acts 2:17) which initially occurred among the one hundred and twenty believers on the day of Pentecost.

> When the day of Pentecost came, they were all together in one place. Suddenly a sound like the blowing of a violent wind came from heaven and filled the whole house where they were sitting. They saw what seemed to be tongues of fire that separated and came to

rest on each of them. All of them were filled
with the Holy Spirit and began to speak in
other tongues as the Spirit enabled them
(Acts 2:1-4).

The people who witnessed this supernatural occurrence responded with a variety of emotions. Some wondered while others mocked.

Amazed and perplexed, they asked one another, "What does this mean?" Some, however, made fun of them and said, "They have
had too much wine" (Acts 2:12-13).

These are typical reactions toward a hippo in a garden.

The second outpouring of the Holy Spirit in the early
days of the church brought the believers together in
unity and released them into their community with boldness and power.

"Now, Lord, consider their threats and enable your servants to speak your word with
great boldness. Stretch out your hand to
heal and perform miraculous signs and wonders through the name of your holy servant
Jesus." After they prayed, the place where
they were meeting was shaken. And they
were all filled with the Holy Spirit and spoke
the word of God boldly (Acts 4:29-31).

God answered their prayer for boldness to preach the
truth in the face of threats and persecution. The dramatic encounter with the Holy Spirit knitted them together into an inseparable family of love, the likes of
which the world has never seen.

> All the believers were one in heart and mind.
> No one claimed that any of his possessions
> was his own, but they shared everything
> they had. With great power the apostles
> continued to testify to the resurrection of
> the Lord Jesus, and much grace was upon
> them all. There were no needy persons
> among them. For from time to time those
> who owned lands or houses sold them,
> brought the money from the sales and put it
> at the apostles' feet, and it was distributed to
> anyone as he had need (Acts 4:32-35).

Since this was the result of the Holy Spirit's being
poured out on only a handful of believers in Jerusalem,
what will it be like when God pours out His Spirit upon
all flesh?

The hippo in the garden is the unusual thing God will
do in places where people have thought that it would not
— or perhaps even should not — be done. First, it is the
Lord returning the power of His prophetic word by His
Holy Spirit into churches that (presumptuously) no
longer have any place for it. To be sure, the "garden" is
lovely, the flowers most fragrant; but the yard is clut-
tered with the toys of children at play while a great
harvest in the fields waits for those who are asleep in
beds of ease. These things will change dramatically
when the hippo arrives.

I realize now why the dream startled me awake as it
did. It was exactly what the Lord intended to happen,
for the uniqueness of what the Lord is about to do will
likewise jar the church from her season of slumber.
Isaiah prophesied, "The Lord will rise up as he did at
Mount Perazim, he will rouse himself as in the Valley of
Gibeon — to do his work, his strange work, and perform his task, his alien task" (Is. 28:21). I refer to this
only to highlight the fact that it is not uncommon for the

Lord to do uncommon things. We tend to think that we can dictate to God what He can and cannot do. But now, as always, God will arise and do His own bidding. He will enter into our docile kingdoms — uninvited, if necessary — and bring His pet *hippo* with Him!

Not only is the hippo in the garden the unusual thing that God will do prophetically *within* His church, but it also heralds His release of a prophetic voice into the world *through* His church, bringing in a great last-days harvest.

> In the last days, God says, I will pour out my Spirit on all people. Your sons and daughters will prophesy, your young men will see visions, your old men will dream dreams. Even on my servants, both men and women, I will pour out my Spirit in those days, and they will prophesy. I will show wonders in the heaven above and signs on the earth below, blood and fire and billows of smoke. The sun will be turned to darkness and the moon to blood before the coming of the great and glorious day of the Lord. *And everyone who calls on the name of the Lord will be saved* (Acts 2:17-21, italics added).

A vast prophetic movement inspired by the Holy Spirit within the church and a validated prophetic message preached through the church in the midst of the world resulting in an evangelistic ingathering — that is the "hippo in the garden."

The vivid imagery of a hippo in my garden and the direct simplicity of what I sensed the Lord say to me truly stirred my mind. I would *never* have thought to compare a hippopotamus to prophetic ministry in the church — or to the prophetic church released into the world — had it not been for this dream. Indeed, why should I? What possible similarities could there be? Yet I know what I saw in my dream, and I am equally certain that the Lord showed me what it meant; so I studied all I could find about the hippopotamus to see what analogies to the prophetic ministry I could discover. I was not disappointed with my research. Both the natural and the biblical sources of information provided me with some fascinating comparisons.

A Few Natural Facts About the Hippo

Reading through a variety of books about the hippopotamus I discovered several facts that clarified the allegory God had given me in the dream. To include them *all* here would be too laborious, but I'd like to draw some of the more apparent parallels to prove my point. Otherwise, I might appear as one who strains out a gnat and swallows a hippo!

The first and most conspicuous thing that struck me was the hippo's *big mouth*. Obviously, the resemblance to prophets speaks for itself! However, while it is funny to say that prophets are like hippos because they both have "big mouths," I know that the dream's insight was more than a joke for the Lord. The inspired allegory of the hippo in the garden has far more to offer than simple humor. For a start, I should at least point out the fact that when the hippo opens its mouth, it is to warn others of danger. I find this very interesting!

One distinctive characteristic of the hippo is that its eyes, nose and ears are all set on the top of its head, enabling it to have full use of all its senses while submerged in the water. Eyes speak of vision, ears of hearing and the nose of discernment. When we "submerge" ourselves fully into the Word of God and the presence of the Holy Spirit, our vision, hearing and discernment become fully activated and alert to whatever happens around us.

Another comparison worth noting is that the awkward, clumsy waddle of the hippo when he is on land is no indication of the creature's power and agility in the water. Similarly, when the prophetic ministry is out of its element, it does seem rather backward and bizarre. But when it is deep in the Word and in the Spirit — suffice it to say you have never seen such an awesome display of grace and beauty!

Possibly the most fascinating correlation to be made between the hippo and the prophetic ministry comes from the vital role which the hippo plays in the eco-cycle of its natural habitat of Tanzania. The daily movement of the hippo through the many waterways maintains a continuous supply of fresh water for the entire region by breaking up the stiff reeds under the surface — thereby preserving the balance of life for all the other animals. By way of comparison, imagine how stagnant and tepid the church would be were it not for the prophetic word of the Lord stirring us with faith and vision unto love and good works.

We need only look into churches who have rejected the word of the Lord to see the drought and death that take place when people no longer hear God's voice.

> "The days are coming," declares the Sovereign Lord, "when I will send a famine through the land — not a famine of food or a thirst for water, but a famine of hearing the words of the Lord. Men will stagger from sea to sea and wander from north to east, searching for the word of the Lord, but they will not find it. In that day the lovely young women and strong young men will faint because of thirst" (Amos 8:11-13).

The hippo in the garden is God's way of keeping "fresh water" supplied to His people.

Shortly after my dream, I watched a televised documentary about the hippopotamus titled "The River of Life." The featured animal was a pregnant female hippo, who was under great duress and anxiety caused by a prolonged drought. Things worsened when she became separated from the herd, unable to travel at the speed of the others making the hundred-mile trek across the drought-stricken land in search of water. Going on pure instinct, she buried herself deep in whatever pockets of mud she could find, waiting to give birth to her pup.

I could see fatigue taking its toll on her. The heightened anxiety brought on by the desperate circumstances produced a frothy pus over her eyes, obscuring her vision. As I watched, I realized that when they are deprived of water, hippos become anxious, separated from the herd, lose their vision and are misdirected by instincts to wallow in mud. This is equally true of drought-stricken prophets!

The hippo's temperament also lends itself well to our analogy. A hippo in the wild must be approached with great care. Tales abound of unprovoked attacks, and each one grows with its retelling. This, too, is allegorical of the prophetic ministry. Stories abound of how churches have been devastated by the unprovoked assaults of uninvited "prophets" and, in some cases, even by those who were initially welcomed but soon wore out the invitation through falsehood or immaturity. False prophets, as well as those who are true but immature, have said and done much to give "hippos" a bad reputation!

But there is another side to this story. Researchers who have taken the time to study hippos carefully have discovered that there is more to Africa's misunderstood giant than meets the eye. One man reported, "In all my years of research I found hippos to be quite gentle creatures which, like many other species, attack only when

molested, cornered or injured." Isn't this the same with
people? Any damage done by "errant prophets" is no
different from that done by any other wounded individual. When cornered, molested or injured, *anybody* not
walking in the Spirit can react wrongfully and do much
damage. As the saying goes, "Hurt people hurt people."

Abuse of the prophetic gift has surely occurred on
many occasions and in many ways and no doubt will
continue until the end. But what sense is there in rejecting the true prophetic word of God simply because false
prophets, or even immature true prophets, peddle their
wares? The gift is true and valid; it is the *individual* who
needs appropriate handling.

In my dream I had noticed the Lord holding the reins
of the hippo firmly in His hand. This speaks of the
Lord's supervision of true prophetic ministers.

> Those who are led by the Spirit of God are
> sons of God (Rom. 8:14).

Prophetic ministry which is of the Lord will *always*
submit to the leadership of the church. It has no agenda
other than that which comes from the Lord, who is not
the author of confusion or rebellion. Discernment, maturity, responsibility and wisdom — these are the
proper tools to employ against the false and with the
immature, as we embrace the genuine.

After I had awakened from my dream, I began to
imagine what would happen if someone actually were to
bring a hippopotamus into his garden. I concluded that
at least three things would take place.

First, there wouldn't be much of a garden left unless
the owner provided *total* management and care for the
creature. Likewise, the prophetic ministry must be handled properly, or else it will unwittingly crush the
"flowers" and make a huge mess of things. The logical
thing to do would be to get rid of the beast, but we don't

have that option. The *Lord* brought the hippo into the garden, and He alone has the prerogative of taking him out! We simply must learn how to care for both the hippo *and* the garden at the same time.

A second obvious fact about having a hippo in your garden is that it would inevitably become the topic of conversation all about town. Restaurants would be abuzz with the chatter of what you had done. People would say, "Did you hear about that silly man with the pet hippo in his garden?"

School children would giggle and make up nursery rhymes: "Let's ask the silly, silly man, 'O sir, we beg your pardon; we think you're strange, but can we see the hippo in your garden?' "

The tabloids would have a banner day with the story: "Eccentric man keeps huge hippo in garden! Says beast is his pet! Wife threatens to leave!"

Most certainly the unveiling of the prophetic ministry within the church and the unleashing of it through the church into the world will *also* give rise to gossip all about town!

> Amazed and perplexed, they asked one another, "What does this mean?" Some, however, made fun of them and said, "They have had too much wine" (Acts 2:12-13).

Scrutiny, ridicule and accusation have *always* accompanied the works of God in the world. Not to worry, however — the *hippo* can handle it.

A hippo in your garden would inevitably result in legal action against you to have the beast removed. The principal charge would be that keeping such a creature in one's garden is a violation of the home owners' neighborhood covenant. The reason for the anger and intolerance of neighbors who are otherwise pleasant and accommodating is the unintentional *offensiveness* of the hippo. The neighbors don't mind smelling your flowers, but the aroma of hippo manure simply does not blend well with morning coffee! Your refusal to yield to their demands for getting rid of the thing would drive them to pursue whatever means necessary to force you to comply.

In the same way, the prophetic moves of God have always been opposed.

> Because your sins are so many and your hostility so great, the prophet is considered a fool, the inspired man a maniac. The prophet, along with my God, is the watchman over Ephraim, yet snares await him on all his paths, and hostility in the house of his God (Hos. 9:7-8).

Those who view themselves as the "home owners' association" will claim that the prophetic movement within the church is a violation of the covenant! But these poor individuals have lost sight of one simple and significant fact. They are *not* the home owners. The house is the *Lord's*, and so is the garden. They, like the hippo himself, are but tenants with little say in what the Lord does with His property!

Biblical Insight About the Hippo

When I looked for the hippo in the Bible, to my surprise I found him there! In the book of Job the Lord calls him "behemoth" which, according to the Strong's Hebrew dictionary, is "of Egyptian derivation; a water-ox, that is, the hippopotamus, or Nile-horse."

> Look at the behemoth, which I made along with you and which feeds on grass like an ox. What strength he has in his loins, what power

in the muscles of his belly! His tail sways
like a cedar; the sinews of his thighs are
close-knit. His bones are tubes of bronze, his
limbs like rods of iron. He ranks first among
the works of God, yet his Maker can approach him with his sword. The hills bring
him their produce, and all the wild animals
play nearby. Under the lotus plants he lies,
hidden among the reeds in the marsh. The
lotuses conceal him in their shadow; the poplars by the stream surround him. When the
river rages, he is not alarmed; he is secure,
though the Jordan should surge against his
mouth. Can anyone capture him by the
eyes, or trap him and pierce his nose? (Job
40:15-24).

The Lord confronts Job's self-righteousness by using
the hippo in an allegorical argument. In so doing, He
ascribes to this gentle giant eleven attributes which parallel the characteristics to be found in those God will
use in prophetic ministry.

Humility

Look at the behemoth, which I made along
with you and which feeds on grass like an ox
(Job 40:15).

The Lord says to Job, "I made the hippo along with
you." This could be taken to mean: Job, what makes you
think you are so special? To Me you are no different
from a hippopotamus!

That surely must have refocused Job's thoughts considerably. But the real point the Lord was making is that
the hippo *obeys* the will of his Creator; he *does* what the
Lord created him to do. The Lord wanted Job to notice

that fact. Indeed, *all* creation obeys the Lord's bidding.

The *ram* ascended the hill to be sacrificed by Abraham in place of Isaac (Gen. 22:13). *Frogs* and *flies*, *lice* and *locusts* invaded Egypt in compliance with God's decree (Ex. 8–10). Tens of thousands of *quail* rained down upon the murmuring Israelites when they complained about not having any meat (Ex. 16:13). Balaam's *donkey* prophesied to him (Num. 22:28). *Two cows*, separated from their calves, delivered the ark of the covenant straight to Israel (1 Sam. 6:7-12). *Ravens* brought Elijah bread and meat in the morning and evening for many days (1 Kin. 17:6). God prepared a great *fish* to swallow up Jonah and then to burp him up three days later (the book of Jonah). Jesus rode a *donkey* on which no man had ever sat (Matt. 21:7). The *cock* crowed after Peter denied the Lord three times, just as Jesus prophesied (Matt. 26:74-75). *All* creation serves the Lord, faithfully and humbly doing His will. All but *mankind*.

The hippo eats grass like an ox. He doesn't complain or wish he was like another creature. He is what he is, and he does what he does. The hippo accepts his lot "in complete agreement with God." That is true humility. A humble man is one who agrees with God.

> He is the Rock, his works are perfect, and all his ways are just. A faithful God who does no wrong, upright and just is he (Deut. 32:4).

By contrast, a proud man argues with the Lord and tries to make himself something apart from what the Lord wants.

> The kings of the earth take their stand and the rulers gather together against the Lord and against his Anointed One. "Let us break their chains," they say, "and throw off their fet-

ters" (Ps. 2:2-3).

The prophet Amos asked, "Do two walk together unless they have agreed to do so?" (Amos 3:3). If we
would walk with God, we must always be in agreement
with Him.

> He has showed you, O man, what is good.
> And what does the Lord require of you? To
> act justly and to love mercy and to walk hum-
> bly with your God (Mic. 6:8).

The foremost quality of true prophetic ministry is
humility. The prophet who is sent by God will act justly,
love mercy and walk humbly with the Lord. He (or she)
will "eat grass like an ox."

Compassion

> What strength he has in his loins, what power
> in the muscles of his belly! (Job 40:16).

In the Scriptures, the "belly" speaks of the inner being — human affections and motivations. The archaic
wording of the King James Version refers to it as "bow-
els of compassion."

> But whoso hath this world's good, and seeth
> his brother have need, and shutteth up his
> *bowels of compassion* from him, how
> dwelleth the love of God in him? (1 John
> 3:17, KJV, italics added).

To be "moved with compassion" is literally to *feel* a
strong surge of emotion deep within you. It is a "gut-
level" response to those who are in anguish.

> When he [Jesus] saw the crowds, he had
> compassion on them, because they were har-
> assed and helpless, like sheep without a shep-
> herd (Matt. 9:36).

As humility is the foundation of fellowship with the
Lord, so compassion is the cornerstone of ministry in
the Spirit.

> When Jesus landed and saw a large crowd, he
> had compassion on them and healed their
> sick (Matt. 14:14).

The strength of prophetic ministry, as with *any* ministry, is when those who minister are "moved with compassion." Those sent by God to speak His words will
surely reveal His heart, for "out of the overflow of the
heart the mouth speaks" (Matt. 12:34). Jesus said,
"Whoever believes in me, as the Scripture has said,
streams of living water will flow from within him"
(John 7:38). The more open we are to the anguish of
others, the greater the flow of God's life and love
through us. And when a true, compassionate prophet of
God speaks the word of the Lord, people will acclaim
his "strength" and "power" as the Lord did of the hippo.

Self-control

> His tail sways like a cedar; the sinews of his
> thighs are close-knit (Job 40:17).

The hippopotamus seems so obese that one would
naturally assume the poor beast could do nothing but
float down the river. Nothing could be further from the
truth. The sheer power in its frame makes it agile and
resourceful. The hippo is in total control of itself and its
environment.

The Bible states that, "The spirits of prophets are subject to the control of prophets" (1 Cor. 14:32). The prophetic anointing of the Holy Spirit does not, as some believe, induce ecstatic fits that compel involuntary and disruptive behavior. The very purpose of the gift of prophecy is to enable us to *communicate* the word of the Lord clearly, which we cannot do if we are disabled by lack of self-control.

Paul lists self-control as one of the fruits of the Holy Spirit (Gal. 5:22-23). To be used by God in prophetic ministry we must exercise restraint over our own impulses, emotions, desires and opinions.

> For we do not preach ourselves, but Jesus Christ as Lord, and ourselves as your servants for Jesus' sake (2 Cor. 4:5).

Those who are sent from God do not seek to exalt themselves; rather they subdue their own agenda for the sake of delivering a true word from the Lord.

God places a high regard for patience and self-control within His prophets by subjecting them to years of seclusion and discipline. John the Baptizer is perhaps our best example. On the occasion of John's birth, his father spoke an inspired utterance over him:

> And you, my child, will be called a prophet of the Most High; for you will go on before the Lord to prepare the way for him, to give his people the knowledge of salvation through the forgiveness of their sins, because of the tender mercy of our God, by which the rising sun will come to us from heaven to shine on those living in darkness and in the shadow of death, to guide our feet into the path of peace (Luke 1:76-79).

What a way to start a life! Who among us would not
want so great a blessing as this spoken over us? But we
sometimes tend to overlook that between this blessing
and its fulfillment, there were years of training in isolation.

> And the child grew and became strong in
> spirit; and he lived in the desert until he ap-
> peared publicly to Israel (v. 80).

The discipline of the desert purges impertinence and
impatience. The pressure of obscurity on a man destined
for visibility is comparable to the making of a diamond
in the recesses of the earth; the intense heat and stress
exerted upon that rock ultimately produce a gem of star-
tling beauty.

> No discipline seems pleasant at the time, but
> painful. Later on, however, it produces a har-
> vest of righteousness and peace for those
> who have been trained by it (Heb. 12:11).

Of course, John was not alone in his seclusion. He
kept company with the likes of *Joseph* (thirty years in
Egypt), *Moses* (forty years in the desert of Midian),
Paul (fourteen years in the tent-making trade) and *Jesus*
(thirty years unaccounted for, except for a brief appearance in the temple at the age of twelve). It seems to be a
regular habit of God's first to set aside in obscurity
those choice servants He has destined for a great work
in His kingdom. It is one way of instilling in them the
self-control engendered by the Holy Spirit.

The issue of self-control affects every area of our
lives — spiritual, mental, emotional, physical, sexual,
social, moral and financial — not necessarily in that order. Lack of self-control in any one area ultimately affects *every* area of our lives, disqualifying us from

God's greater purposes for us.

> See that no one is sexually immoral, or is
> godless like Esau, who for a single meal sold
> his inheritance rights as the oldest son. After-
> ward, as you know, when he wanted to in-
> herit this blessing, he was rejected. He could
> bring about no change of mind, though he
> sought the blessing with tears (Heb. 12:16-
> 17).

The hippo's muscles are so well developed that he
has full control over his massive body. That same level
of self-control is crucial to prophetic ministry. As God
said of the hippo, so it will be said of those whom God
raises up to speak His words: "He bends his tail like a
cedar; the sinews of his thighs are close-knit."

Integrity

> His bones are tubes of bronze, his limbs like
> rods of iron (Job 40:18).

The hippo's internal bone structure supports its great
bulk. Even the slightest fracture could render the creature completely dysfunctional. The same can be said of
prophetic ministry. Without integrity it topples like a
house of cards.

Webster defines integrity as "an unimpaired condition; incorruptibility; the quality or state of being complete or undivided." Manufacturers use this word to
describe a product that keeps its strength and consistency throughout the testing process — it has "integrity." Look at a desk or other well-made piece of
furniture near you. Make your hand into a fist and tap at
random on it. You will find that it is the same *no matter
where you knock on it.*

The same is true for men and women of integrity;
they are the same no matter where you knock on them!
They keep their strength and consistency through the
test. You will find no duplicity in their lives. The Bible
says, "The integrity of the upright guides them, but the
unfaithful are destroyed by their duplicity" (Prov. 11:3).

God guides the upright by the integrity of their
hearts.

> Delight yourself in the Lord and he will give
> you the desires of your heart (Ps. 37:4).

Paul said, "It is God who works in you to will and to
act according to his good purpose" (Phil. 2:13). The
Lord puts His desires within those prophets who have
hearts of integrity. They can trust their hearts to guide
them to the will of God.

> In my integrity you uphold me and set me in
> your presence forever (Ps. 41:12).

Like the hippo, whose sheer mass speaks of its inner
strength, so the true prophets of God are such "whose
bones are tubes of bronze, and whose limbs are like rods
of iron."

Authority

> He ranks first among the works of God (Job
> 40:19).

"First in rank" speaks of authority. All of the preced-
ing qualities of our allegorical hippo combine to lend
themselves to the strength of this one characteristic. Humility, compassion, self-control and integrity make for
authority in ministry. Without these things a man will
not have any voice to speak for God.

The Lord said the hippopotamus "ranks first among the works of God." This admittedly is somewhat of a puzzle, particularly when we consider the hippo as a type of the prophetic ministry. Are we to assume by this that prophetic authority in any way denotes separation from, or superiority over, all other works of God? Absolutely not! Such an assumption would be a serious mistake.

As we have seen, the giftings of God are equally essential within the church, and each is dependent upon the other for complete success.

> There are different kinds of gifts, but the same Spirit. There are different kinds of service, but the same Lord. There are different kinds of working, but the same God works all of them in all men (1 Cor. 12:4-6).

God diversified the spiritual gifts "so that there should be no division in the body, but that its parts should have equal concern for each other" (1 Cor. 12:25).

Anyone who claims that prophets are better than pastors and teachers, or vice versa, is in error. We are each to do what God has called us to do, hand in hand with one another, building up the body of Christ. As we do our part with faithfulness, the Lord will commend us with fruitfulness.

> "Let him who boasts boast in the Lord." For it is not the one who commends himself who is approved, but the one whom the Lord commends (2 Cor. 10:17-18).

The Lord "commended" the hippo when He said to Job, "He ranks first among the works of God!" In much the same way, the Lord also endorses the true prophetic word with His own unquestionable authority.

> The Lord was with Samuel as he grew up,
> and he let none of his words fall to the
> ground. And all Israel from Dan to Beersheba
> recognized that Samuel was attested as a
> prophet of the Lord (1 Sam. 3:19-20).

Samuel was indeed an impressive "hippo"!
Notice that the hippo himself did not claim to be first
among the works of God; the Lord did.

> Many a man claims to have unfailing love,
> but a faithful man who can find? (Prov. 20:6).

A faithful messenger, a trustworthy man, is set with
rank among the workers of God.

> Who then is the faithful and wise servant,
> whom the master has put in charge of the
> servants in his household to give them their
> food at the proper time? (Matt. 24:45).

Moses was such a man, and God bestowed great
authority on him.

> [My servant Moses] is faithful in all my
> house. With him I speak face to face, clearly
> and not in riddles; he sees the form of the
> Lord. Why then were you not afraid to speak
> against my servant Moses? (Num. 12:7-8).

King David is yet another example of a faithful man
to whom authority was given.

> Who of all your servants is as loyal as David,
> the king's son-in-law, captain of your body-

guard and highly respected in your household? (1 Sam. 22:14).

God took David from the fields where he faithfully
tended a small flock of sheep and made him king of
Israel. Faithfulness before God results in authority before men.

There are those today, like Samuel, Moses and David
of old, whom God commends. But there are also those
who commend themselves, who presumptuously boast
of authority not given them, claiming a ministry they do
not perform. They are aptly described by Solomon:

Like clouds and wind without rain is a man
who boasts of gifts he does not give (Prov.
25:14).

Authority cannot be seized by a man; it can only be
bestowed by God. When this happens, it will be hon-
ored by others. Undoubtedly the Lord desires to say of
you and me, "Well done, my good servant!...Because
you have been trustworthy in a very small matter, take
charge of ten cities." (Luke 19:17). Matthew's Gospel
adds one significant phrase to this story, "Come and
share your master's happiness!" (Matt. 25:21). What
joy it brings the Lord when we are faithful in what He
gives us to do.

Like the coolness of snow at harvest time is a
trustworthy messenger to those who send
him; he refreshes the spirit of his masters
(Prov. 25:13).

Submission

His Maker can approach him with his sword
(Job 40:19).

Though the hippo is first in rank among the works of
the Lord, nevertheless his Maker "can approach him
with His sword." This displays submission to divine
authority. Those whom God uses in prophetic ministry
will consistently exhibit this virtue. Submission is not
weakness or passivity or softness. It is controlled power
— intelligent composure and compliance for the purpose of deriving the maximum benefit from any trying
circumstance.

> During the days of Jesus' life on earth, he
> offered up prayers and petitions with loud
> cries and tears to the one who could save him
> from death, and he was heard because of his
> reverent submission (Heb. 5:7).

Submission grants authority in turn to those who submit. The logic here is obvious. To have authority, one
must be *under* authority. If the Lord cannot approach us
with the sword, He will never send us forth with His
words. Submission makes a man approachable, not only
by others, but by God Himself.

The Roman centurion impressed Jesus with his great
sensitivity and faith when he asked the Lord to heal his
servant. He certainly did not fit the stereotype of a hardened, Roman military officer. He was tender, yet strong.
He was a caring commander, having compassion for
one beneath him. " 'Lord,' he said, 'my servant lies at
home paralyzed and in terrible suffering' " (Matt. 8:6).
He genuinely cared about what was happening to his
servant. Such empathy is the cornerstone of true leadership.

This soldier also exhibited insight into how Jesus
healed the sick by comparing it with his own chain of
command.

> But say the word, and my servant will be

> healed. For I myself am a man under author-
> ity, with soldiers under me. I tell this one,
> "Go," and he goes; and that one, "Come,"
> and he comes. I say to my servant, "Do this,"
> and he does it (Luke 7:7-8).

The centurion understood that because Jesus was *under* authority to God, He *had* authority to heal. Jesus
therefore needed only to give the commandment and the
healing would occur — as, in fact, it did.

> When Jesus heard this, he was amazed at
> him, and turning to the crowd following him,
> he said, "I tell you, I have not found such
> great faith even in Israel." Then the men who
> had been sent returned to the house and
> found the servant well (Luke 7:9-10).

Faith

> The hills bring him their produce (Job
> 40:20).

Because the hippo dwells in valleys, his food supply
naturally comes from above him. The rains from
heaven, the streams from the mountains and the abundance from the hills — the hippo looks to them all for
his nourishment. This illustrates the faith that supplies
the prophetic ministry with revelation from heaven.

> The eyes of all look to you, and you give
> them their food at the proper time. You open
> your hand and satisfy the desires of every
> living thing (Ps. 145:15-16).

Those who humble themselves in the valley and look
expectantly to the heavens above will surely receive a

gracious supply from the Lord.

> Every good and perfect gift is from above,
> coming down from the Father of the heav-
> enly lights, who does not change like shifting
> shadows (James 1:17).

The Lord said to Isaiah,

> As the rain and the snow come down from
> heaven, and do not return to it without water-
> ing the earth and making it bud and flourish,
> so that it yields seed for the sower and bread
> for the eater, so is my word that goes out
> from my mouth: It will not return to me
> empty, but will accomplish what I desire and
> achieve the purpose for which I sent it (Is.
> 55:10-11).

God supplies us with seed and bread by sending His
Word from above. This is the favorite diet of those who
are called to prophetic ministry. Indeed, without it we
perish. What sort of person will receive this rain from
heaven, this abundance of produce from the hills?

> He who walks righteously and speaks what is
> right, who rejects gain from extortion and
> keeps his hand from accepting bribes, who
> stops his ears against plots of murder and
> shuts his eyes against contemplating evil —
> this is the man who will dwell on the heights,
> whose refuge will be the mountain fortress.
> His bread will be supplied, and water will
> not fail him. Your eyes will see the king in
> his beauty and view a land that stretches
> afar (Is. 33:15-17).

This seems so idealistic, like a fairy tale. But Isaiah's vision of the Lord had impressed him with the reality of what he was speaking about:

> I saw the Lord seated on a throne, high and exalted, and the train of his robe filled the temple (Is. 6:1).

The Lord is pleased to bless His prophets in much the same way that Isaac blessed Joseph:

> May the Lord bless his land with the precious dew from heaven above and with the deep waters that lie below; with the best the sun brings forth and the finest the moon can yield; with the choicest gifts of the ancient mountains and the fruitfulness of the everlasting hills; with the best gifts of the earth and its fullness and the favor of him who dwelt in the burning bush. Let all these rest on the head of Joseph (Deut. 33:13-16).

Of course, this is by no means limited to prophetic ministry. It shows the rich produce which the hills bring to all who look to the Lord for His blessing.

The hippo has instinctive confidence that the hills will "bring him their produce." Those who are called to prophetic ministry likewise rest in the assurance of receiving true words from the Lord.

> He [the Lord] gave a command to the skies above and opened the doors of the heavens; he rained down manna for the people to eat, he gave them the grain of heaven. Men ate the bread of angels; he sent them all the food they could eat (Ps. 78:23-25).

Gentleness

All the wild animals play nearby (Job 40:20).

The hippo is a herbivore, so other animals are safe in his presence. He is not threatened by their intrusion into his domain, nor does he threaten them with his bulky presence. The hippo only attacks to protect those about him. Similarly, those mature in prophetic ministry do not attack others. They have no agenda for doing harm to any person.

Hearing God's voice instills peace deep in the heart of the listener, removing any need for self-promotion.

> Here is my servant whom I have chosen, the one I love, in whom I delight; I will put my Spirit on him, and he will proclaim justice to the nations. He will not quarrel or cry out; no one will hear his voice in the streets. A bruised reed he will not break, and a smoldering wick he will not snuff out, till he leads justice to victory (Matt. 12:18-20).

When God gives us insight to share with others, He also gives us the tenderness to share it in ways that build them up rather than tear them down.

> But the wisdom that comes from heaven is first of all pure; then peace-loving, considerate, submissive, full of mercy and good fruit, impartial and sincere (James 3:17).

Again, the express purpose for which the prophetic gift is manifested within the church is to "strengthen, encourage and comfort." The apostle Paul gave specific instructions concerning how we are to convey truth to one another:

> And the Lord's servant must not quarrel; in-
> stead, he must be kind to everyone, able to
> teach, not resentful. Those who oppose him
> he must gently instruct, in the hope that God
> will grant them repentance leading them to a
> knowledge of the truth, and that they will
> come to their senses and escape from the trap
> of the devil, who has taken them captive to
> do his will (2 Tim. 2:24-26).

Other animals can play before the hippo feeling no
dread in his presence. Likewise, the hearts of those who
draw near for a word from the Lord are put at ease by
the loving demeanor of mature prophetic ministry.

Hiddenness

> Under the lotus plants he lies, hidden among
> the reeds in the marsh. The lotuses conceal
> him in their shadow; the poplars by the
> stream surround him (Job 40:21-22)

The hippo loves to hide in the shade provided for him
in the stream, and the prophet loves to seclude himself
with the Lord in the secret place of prayer.

> He who dwells in the shelter of the Most
> High will rest in the shadow of the Almighty
> (Ps. 91:1).

The idea of being in God's "shadow" speaks of our
nearness to the Lord — close enough even to hear Him
whisper. The Lord asked Jeremiah, "But which of them
has stood in the council of the Lord to see or to hear his
word? Who has listened and heard his word?" (Jer.
23:18). According to Strong's concordance, the Hebrew
word translated as "council" means a session, a com-

pany of persons in close deliberation. By implication, it speaks of intimacy, consultation and the sharing of a secret.

Like the hippo submerged in the water beneath the shadows of the poplar trees, we must hide in the secret place of prayer to see or hear God's words to us.

> The Lord confides in those who fear him; he makes his covenant known to them (Ps. 25:14).

We must first receive a word from God in order to speak a word for God. Jesus said to His disciples, "What I tell you in the dark, speak in the daylight; what is whispered in your ear, proclaim from the roofs" (Matt. 10:27). When we speak the words God gives us as we draw near to Him, they will turn many away from sin to God.

> If they had stood in my council, they would have proclaimed my words to my people and would have turned them from their evil ways and from their evil deeds (Jer. 23:22).

The hippo finds renewal as he rests beneath the shadows at the river's edge. Often we can become overloaded with a sense of responsibility in the *work* of the Lord. To avoid burnout we must find repose in the *shadow* of the Lord. When Moses felt overwhelmed with all the details of the tabernacle, the Lord assured him that one named Bezalel would be his helper. The name means "in the shadow of God," and the Lord appointed him as the foreman for the building of the tabernacle. God said to Moses,

> I have filled him with the Spirit of God, with skill, ability and knowledge in all kinds of

> crafts — to make artistic designs for work in gold, silver and bronze, to cut and set stones, to work in wood, and to engage in all kinds of craftsmanship (Ex. 31:3-5).

When we stay in the shadow of God, the secret place of prayer, we, too, are filled with the Holy Spirit, with skill, ability and knowledge in all kinds of crafts in the kingdom of God!

> Your love, O Lord, reaches to the heavens, your faithfulness to the skies. Your righteousness is like the mighty mountains, your justice like the great deep. O Lord, you preserve both man and beast. How priceless is your unfailing love! Both high and low among men find refuge *in the shadow of your wings.* They feast on the abundance of your house; you give them drink from your river of delights. For with you is the fountain of life; in your light we see light (Ps. 36:5-9, italics added).

In the shadow of His wings we find refuge in God's unfailing love. We find security and preservation of our lives from the heat of persecution. We find an abundance of delights in the house of the Lord, which is a house of prayer. And we have the light of revelation to see all things as they truly are. How accurately did the psalmist say, "Those who are planted in the house of the Lord shall flourish in the courts of our God" (Ps. 92:13, NKJV).

We must frequent the secret place of prayer if we want to stand on the public platform of prophetic ministry. Like the hippo, we must take the time to be "hidden among the reeds in the marsh, concealed in their shadow, surrounded by the poplars at the river's edge."

Courage

> When the river rages, he is not alarmed; he is
> secure, though the Jordan should surge
> against his mouth (Job 40:23).

The hippopotamus is not intimidated by a flood; the
onslaught of many waters does not cause him any
alarm. Likewise, when God raises up a prophet, He
gives him the security of knowing the truth. "Then you
will know the truth, and the truth will set you free"
(John 8:32). This, and sometimes this alone, enables
those who speak the truth to stand firm even though a
host should surge against their words.

Peter and John stood courageously against the intimidation and threats of the Jewish leaders because they
were armed with truth. When they were commanded not
to preach or teach in the name of Jesus, they replied,
"Judge for yourselves whether it is right in God's sight
to obey you rather than God. For we cannot help speaking about what we have seen and heard" (Acts 4:19-20).
The Living Bible relates,

> When the Council saw the boldness of Peter
> and John, and could see that they were obvi-
> ously uneducated non-professionals, they
> were amazed and realized what being with
> Jesus had done for them! (Acts 4:13).

Courage is the fruit of fellowship with Jesus Christ.
The Lord said to Joshua,

> No one will be able to stand up against you
> all the days of your life. As I was with Moses,
> so I will be with you; I will never leave you
> nor forsake you. Be strong and courageous,
> because you will lead these people to inherit

> the land I swore to their forefathers to give
> them. Be strong and very courageous. Be
> careful to obey all the law my servant Moses
> gave you; do not turn from it to the right or to
> the left, that you may be successful wherever
> you go. Do not let this Book of the Law de-
> part from your mouth; meditate on it day and
> night, so that you may be careful to do every-
> thing written in it. Then you will be prosper-
> ous and successful. Have I not commanded
> you? Be strong and courageous. Do not be
> terrified; do not be discouraged, for the Lord
> your God will be with you wherever you go
> (Josh. 1:5-9).

Jeremiah was a young lad when the Lord called him
to be His prophet. Naturally, he expressed youthful fear
and reluctance. "Ah, Sovereign Lord," he said, "I do not
know how to speak; I am only a child" (Jer. 1:6). But the
Lord said to him, "Do not say, 'I am only a child.' You
must go to everyone I send you to and say whatever I
command you. Do not be afraid of them, for I am with
you and will rescue you" (Jer. 1:7-8). Jeremiah understood his call and received the touch of God that put the
Lord's words in his mouth.

> Then the Lord reached out his hand and
> touched my mouth and said to me, "Now, I
> have put my words in your mouth" (Jer. 1:9).

Once God's words are put in our mouths, there can be
no compromise in speaking the truth.

> Get yourself ready! Stand up and say to them
> whatever I command you. Do not be terrified
> by them, or I will terrify you before them
> (Jer. 1:17).

Sometimes, one must go against the stream of public opinion in speaking the word of the Lord. Truth has no enemies but those who love falsehood. Jesus said,

> This is the verdict: Light has come into the world, but men loved darkness instead of light because their deeds were evil. Everyone who does evil hates the light, and will not come into the light for fear that his deeds will be exposed (John 3:19-20).

Speaking the truth — even when motivated by love — is not always welcome and sometimes incurs great wrath. The spokesperson of the Lord will nevertheless deliver the word undaunted.

> We say with confidence, "The Lord is my helper; I will not be afraid. What can man do to me?" (Heb. 13:6).

Alertness

> Can anyone capture him by the eyes, or trap him and pierce his nose? (Job 40:24).

The hippopotamus can be totally submerged under water, hidden from sight, and yet have his nose, eyes and ears slightly above the surface — keenly alert to all that is going on about him. He is the epitome of discernment and vigilance. His sharp senses of hearing, smelling and seeing uncover and frustrate any trap set for him or others. The parallel this has to the prophetic ministry speaks for itself. God has given us eyes to see, ears to hear and discernment that we might know the devil's schemes.

Peter said, "Be self-controlled and alert. Your enemy the devil prowls around like a roaring lion looking for someone to devour" (1 Pet. 5:8). David proclaimed, "As for the deeds of men — by the word of your lips I have kept myself from the ways of the violent" (Ps. 17:4). The word of the Lord will also deliver us from the snares of men and devils.

The Hippo in the Garden

This biblical reference to the hippo in the book of Job has provided us with a fascinating allegorical model for prophets. The characteristics of the hippo are typical of those found in people the Lord is raising up in prophetic ministry in these last days: humility, compassion, self-control, integrity, authority, submission, faith, gentleness, hiddenness, courage and alertness.

The Lord's principal purpose for bringing the hippo into the picture with Job was to confront Job's self-righteousness by way of comparison with the behemoth. And when the Lord brings the "hippo" into the garden, He will *again* confront the self-righteous in the church and in the world. Someone has rightly said, "God often offends our minds to reveal our hearts." The hippo in the garden can accomplish this rather easily.

Regardless, the Lord will do His work in this generation, though it may seem strange and out of place. He will bring forth the prophetic movement of His Spirit within the church like a hippo in a garden. Men and women will be filled with the Holy Spirit to speak words from God. They will bear the characteristics of the hippo as seen in the allegory of Scripture. While there will be much ado about this, God will nevertheless do His work, His strange work, and bring to pass His unusual act.

The prophetic movement will surely be established in the midst of the church, like a hippo in the midst of a garden. And — mark this, for it surely follows by reason of the inevitable — the church will be found in the midst of the world, speaking forth the words of God to a crooked and perverse generation, among whom we will shine as light, holding forth the word of life. The hippo in the garden is the indefinable, unexpected, strange and extraordinary work of God! Yet, though it seems so out of place, it nevertheless is *exactly* what the Lord wants. The hippo is His pet, and it is here to stay.

One author suggests that by the year 2000, the church, left to itself on its present course, might very well become like "the frog in the kettle" — cooked alive in a pot of water which is slowly, imperceptibly heated to a full boil. This could be true, *if* God left us to ourselves. But the Lord will arise and have compassion on us and stir us to seek His face. The Scripture says that He will pour His Spirit upon all flesh, and our sons and daughters will prophesy, our old men will dream, and our young men will see visions. And the great, unfailing mercy of God will provide for all who call upon the name of the Lord to be saved!

Therefore, I say that by the will of God the church will *not* end up as the frog in the kettle — but will instead be *the hippo in the garden!* ❀

Chapter Three

1. Charles H. Spurgeon, *The Treasury of David*, vol. 4 (Grand Rapids, Mich.: Guardian Press, 1976), p. 30.

Chapter Four

1. John Wesley, *The Works of John Wesley*, vol. 1 (Weimer Edition, 1872), p. 1030.

Chapter Five

1. Charles Emerson, quoted in Compact Classics Library, vol. 3, A2, s.v. "quotes and anecdotes."

Chapter Seven

1. From the hymn "Great Is Thy Faithfulness," by Thomas Chisholm, copyright © 1923. Renewal extended by Hope Publishing Co., Carol Stream, IL 60188. All rights reserved. Used by permission.

2. Charles H. Spurgeon, *The Treasury of David*, vol. 1 (Grand Rapids, Mich.: Guardian Press, 1976), Psalm 8, p. 89.

3. Adapted from the cartoon strip *For Better or for Worse*, by Lynn Johnston, United Press International (UPI) Syndicate.

If you enjoyed *Hippo in the Garden*,
we would like to recommend
the following books:

the SOUND OF HIS VOICE
IT SAME

God Has a Word for You
by Kim Clement
Author Kim Clement shares that prophecy did not
end in Bible times and that it has been the
forgotten ministry of the church. He gives
practical principles for hearing the voice of God.
God Has a Word for You is a call for prophecy
to come alive in every believer.

ALMAWD
means BRANCH
God is
WATCHING

On the Ash Heap With No Answers
by Iverna Tompkins
Is God speaking? Are we hearing?
Author Iverna Tompkins digs into the book
of Job to unearth a powerful — and hopeful —
teaching on God's desire to reveal Himself
to His people through personal prophecy.

Prophetic Destinies
by Derek Prince
How does the church relate to the Jews
and the state of Israel? Author Derek Prince
answers that question based on a lifetime
of study and experience. You will discover
how the prophetic destinies of Israel
and the church are intertwined.

Available at your local
Christian bookstore or from:

Creation House
600 Rinehart Road
Lake Mary, FL 32746
1-800-451-4598